D1156837

A MONUMENT TO ST. JEROME

A MONUMENT
TO
SAINT JEROME

ESSAYS ON SOME ASPECTS OF HIS
LIFE, WORKS AND INFLUENCE

Edited by

FRANCIS X. MURPHY, C.SS.R.

Foreword by

CARDINAL TISSERANT

SHEED & WARD — NEW YORK — 1952

Testimonia

"Scriptor Mirificus . . ."
"Totius ecclesiae simmistes, theca sophiae . . ."

Interpresque sacer fuit hostis et hostibus acer
Dogmatis ac fidei nostrae pacis requiei
Illum vesanus pavet hostes Iovinianus
Arrius et Photinus, Origenes atque Rufinus.
Non abiit immunis quem tu, Ieronime, punis.
Tu pestes rabidas verbi mucrone trucidas.
Omnes lascivi, nebulones atque nocivi
Te detestantur, metuunt et amara precantur.
Lubrica te tellus, iuvenes cunctusque popellus,
Teque proci matrum, te matres teque theatrum
Urbes et vici, portus tibi sunt inimici.

Te posuit lumen sapientia, dans tibi flumen
Quo flueres vivo felix septemplice rivo;
Nempe tuo vivi septem de pectore rivi
Insimul emanant qui languida pectora sanant.
Et cibus est menti doctrina tui documenti
Palladis ad cenam cupienti scandere plenam.
Tu iam duxque viae, tu fons splendorque sophiae
Monstrans namque viam cupidus potare sophiam.

—Preface to the *Vita Malachi*
of Reginald of Canterbury (1050–1109)
(ed. L. R. Lund, Urbana, 1942).

(A translator of holy writings was he, and a terrible foe;
To the foes of our faith, of our creed, of our peace and our rest, a
     merciless goad;
The wild Jovinian feared him fully
As did Arius and Phontius, Origen and Rufinus.
He goes not unscathed, whom you, Jerome will punish.
For the sword of your tongue disembowels pestiferous beasts.
All the lascivious, the crass, the harmful detest you:
They fear and call down curses upon you.
The sinful world, youth, and the shadowy people,
The wooers of wives, bad mothers, theatrical fools,
The ports, the cities and towns all repulse you.

Wisdom holds you up as a light, granting you eloquence
Wherewith, in sevenfold stream, you happily gleam:
From your heart seven living rivers flow,
Curing the hearts of the languid.
The knowledge of your wares is a food for the mind; a banquet
For one desiring to approach the full table of knowledge.
You are a guide, and a leader on the way;
You are a fount, and the splendor of wisdom
Lighting the path before those desirous of devouring wisdom.)

"Nec sanctum Hieronymum, quia presbyter fuit, contemnendum
arbitreris, qui Graeco et Latino insuper et Hebraeo eruditus eloquio
ex occidentali ad orientalem transiens Ecclesiam, in locis sanctis
atque in litteris sacris usque ad decrepitam vixit aetatem . . ."
                        —St. Augustine, *Contra Julianum* I, 7, 34.
(Nor are you to disdain the blessed Jerome because he was a priest;
for well versed in Greek and Latin, and above all in Hebrew eloquence, he passed over from the western to the eastern Church, and
lived to an advanced age amid the Sacred Scriptures in the Holy
Lands . . .)

    "Hieronymus Catholicorum magister, cuius scripta per universum
    mundum quasi divinae lampades rutilant . . . fuit enim Hier-
    onymus vir sicut maximae scientiae ita probatissimae, puraeque
    doctrine. . . .")
                        —J. Cassianus, *De Incarnatione* lib. vii.

(Jerome, a teacher of Catholics, whose writings, as it were, divine lights shone brightly on all the world. . . . Of the highest learning, Jerome was likewise a man of the most approved and pure doctrine. . . .)

"Beatus etiam Hieronymus latinae linguae dilatator eximius, qui nobis in translatione divinae Scripturae tantum praestitit, ut ad Hebraeum fontem pene non egeamus accedere, quando nos facundiae suae multa cognoscitur ubertate satiasse, plurimis libris copiosis epistolis fecit beatos, quibus scribere, Domino praestante, dignatus est. Planus, doctus, dulcis. . . ."
— Cassiodorus, *Divin. lect.* cap. xxi.
(And the blessed Jerome, a most outstanding propagandist of the Latin tongue, who so greatly excelled us in the translation of the divine Scriptures since we could scarcely approach the Hebrew source; while it is well known that he overwhelmed us with the great richness of his learning, he blessed us with many books and copious letters, which he deigned to write with the aid of the Lord. Simple, learned, kind. . . .)

"Hieronymus divina et seculari doctrina praecipuus et velut quidam parens cum Augustino ecclesiasticae philosophiae, quae humanam nec multum appetit, nec in omnibus contemnit, Pelagianam haeresim recens exortam potenter debellans. . . ."
— Servatus Lupus, *De. trib. quaest.*
(Jerome, outstanding in his knowledge of divine and secular things, and as it were, a founder with Augustine of ecclesiastical philosophy, which neither seeks much after what is merely human, nor contemns it in all things . . . a powerful opponent of the newly arisen Pelagian heresy. . . .)

Foreword

WHEN I ARRIVED at the Biblical School of the Dominican Fathers in Jerusalem, on October 22, 1904, and I asked Father Hughes Vincent for suggestions about reading useful for a man who wished to devote his life to the study of the Old Testament, he recommended three titles: Schuerer's *History of the Jewish People at the Time of Christ*, Darmestetter's *Annotated French Translation of the Zend-Avesta,* and St. Jerome's *Letters*. I chose two of these titles, Schuerer's three volumes and St. Jerome's *Letters*.

When, four years later, I became a *Scriptor orientalis* at the Vatican Library and I asked my senior colleague, Pio Franchi de'Cavalieri, what I ought to read in order to find a suitable Latin style for my work of cataloguing the Oriental manuscripts, he answered, St. Jerome's *Letters*. And again I took in hand Vol. XXII of Migne's *Patrologia Latina*.

Later, I bought Hilberg's edition in the *Corpus Scriptorum ecclesiasticorum latinorum*, published by the Vienna Imperial Academy of Letters—the first two volumes appeared before World War I, and the third volume was purchasable for a few *centesimi* when the Austrian schilling was at its lowest. But the index never did come out; nor is it to be hoped for now, when World War II has completed the ruins of World War I. *Multa flagella peccatorum,* as the old warrior himself wrote in the exordium to his last letter to Donatus (Hilberg 154).

St. Jerome's *Letters* are important, of course, for their style and for their contents; they are the most interesting of his works for people who wish to become acquainted with his personality, his world and his age.

Educated in accord with the best traditions of classical antiquity, with an excellent knowledge of the classical authors, both
Greek and Latin, Jerome was able to write in true classical, almost
Ciceronian style. But Jerome was a Christian; moreover he was a
monk and a priest. As the Romans of his time no longer used
classical Latin, Jerome indulges in new moods and uses ecclesiastical language, not only in his translations of the Biblical texts but
wherever he speaks about religious matters. St. Jerome's works are
milestones for a study of the transformation of Latin style and
language at the end of the ancient times. A classical scholar may
read them without being offended, while they form a prelude to
the best mediaeval compositions. St. Jerome's works had great
influence on the Middle Ages, as Professor M. L. W. Laistner
shows in his important contribution to the present book.

From earliest boyhood Jerome was avid for knowledge. He desired to be informed about everything. Amongst his contemporaries he enjoyed an extraordinary reputation; not only was he the
first authority in the West on Holy Scripture, but as we see from
the Letters, he was consulted on many other subjects besides.
St. Augustine, who did not always agree with St. Jerome's
ideas, proclaimed that he had read all the Christian authors who
wrote before him. On the other hand, we can verify from his
quotations that he had a good knowledge of Greek and Latin
literature. Rufinus, in controversy with Jerome, asserted that he
paid for a copy of Cicero's *Dialogi* more than he used to pay
for copies of sacred books. Even after the famous dream in the
desert of Chalcis, Jerome kept an interest in classical literature.
Near the end of his life he taught Latin language and literature
to young people in Bethlehem.

The Bible is a most important book for Christians because it
contains God's word. St. Jerome had a strong faith and his love
of Christ was the love proper to a saint. He knew the unique
value of the New Testament, but he chose the Old Testament as
a favorite matter of study—perhaps because the Old Testament
was not so well known as the New, but perhaps also because it
was more difficult to write about it, for he liked to tackle difficult

tasks. It is well known how St. Jerome strained every nerve in order to obtain a true knowledge of the Hebrew language. Certainly we may criticize his translations and improve them, but we are obliged to admit that he knew Hebrew grammar and vocabulary as well as it was possible to do at his time. St. Jerome was interested in history and intended to prepare a continuation of Eusebius' *Chronicle,* which he translated from the Greek and completed briefly. He knew the works of the best profane historians and he borrowed from their works a good part of his additions to this chronological epitome of the 'Father of Church History'; he intended to compose a detailed account of the attacks by the Barbarians against the Empire and Rome, but he did not accomplish this. The biographies written by St. Jerome are lively; he excels in describing the environment of his heroes. When he travelled, he was interested in the customs of the nations he was passing through, in their religious practices, in their folk-lore. Therefore he was able to captivate his audiences, distinguished patrician women of Rome, or Eastern monks.

Nobody was better equipped than St. Jerome to build a bridge between East and West; for it was a century since the division of the Roman Empire by Diocletian, and Easterners and Westerners were beginning to be strangers. But, although he knew personally some of the prominent Greek prelates and laymen, he was not much interested in them. St. Jerome wanted to adapt pagan classicism to Christian teaching, and since Christian writers of the East had already tried to do something similar, he decided to translate a number of their works. But the Greek Fathers had written on philosophical and theological questions, which were not of major interest for Jerome himself or for most of the Roman churchmen, who were concerned with the practical problems of Christian life. Jerome preferred the more technical works of such Christian scholars as Origen, Didymus and Eusebius of Caesarea.

It is an encouraging feature of our time that interest has grown, among the educated laity as well as the clergy, in the treasures of ancient Christian literature. St. Jerome is one of the Fathers of the Church who is more likely to interest modern readers. He was not a bishop, and he had no occasion to explain Holy Scripture in practical homilies. He spoke almost exclusively for selected audiences. But his writing aimed at a wider influence. His letters were written not for his correspondent alone, but for the general public as well.

The present book is an excellent introduction to the reading of St. Jerome's works, especially of his *Letters,* because the reader will find here discussions of many aspects of the person and works of St. Jerome. To anyone genuinely interested in St. Jerome, I must say: *Tolle, lege.*

Rome, January 8, 1952

✠ Eugene Card. Tisserant
Bp. of Ostia, Porto and Santa Rufina

EDITOR'S NOTE

In keeping with the more acceptable of modern scholarly calculations, Jerome of Stridon was born in A.D. 347. Accordingly it was planned to issue a volume of commemorative essays, as much by way of tribute to the *Doctor Maximus in Interpretandis Scripturis Sacris* as to supply a long-standing want among Patristic studies in English. Circumstances that will be easily understood, these days, rendered impossible the appearance of this volume in time to call attention to the Centenary. It is felt, however, that the group of essays here presented will prove of sufficient interest to scholars and to the reading public generally to warrant their publication now. For many facets of Jerome's personality, his life and influence are here presented by a group of men who need no introduction to the historically or Scripturally minded world.

It but remains for me to render special thanks to Dr. Martin R. P. McGuire for his interest from the inception of this undertaking, and to Miss Ruth Reidy and Mr. Frank Sheed for their long-suffering interest and editorial aid in preparing it for publication.

FRANCIS X. MURPHY, C.SS.R.

In festo S. Hieronymi,
1951

Contents

St. Jerome: The Irascible Hermit
FRANCIS X. MURPHY, C.SS.R.

St. Jerome: The Irascible Hermit

THE AGE into which St. Jerome was born was, in Arnold Toynbee's phrase, "a time of troubles." The fourth century of the Christian era found the vast, ordered Roman Empire on its knees about to succumb before the barbarian pressure from without, and a hopelessly enervated economic and political situation within. A new world was being born. And the pains and dangers inherent in such a gestation were reflected in the turbulent careers not only of its military and political figures, but even in the lives of its scholars and men of the Church. Hence we find the outstanding figures of the emergent Christian civilization men of nervous mettle, strong of language, severe of morals, and implacable in their opposition to the dying paganism and the social corruption that faced them on every side.

It is thus not exactly invidious to call St. Jerome an irascible hermit at the very start of a Monument in his honor. For, although he was not always irascible, nor always a hermit, he did make great effort to cope with the turbulence of his times; and in so doing, he not infrequently reacted irascibly, at least twice betaking himself to what he thought would be the solitude of a hermitage in an effort to stabilize his own sanity before the onrush of political and ecclesiastical storms raging about him. But though a true hermit at heart, he was at once too talented and too prominent to escape the burdens of the hour. From the desert of Chalcis as a young man, from the solitude of Bethlehem during the whole course of his old age, he played so vital a part in theological and ecclesiastical affairs that he has well merited the title of a "Founder of the Middle Ages." [1]

In keeping with the career of the man himself, the biography of St. Jerome is studded with controversy.[2] Scholars and writers of the Renaissance and the Reformation—from Erasmus and Basnagius to Cave and the Bollandists—indulged in the most vitriolic of polemic when discussing St. Jerome, for the most part exaggeratedly praising or damning one another along with the subject of their labors. In the nineteenth century, likewise, opinion favoring Jerome or belittling him ran full current. One has to go back to Lenain de Tillemont in the eighteenth century to find a calm, judicious, and tempered estimate of the man and of the problems connected with the investigation of his career.[3]

Strangely enough, though the knowledge we have of his life is minute and vast, we do not actually know just when St. Jerome was born, or where; nor are we completely certain of the date of his death. Jerome himself tells us that he was "of Stridon, a town since destroyed by the Goths, which was located on the *confinium* of Dalmatia and Pannonia." [4] Unfortunately the topography of the place has been lost to history.

Jerome likewise gives frequent indication of himself as a boy, a youth, a young man and old; but the latitude he allows himself in these various stages is such as to make a precise dating all but impossible.[5] Though he was in frequent epistolary and other contact with the great personages of his era—Augustine, Paulinus of Nola, Damasus, Theophilus of Alexandria, the two Melanias, Palladius of Helenopolis, to name but a few—the chronological problems encountered in much of the history of the fourth and fifth century have still to be mastered.[6]

F. Cavallera has conjectured that the year 347 was Jerome's date of birth; he has traced Stridon, in Italy, to a small finger of land extending the province of Venetia-Istria (formerly the tenth region) as a wedge between modern Austria and Jugoslavia, close by the ancient sites of Aquileia and Hemona.[7] On well-founded hypotheses, Cavallera has thus cut through an ancient legend, traceable to Prosper of Aquitaine, which placed the date of Jerome's birth in 331,[8] and which was given verisimilitude by Jerome's frequent reference to Augustine in their correspondence as a 'young man.' [9] In making Jerome out a provincial Roman, Father Cavallera has likewise invalidated the claims that would make him an Italian, an Istrian, a Slav, a Bohemian, or even a Spaniard.[10]

We get but a fleeting glimpse of Jerome's early youth, involving his dealings with the household slaves, and a grandmother who not infrequently saved him from the savagery of his schoolmaster, Orbilius (the name is filched from Horace).[11] He likewise makes an unsavory reference or two to the doughty citizens of Stridon and their bishop.[12]

At twelve, Jerome was sent to Rome for further classical studies, with his townsman Bonosus as a companion. There, besides sitting at the feet of Donatus and other eminent schoolmen, he took part in the outrageous if not obscene vandalisms of the school-boys—*eversores* (destroyers), Augustine calls them— and was overawed by his experience in the catacombs and in the great Christian churches. He was baptized at 20; [13] then set out on a *wanderjahr* that took him north to Treves and over vast portions of Gaul,—we do not know why he made this journey. It did, however, result in both scholarly and religious contacts. For he made copies of Hilary of Poitiers' *On the Psalms* and his *On the Synods* in Treves. There too he seems to have learnt something of the hermits of Egypt—for twenty years earlier Athanasius had been in exile here—and neatly incorporated this knowledge into his *Life of St. Anthony the Hermit*.[14] In any event by A.D. 369 Jerome was back in the vicinity of Stridon, anxious to make contact with an Aquileian group of ascetics gathered round their Bishop Valerian, and the priests Chromatius, Jovinus and Eusebius—all three to be, as Rufinus would write of them in A.D. 400, *"opinatissimos et probatissimos in Ecclesia Dei episcopos."* [15]

Jerome first met Rufinus of Aquileia in Rome as a school boy. He renewed contact with him upon returning from the north, probably in A.D. 370, finding him an ardent member of what Jerome himself would term in his *Chronicle* "a choir of the blessed." [16] Too restless to join the group formally, Jerome seems eventually to have got involved in some unpleasantness over this new Christian ascetic movement. For in 372 a "sudden whirl-wind" shook him from the side of Rufinus and the Aquileian ascetics. He set out on "an uncertain pilgrimage through Thrace, Bithynia, Pontus, through Galatia and Cilicia, until he reached Syria" and the home of Evagrius of Antioch.[17] Sick of soul and body, he retired for a while to the desert of Chalcis, but found neither spiritual nor ecclesiastical peace there. He could not entice his friends to join him—Rufinus, or Nicetas, or Chryso-comas. Nor even by twice appealing to Pope Damasus in Rome could he cut through the doctrinal disputes and ecclesiastical entanglements that menaced the peace of the desert as a result of a schism in Antioch. In disgust, he returned to that city for a time.

It was there, it seems, that he was ordained a priest in A.D. 378. It was there too that he began his literary career, following his letters from the desert with several minor compositions includ-ing the *Life of Paul the Hermit*.[18] There he must likewise have listened to the lectures and scriptural commentaries of Apollinaris of Laodicea, and thus renewed a determination he had formed in the desert to devote himself to scripture studies. For it was with some such resolution in mind that, while struggling with his temper and his passions in the desert, he had perfected his knowl-edge of Greek and enmeshed himself in the difficulties of Hebrew.[19]

Jerome was in Constantinople in 379. He made the acquaint-ance, there, of one of the outstanding theologians of the East, Gregory Nazianzen, along with many of the prominent Oriental prelates and exegetes. Inexplicably, he says nothing of the Council of Constantinople held in 381, where the divinity of the Holy Ghost was defined and other pressing theological and ecclesiastical problems of the hour discussed. It was at Constantinople, how-ever, that he seems to have inaugurated the main current of his productive activity, beginning with a translation and continua-tion of the World Chronicle of Eusebius of Caesarea, of fourteen of Origen's homilies on the prophet Jeremias, of a similar series on Ezechiel, and nine on Isaias. By this time he had come to a decision with regard to the art of the translator, deciding to follow the Ciceronian pattern of bringing over ideas from one language to another, instead of betraying the original text by attempting to transpose it word for word. His discovery of Origen was a decisive influence in his life and career. It shaped his scriptural outlook, becoming a mainstay of his competence; but it involved him in troubles innumerable as well.[20]

In 382, Jerome was in Rome, serving as secretary to Pope Damasus, and enkindling an ascetical spirit among the noble Roman ladies living on the Aventine hill and the Villa Scaurus—Marcella and Blesilla, Paula and Eustochium, Melania and Asella. But his influence on these well-born, spirited women was envied; and when he turned to ridiculing the antics of his clerical critics and calumniators, a whispering campaign was started against him. It included the charge that the excessive mortification indulged in by Blesilla under his guidance had brought about her untimely death.[21]

Jerome engendered further misunderstanding by his determination, under the Pope's direction, to co-ordinate the Latin translations of the Scriptures, beginning with the Gospels.[22] Nor did the devastating satire and mordant caricatures that formed part of his refutation of the heretic Helvidius' strictures on virginity and the Virgin Mary, help matters.[23] Hence upon the death of Pope Damasus in December of 384, he began making preparations for a return to the East. This time, he decided to take up residence in Bethlehem, to be in contact with the biblical sites whereof he would write, and to be close to the localities sanctified by the actual presence of the Savior. Departing from Ostia in August 385 with his brother Paulinian and several monks, Jerome stopped at Crete and at Antioch; then, together with a party of virgins under the guidance of his former pupil Paula, he made a sweeping pilgrimage through the deserts of Egypt and the whole of Palestine, making contacts with the ascetical heroes of the hour, and developing his knowledge of biblical geography.[24]

A full year later, he was at Gaza in Palestine, on the way to Bethlehem. There a double monastic foundation was established, with Paula, whose fortune subsidized the enterprise, as superior of the women's monastery, and Jerome as head and guide of the whole. Cordial relations were established with a similar foundation in Jerusalem presided over by Rufinus and Melania the Elder. But in 393, an anti-Origen movement broke out in the East. It was promoted in Palestine by an otherwise unknown monk, named Atarbius. It was further agitated by the influence of Bishop Epiphanius of Salamis in Crete.

When Rufinus, in consort with his bishop, John of Jerusalem, refused to condemn the great Alexandrian scripture scholar and exegete, a quarrel was promoted between Rufinus in Jerusalem and Jerome in Bethlehem. It resulted in the estrangement of the two groups, the depriving of Jerome and his associates of the spiritual ministrations of the Jerusalem clergy, and the interference by Bishop Theophilus of Alexandria on Jerome's behalf in matters outside his jurisdiction.[25] It was only patched up on the eve of Rufinus' departure for the West, at Easter of 397, but not before Jerome had delivered himself of a devastating *Against John of Jerusalem*.[26]

The quarrel between Jerome and Rufinus broke out once again in 399, a year or so after the latter's return to Italy. Jerome's friends in Rome objected to Rufinus' claim that, in translating Origen's "On the First Things" for the philosopher Macarius, he was following the lead and the method of Jerome in bringing the Alexandrian master's works over into Latin. Unfortunately Origen was now looked upon with great suspicion in orthodox circles. Hence Jerome was informed that his reputation was at stake. He thundered forth in letters of warning.[27] To protect himself, Rufinus prepared an Apologia, which appeared early in 401. And Jerome, in considerable agitation, tried to answer the book, even before he got his hands on it.[28] In the spring of 401, he completed "Two Books against Rufinus"; and then, upon the reception of a letter of the latter in reply, he boomed back with a third invective.[29] Informed of the proportions of the quarrel, Augustine, in far off Africa, was genuinely shocked. "Is there any friend," he wrote, "is there any friend one will not now dread as a future foe, when this that we bewail has raised its head between Jerome and Rufinus . . . men so closely knit in study and in friendship . . . ripe in years, and together in the very land our Lord once trod." [30]

Once aroused, Jerome's anger was implacable. Though his adversary dropped out of the controversy completely, Jerome in the prefaces to his subsequent scriptural commentaries, all unmistakably influenced by, if not based upon Origen, continued to scarify his erstwhile friend.[31] Even in 411 on hearing of Rufinus' death, Jerome wrote: "Now that the scorpion lies buried in Trinacria (Sicily) . . . and the hydra with its numerous heads has ceased its hissing against us, and time is given for other things than answering the iniquities of heretics . . . I will tackle the prophet Ezechiel." [32]

Controversy was, of course, the man's avocation. At the very start of his literary career he had splintered shafts with, and vanquished, the followers of Bishop Lucifer of Calaris in his *Altercatio Luciferiani et Orthodoxi* written most probably in 378.[33] In Rome in 383, he demolished Helvidius. In 393 from Bethlehem he lashed and pilloried Jovinian because the latter had had the gall to call into question the superior virtue of a monastic way of life, belittling likewise the veneration of saints and their relics.[34] In 406, it was the turn of Vigilantius.[35] Before death sounded its call, he was to rouse the West to the dangers of the heretic Pelagius, in 415 publishing his Dialogues against the Pelagians.[36]

Meanwhile he had roamed through the whole of the Old Testament, supplying new versions of faulty or meaningless translations, justifying the Church's stand in regard to the canon of the scriptures,[37] and clarifying the interpretation of the prophets of old by his homilies and commentaries. Upon the death of dear friends, he supplied fitting and generous eulogies—for Nepotian, for Paula, for Pammachius and Marcella.

As old age grew upon him, he undertook tasks that would have taxed the strength and patience of a young man—teaching the classics in a school he started for the children of Roman officials and exiles in Palestine; giving simple, ascetic homilies to his monks and followers in Bethlehem; [38] consoling friends in Italy and Rome after the barbarian devastations of 410, and the raids that continued to upset the dying civilization of which they were part.[39]

But even in death, Jerome left a controversial mark upon the world. For there is a problem with regard to the date of his demise, Cavallera resorting to the findings of the Bollandist Stilting, and placing it in A.D. 419,[40] while Vaccari and most of the modern authorities adhere to the more traditional A.D. 420.[41] Even the resting place of his bones is in doubt. Originally placed in the grotto at Bethlehem, they are now supposed to repose beneath an altar in St. Mary Major's in Rome.[42]

Finally, there is a problem with regard to the estimate of Jerome's character, and the quality of his heroic virtue. The early Protestants pounced upon him for his unrelenting polemic, and his intransigent enmities, as well as for his exact Catholicity in the matter of the Virginity of the Mother of God, the cult of relics, and the practice of bodily mortification; but above all for his having so explicitly championed the primacy of the papacy of Rome. On the other hand, many of his Catholic apologists have tried to deny, or at least to cover up—usually at the expense of some innocent party—his exaggeration and vituperation.

That he was irascible, that he made enemies, that he flayed innocent people as well as heretics is unfortunate. It need not, however, be taken as an indication that the man was not a saint. He was a strong-minded individual, given to the hyperbole of a literary tradition in which he had been educated. But at the same time he was a relentless ascetic who practised mortification incessantly, who lived in the realm of the supernatural, and who helped to form a truly Christian mind in hundreds of his friends and followers.[43]

It was a Renaissance pope who, seeing one of the numerous paintings in which Jerome is portrayed as a cadaverous ascetic, beating his breast with a rock, exclaimed: "Ah Jerome! and had you not been discovered in that attitude, you would not be on the altars of the Church today!"

But the point of the matter is that he was discovered in that

attitude. It is quite evident that the contemplative life to which
he gave himself so assiduously for well over forty years well compensated for his faults, however unpleasant and numerous they
may have been. For, despite the problems regarding his age and
fatherland, his polemics and present resting place, there is no
problem as to the vividness with which he affected the imaginations of the Middle Ages and the Renaissance.[44] Nor is there any
question of the effect his inspiration and memory have had on
the pursuit of Scripture studies, and of the higher life right down
to our own day.

[1] Cf. E. K. Rand, *Founders of the Middle Ages* (Camb., Mass., 1928), 102-134.

[2] Cf. F. Murphy, "The Problem of St. Jerome," *Amer. Eccl. Rev.* 117 (1947), 102-107.

[3] L. de Tillemont, "Saint Jérôme. Abbé Solitaire," in *Mémoires pour servir à l'Histoire ecclés. des six premiers siècles*, t. XII (Paris, 1907), 1-265; 616-662. In solving both the chronological and personality problems connected with the life of St. Jerome, Tillemont is still an indispensable source as attest A. Vaccari (*S. Girolamo, Studi e schizzi*, Rome, 1920) and F. Cavallera (*Saint Jérôme*, Paris, 1922) along with his most recent biographers, A. Penna, (*S. Girolamo*, Rome, 1949) and P. Antin (*Essai sur S. Jérôme*, Paris, 1951).

[4] *De viris illustribus*, 135.

[5] Cf. F. Cavallera, *S. Jérôme* II, 10-11.

[6] Cf. C. Favez, "Trois disciples . . .: Marcella, Fabiola, Paula," *Études de lettres* 12 (1938), 219-232; P. Courcelle, "Paulin de Nole et S. Jérôme," *Revue des études lat.* 25 (1947), 250-280; D. Gorce, *Lectio divina* I. S. Jérôme (Paris, 1925).

[7] Cavallera, II, 67-71; See the map in Fliche et Martin, *Histoire de l'Église*, III (Paris, 1936), 326.

[8] Prosper of Aquitaine, *Chronicon* (ed. T. Mommsen, *Chron. minora*, Berlin, 1894), I, 451.

[9] Jerome was Augustine's senior by seven, at the most ten years.

[10] Cf. Cavallera, "La patrie de S. Jérôme," *Bull. de litt. ecclés.* (1946), 60-64, where he gives an account of the most recent controversy over the birth place of Jerome.

[11] Jer., *Apol. in Rufinum*, I, 30 (PL 23, 422).

[12] Jer., *Ep.* 7, 5.

[13] F. Cavallera, *S. Jérôme* I, 16; II, 10. He dates Jerome's baptism somewhere between 365 and 367, on the supposition that Jerome had then begun his philosophical studies. Cf. Jer., *Apol.* III (*PL* 23, 484-485): "Sed fac me erasse in adulescentia et philosophorum, id est gentilium, studiis eruditum in principio fidei ignorasse dogmata christiana . . ." P. Monceaux (*S. Jérôme*, Paris, 1922, 63) elects for Easter 366, which would make Jerome 19 at the time.

[14] Cf. G. Bardy, *S. Athanase* (Paris, 1924), 44, 48-49.

[15] Ruf., *Apol.* I, 4 (*PL* 21, 544).

[16] Jer., *Chronicle* (ed. Fotheringham), 329. Cavallera dates this entry as of 374 (*S. Jérôme*, I, 20; II, 12–13); but it is Jerome's own dating that seems to be faulty. See F. Murphy, "Melania the Elder: A Biographical Note," *Traditio* 5 (1947), 65–67.

[17] Jer., *Ep.* 3, 3. For the date, see F. Murphy, *op. cit.*, 67.

[18] Cf. H. Delehaye, "La personnalité historique de S. Paul de Thèbes," *Anal. Bolland.* 44 (1926), 64–69; W. A. Oldfather, *Studies in the Text Tradition of St. Jerome's Vitae Patrum* (Urbana, 1942).

[19] Cf. "St. Jerome as an Exegete," below, pp. 35ff.

[20] Cf. "St. Jerome as an Historian," below, pp. 113ff.

[21] Jer., *Libellus de optimo genere interpretandi* (*Ep.* 57, *CSEL* 55, 503ff.); M. Villain, "La quarelle autour d'Origène," *Recherches de sci. religieuse* 27 (1937), 5–37; 165–195.

[22] Cf. "St. Jerome as an Exegete," below, pp. 35ff.

[23] Jer., *Adv. Helvidium.* Cf. P. Courcelle, *Les lettres grecques en occident* (Paris, 1948), 79–81.

[24] Cf. F. Cavallera, *S. Jérôme* I, 123–127.

[25] Cf. F. Murphy, *Rufinus of Aquileia* (Wash., 1945), 68–80.

[26] Jer., *Contra Johannem Hier.* (*PL* 23, 355–396). It was written in the autumn of 396 (cf. Cavallera, II, 94–96).

[27] Jer., *Ep.* 81 (*CSEL* 55, 106); *Ep.* 84 (*ibid.*, 121–134).

[28] Rufinus, *Apol.* (*PL* 21, 541–624).

[29] Jer., *Apol.* I, 1 (*PL* 23, 397): "Ex vestris (Pammachii) et multorum litteris didici, objici mihi in schola Tyranni (Rufini) . . . scribuntur contra me libri. Ingeruntur omnibus audiendi et tamen non eduntur ut et simplicium corda percutiat et mihi facultatem pro me auferant respondendi." *Apol.* III, 3 (*PL* 23, 459): "Illis eruditissimis libris quos antequam legeram confutavi."

[30] Aug. *Ep.* 73, 6–10 (*CSEL* 34, 270ff.). Cf. D. DeBruyne "La correspondance échangée entre Augustin et Jérôme," *Zeit. neut. Wissensch.* 31 (1932), 237–240.

[31] F. Cavallera, *op. cit.* II, 131–135.

[32] Jer., *Praef. ad Ezech.* (*PL* 25, 16–17).

[33] Cf. P. Batiffol, "Les sources de l'Altercatio Luciferiani et Orthodoxi," *Miscel. Geronimiana* (Rome, 1921), 97ff.; Cavallera, S. Jérôme, II, 18–19.

[34] Jer., *Contra Jovinianum* (*PL* 23, 220f.). Cf. P. Courcelle, *Lettres grecques,* 60–62.

[35] Jer., *Contra Vigilantium* (*PL* 23, 339ff.).

[36] Jer., *Contra Pelagianos* (*PL* 23, 495ff.); cf. G. de Plinval, *Pélage. Ses écrits, sa vie et sa réforme* (Lausanne, 1943).

[37] Cf. "St. Jerome and the Canon of the Scriptures," below, pp. 257ff.

[38] Cf. G. Morin, *Les monuments de la prédication de S. Jérôme, Analecta Maredsolana* III (Maredsous, 1903), 2 and 3.

[39] Cf. "St. Jerome and the Barbarians," below, pp. 171ff.

[40] Cf. F. Cavallera, *S. Jérôme* II, 56–63.

[41] A. Vaccari, *S. Girolamo* (Rome, 1920), 133.

[42] Cf. P. Antin, *Essai sur S. Jérôme* (Paris, 1951), 219–220.

[43] Cf. "St. Jerome as a Spiritual Director," below, pp. 143ff.

[44] Cf. "St. Jerome and the Middle Ages," below, pp. 233ff.

The Personality of St. Jerome

FERDINAND CAVALLERA, S.J.

The Personality of St. Jerome *

F<small>OR A STUDY</small> of the character and personality of St. Jerome, the few facts concerning his early life that we do possess actually pose more problems than they solve. Jerome himself would have declared that this is a matter of little importance. Once arrived at the age of manhood, he looked upon Rome, the city in which he had been baptized and in which he had received his literary training, as his true home. Despite bitter memories which his second stay in the Eternal City would engender, and even in spite of the maledictions he would eventually call down upon this "sinful Babylon," Rome impressed itself lovingly in his thoughts and in his heart. This became most evident when news reached him of the sack of the ancient city by Alaric in A.D. 410. A sudden distressful cry escaped him: *"Domine, venerunt gentes in hereditatem tuam!"* (Ps. 78:1). Prostrate with grief, he had to lay aside his pen for several days.

Jerome's vivid imagination and his natural curiosity found in Rome a haven of delight. There he came in contact with teachers of the very first rank to whom, in after years, he frequently pays homage, and who in turn had the satisfaction of discovering in him a most enthusiastic pupil. It is not without good reason that the humanists of the Renaissance recognized in Jerome a man after their own hearts, and heaped upon him fulsome praise.

Roman education was primarily of a literary nature, giving exceptional advantage to the student with a good memory and a spark of genius. Jerome possessed both these aptitudes and was

* Cf. F. Cavallera, *S. Jérôme, sa vie et son oeuvre* (Louvain, 1922) I & II.

soon busy storing his memory with an inexhaustible supply of quotations from the famed poets and prose authors of classical antiquity. This helped to shape his literary tastes and to awaken in him a preference for intellectual pursuits. Exercises in composition and in declamation helped him to assimilate the models upon which he fashioned his literary style. Thus he developed a deep personal charm. It betrays itself in his normal eloquence; it is evident from the ease with which he continually produces neat phrases and finely polished expressions.

Jerome would always be extremely conscious of literary excellence. Nor did he spare himself in assuring his writings, and in particular his letters, a unique stylistic tone. Even in his translations, while striving for exactitude, he seemed ever on the alert for an harmonious phrase, such as would be bound to please the word-conscious reader. This brilliant student of the grammarian Donatus never forgot the lessons taught him by that exacting pedagogue. Jerome became the leading litterateur among the Christian writers of his times. He proved to be the least affected by the literary foibles of the age, and though not completely devoid of current rhetorical fancies, he managed best to overcome the pitfalls that snared his contemporaries.

Jerome was no Augustine. He did surpass the latter in the extent and universality of his knowledge. His curiosity was extensive and far-reaching, but it was the curiosity of the erudite scholar, not that of the profound thinker. Jerome had universal interests; and although he wrote on almost any subject, he did not seem to assimilate that which he read and to make it part of himself. There is no great mind less speculative than his. In spite of his remarkable literary qualities, entire pages of Jerome offer less material for meditation and reflection than several lines of Augustine. In general, Jerome was intent upon exactitude and precision in expressing common theological doctrines. He knew his philosophy well, and was capable of enumerating different species of syllogisms, and of characterizing diverse schools of thought; but he was not interested in philosophy for itself. The orthodoxy of a man of the Church, expressing himself in precise terms, was the extent of his interests.

Long years spent in Rome studying grammar, literature, philosophy and law made a lasting imprint on the man's character. It would be most satisfying could we follow his early career, during which time the exceptional qualities with which he was endowed by divine Providence came to maturity. Jerome had great qualities of the heart—an extreme and delicate sensitivity—which led him into passionate friendships, but which, at the same time, easily betrayed him into jealousy and suspicion. His intimacy could be precious; but it was frequently spoiled by exhibitions of ill humor. Jerome was irascible, and greatly exaggerated petty incidents. His resentments were long-lasting and, despite his disavowals, he did not easily forgive wrongs, real or fancied. He was passionately faithful. His letters are true testimonials of his tender affections, particularly those addressed to Paulinus of Nola, Lucinus, Castricianus, and Heliodorus; and also those to the great Roman ladies whose fidelity consoled him amid the calumnies and deceptions of which he was later victim.

In his letters are preserved a unique gallery of truly great souls. There live eternally a great number of gracious and austere fourth-century figures, each vividly and sympathetically portrayed. In particular, there are his pen pictures of young men and young women taken suddenly to their eternal destiny—a Blesilla or a Nepotianus—reminding us so strongly of the Innocents praised by St. Ambrose. In these immortal pages which do equal honor to their author and his heroes, Jerome reveals the striking kindliness of his own character. He thus brings into focus the moment in which Christianity transformed the soul of antiquity, endowing it with a new and priceless nobility.

But unfortunately, there is another side to Jerome's character. This great soul is given to moments when he is all but unbearable. The education he had received in the schools of rhetoric served but to aggravate his mordant tendencies instead of helping him remedy them. At times, he seemed unable to master himself, or to keep his passions within reasonable limits once his ire had been fully roused. It is only in our day that attention is being given to this aspect of Jerome's character, with many a severe though just word being spoken on the subject.

It is easy, of course, to speak of the man's faults: they are identical with those of the fifteenth- and sixteenth-century humanists. Hence it is imperative not to gloss them over, when attempting to assess the man's achievements, and particularly when dealing with Jerome's judgments of his contemporaries.

The literary habits which Jerome contracted in the course of his studies in Rome, and from which he never seems to have even considered unshackling himself, had done him a bad turn. They have likewise tended to weight the judgment of posterity in his favor. There has always been a great temptation to take at their face value pronouncements and affirmations of Jerome's, which a better knowledge of his literary ethics, and of those of his con-' temporaries, would tend to place in a much different light—his strictures on St. Basil, for example, on St. Ambrose, Rufinus of Aquileia, Melania the Elder, and many another of his less well-known acquaintances, or opponents.

There is reason to believe that Jerome was not unconscious of the difficulties to which a temperament such as his gave rise; the irascibility that accompanied his brillance, his rancors and his favoritisms. He indulged a tendency to jealousy, suspicion, brooding anger, and even a certain self-centeredness. We know that Jerome wrestled with himself to check and control these passions, but we must also recognize the fact that he was often far from successful.

Jerome was never able to rid himself of a tendency to exaggeration, to a lack of exactness, to a penchant for biting satire, to which he was tempted by nature, and which the histrionic exercises of the schoolroom and legal chambers he frequented as a youth but fortified and developed. His striving after the charity of a true Christian was not always powerful enough to overcome these literary extravagances. The older he grew, the more he experienced an ability to overawe and dominate his contemporaries. Contradictions merely tempted him to give free rein to these propensities.

He was forever mixing himself in controversies and ecclesiastical affairs not necessarily concerning him. By his exaggerations, he was constantly magnifying the difficulty of the labors he undertook. He belittled his opponents mercilessly, excoriating their mistakes. Thus he assured himself of victory over them no matter what the cost. He admits this: "Polemics have nothing to do with truth," he enunciates blandly, "their only objective is to conquer, to crush one's adversary." So absorbed, he gave little thought to the niceties of proof. The more one exaggerated, the better: for then, the sooner would one's adversary be forced to yield the field. These were the attitudes met with in the profane authors of the age, and only too often, the same approach is discerned in Jerome. The fact that his enemies were guilty of similar tactics does not excuse him.

It can only be regretted that he yielded to his feelings so frequently in these matters—particularly that, once the controversy had ended, he did not manifest a grandeur of soul. It is most difficult not to regard as the true measure of his feelings certain phrases which should never have escaped his lips: the gross caricatures he drew of Rufinus and of Origen—such, for example, as his announcement that only the death in Sicily of (Rufinus) "the Scorpion" and the "hydra with its multitude of heads" had been capable of awakening him from the torpor into which he had fallen upon hearing of the sack of Rome; and had enabled him to arouse himself sufficiently to take up anew works he had long neglected.

Finally there is the matter of his gross exaggerations in reference to the time and trouble involved in his own productions, which make the task of dealing with his life and times, his likes and dislikes, so difficult.

Yet, all things considered, these are but the blemishes that are bound to manifest themselves in the close scrutiny of a character at once so brilliant and so admirable.

There is, of course, another influence that was paramount in

Jerome's life, and which effectively balanced the traces of a pagan literary spirit upon which he had been nurtured. This was likewise a result of his sojourn in Rome. For the Eternal City had become the true home of his soul, and wielded the final, formative influence that colored his striving for sanctity. Jerome was well aware of this fact. It is he himself who so strongly insisted that it was in Rome that he had been baptized, and first donned the white robes of the catechumen and neophyte. It was there he became a Christian, and there that he had early determined to be, before all else, and if necessary, despite all else, a *vir ecclesiasticus,* solely attached to the Catholic Church. Putting aside all human consideration, he had determined to allow nothing to come before his fidelity to the institution given by Christ to the world. He was to have ever uppermost in his thoughts the doctrinal truths of which that Church alone was the embodiment.

It would be most encouraging to know what were the immediate influences that caused Jerome to seek Baptism, and to be able to trace the steps leading up to that decision. The evidence to be gleaned from his own declarations points merely to his acquaintance with the Christian life as it was practiced in mid-fourth-century Rome. It can be reduced to the high regard he had for the faith of the Romans—already praised by the apostle St. Paul, as a simple but burning expression of belief. As an instance, he cites the thunderous "Amen" that re-echoed through the streets in answer to the prayers of the celebrant.

Jerome has recounted the story of his Sunday pilgrimages to the catacombs in company with some young friends animated with a conviction similar to his own—and the impression of awe that dogged them while stumbling through these dark, sepulchral alleys, lighted only here and there by an occasional ray of sunshine from above. His impressions reveal the extent to which he was struck by the boldness of belonging to a church wherein fidelity to Christ had been manifested with such true courage and generosity.

The sudden death of the Emperor Julian, the Apostate, coming so quickly after his military triumphs, struck Jerome and his contemporaries as evidence of Divine intervention favoring Christianity against the civil power. He makes note of the bitterness with which his pagan associates received news of the Emperor's tragic end. They were jarred by the promptness and dispatch with which God had struck down the renegade.

From several remarks made in the course of letters, and of his Scriptural commentaries, it is evident that Baptism, which Jerome received at the age of twenty, started him on a new life. The boldness of his decision startled him, and though still a good distance from the achievement of his spiritual ideals, he felt himself on the right path.

At the same time, in Rome and Italy a certain slowing-down of Christian vigor could be noticed among the clergy and laity. Later Jerome was to castigate these weaknesses, which were used to justify laxities among many of the faithful. A growing series of superstitious practices met with in the imperial city were hardly conducive to the leading of an interior life. Rather than turning Jerome from fervor, these defections awakened in him—once he had given himself to his Maker completely in the self-surrender of Baptism—a pressing desire to dedicate himself fully to the actualization of this new way of life. While still absorbed in the pursuit of studies and in enjoying the pleasures of learning, he gradually came to give increasing attention to a stricter practice of the Christian life.

Jerome left Rome at the age of twenty, in accordance with an imperial law then obliging foreign students to seek asylum elsewhere. Without knowing whether he was in search of an official position, or simply on a journey of study and travel—we suddenly find him at Treves, copying the works of early and contemporaneous Christian writers for his own and his friends' libraries. It was here in Treves that, together with Bonosus, he first took notice of a growing desire for further perfection, for the attractions of the monastic way of life, a knowledge of which was then making its way through Western Europe. For it was at Treves that he caught the spirit of those youthful imperial officers whose conversion, as narrated by Pontitianus, had so impressed St. Augustine. This is the reason, no doubt, that upon his return to Italy, Jerome joined the "choir of clerics" grouped about Valerianus, Bishop of Aquileia, who appeared to be already "living a heavenly life." Unfortunately, Jerome has not recorded the difficulties that disturbed the blessed there and prompted his own departure from Aquileia. But it is certain that it was for him an instructive experience, and forced him to a decision. He now sought in the East the peace and solitude that he could not find in his own land.

His friendship with Evagrius of Antioch was certainly an element in the matter. But Jerome did not stop with him for very long. We soon find him in the harsh desert of Chalcis "on the very borders between the civilized world and that of the barbarians," seriously assuming his new obligations as an ascetic. Labor, prayer, mortification—by day and by night—fully occupied his time, in the midst of a group of monks of whose affronts he would soon find himself the victim. He was surrounded by a few Latins desirous like himself of fleeing the world and of living exclusively for God. But it is difficult to determine, in the pathetic description he has left of his stay in the desert, just what type of existence he experienced there. He surely had his hours of exaltation, moments when like St. Paul, he tasted the delights of heaven. But there were also days of distress when everything disgusted him —his own self as well as his companions. There were times when temptations assailed him, when the remembrance of his follies in Rome forced themselves in upon him, when the malice and folly of men gave him full cause to make use of his penchant for satire and invective. Peace and forgetfulness, for which he had come into the desert, there fled him. Soon life itself became impossible because of perpetual wranglings. Once again he was forced to modify his plans and change his mode of living.

But this change was more in appearance than in reality. For from now on, he would be continually dedicated to the life of the monk, of the Christian detached from the things of the world. He even tried to avoid the external obligations attached to the life of a priest, which office he was about to take upon himself. Paulinus, the Eustathian Bishop of Antioch, was given this to understand when he offered to ordain Jerome, who had no intention of losing the monastic liberty for which he had fled the world. He knew exactly what he desired, and nothing would turn him from it. He would be a monk until the end of his days, and a monk dedicated to intellectual labor in the service of Christ and of his Church. He would force himself to use the talents he had developed for the glory of the faith he had embraced. By his literary labors he sought to endow the Church with the prestige enjoyed by pagan literature. He would be one of the *scriptores ecclesiastici* whom he would soon carefully address himself to catalogue.

Jerome envisioned various projects which would help him to realize this ideal; but little by little they were put aside in favor of his Scriptural studies, although he never fully abandoned them. Translation and original composition would come side by side. In the desert he had perfected his knowledge of Greek, and had even begun a study of the Hebrew language, with which he was to become more and more familiar.

In Constantinople he embarked on a life of incessant labor. He translated and brought up to his own times the *World Chronicle* of Eusebius. He considered supplementing it with a composition of greater scope in which he would also recount the history of his own times. But Gregory Nazianzen, the bishop whose disciple he had become, succeeded in opening up for Jerome a whole new discipline, still but poorly comprehended in the West. It was the immense Scriptural literature which starts with Origen, and which proved capable of slaking a thirst for the study of the word of God that had begun to possess Jerome. Even though we do not know what prompted him, we find him studying Hebrew most attentively, and passionately reading Origen, and they molded forever his scientific bent. If after long years spent in intimacy with the great Alexandrian, Jerome appeared to forsake Origen and to allow himself to belittle the man whom he had until then so fervently admired, it will be really only in appearance. It is hard to believe that Jerome renounced this great master. In reality he continued in his indebtedness to Origen, from whom he had always helped himself to what was worth while in his exegetical works. Nor had Jerome the power of always being able to reach in his own commentaries that spontaneity, that richness of thought or succinctness of Christian feeling which the homilies of his master Origen still offer us.

Jerome gave himself to the study of Hebrew unremittingly, not allowing the harshness of the language, nor a weakness of the eyes about which he complained, nor even the sarcasm and the incomprehension of his enemies to deter him. It is really a matter of astonishment that the impatient Jerome was able to persevere for so many years in a study which had broken many more patient than he, and which afforded him more mortification than satisfaction.

It was thus that Jerome prepared himself somewhat unwittingly for a task which God had evidently assigned to him—an exhaustive study of the Scriptures—to which he would devote himself with the assistance of all the resources which the original language and the Christian tradition would afford him. From his labors the Western world would profit until the end of time.

The monastic life, however, to which he was so firmly attached, did not and would not ever mean for him—even when settled in his monastery at Bethlehem—a complete break with his contemporaries. He intended to continue interesting himself in all that concerned the life of the Church. He applied himself to this task with that broad curiosity that was his; but also with his *parti pris,* and his passionate way of looking at things. This, of course, hardly permitted him to remain an objective and disinterested spectator of world events. He threw himself avidly into the doctrinal and disciplinary quarrels of the day, making of himself a redoubtable adversary for anyone who, in Jerome's regard, abandoned the only path open to the *vir ecclesiasticus* preoccupied solely with orthodoxy. This is why in 382, no longer able to attend the classes of Gregory Nazianzen at Constantinople when that bishop fled his see in disgust over local intrigues, Jerome went up to Rome in company with Bishops Paulinus and Epiphanius, who were on their way to a Roman council convoked by Pope Damasus.

Jerome returned to Rome with very definite ideas. Age had matured him; and his dealing with diverse peoples and situations had crystallized his opinions both of men and of affairs. He had now two abounding passions: to make of himself an indefatigable apostle of the monastic way of life, and to place within easy reach of all, the sacred books whence he himself had come to such an impressive knowledge of the interior life. He found in Rome a Pope who immediately understood and encouraged him; who by his example and by the confidence he placed in Jerome gave him the assurance of being on the right path; and who finally consoled him amid the incomprehensions, the attacks and calumnies which were speedily heaped upon him. Jerome, of course, brought many of these upon himself by his sharp, pitiless criticisms. In the aged Pope Damasus, a poet of mediocre talent but a man of taste— like Jerome himself, attached to the cult of the martyrs—he found a sympathetic and close friend who stimulated him, and provided the best motivations for his labors and his apostolate.

In return for the services Jerome afforded him in his daily correspondence and in his administration of the Church, Damasus manifested a sincere interest in Jerome's Scripture endeavors. He put questions to him, encouraged him to undertake new research projects, finally insisting that he revise the older versions of the Gospels and produce a text at once elegant and faithful.

Jerome found himself ideally situated. Added to the confidence which the octogenarian Pope placed in him, he received abundant evidence of affection and good will from the more fervent souls then living in the Eternal City. His insistence on a strictly religious way of life for many of the capital's more cultivated citizens met with considerable success. Many of the noble Roman women, strengthened in adversity, took upon themselves the service of God, and were prepared to follow him to the very ends of the promised land.

The Aventine resounded with the chanting of Psalms in their original language. Marcella ceased not to pester him with the difficulties which she encountered in the course of her perusal of the Scriptures. Nor was she alone in this. For others grouped themselves about her—friends of all ages—who also became the disciples of Jerome in the ways of perfection and in the reading of the Sacred Scriptures.

While Damasus lived, this fervor compensated Jerome in good part for the attacks which continued to be heaped upon him, and which incited him to spirited replies. He poured out mordant criticisms against the worldly life of a large number of monks and clerics who had seemingly forgotten the obligations of their state in life. But once again, a tempest gathered and cast its violence upon his work. And by this time, Damasus was no more. Jerome at first made up his mind to face his enemies and critics in Rome, who were accusing him of an irreligious rigor in his guidance of the saintly souls gathered round him. But almost immediately he perceived that a return to Palestine, this time for good, was really the only logical solution. The Rome that he loved as a youth had become a "sinful Babylon." He could do nought but shake its dust from his sandals. In August 385, then, he left his abode in Rome, betook himself to Ostia, and there embarked for the East.

Settled in Bethlehem, he came face to face with a new task, which hitherto he had not considered of much importance. From now on, an increasing number of people would seek him out and commandeer his time, over and above that which he had allotted for the founding of his monastery and the construction of his chapel. Intermingled with his studies and prayers, the direction of his monks and of the religious women who had settled with Paula and Eustochium in a corresponding monastery close by, there arrived pilgrims and travellers, who in increasing numbers came to visit with him for a few days, a few weeks, or even months; who pestered him with their questions and difficulties; spoke to him of the friends whom he left behind; bothered him with their letters; but at the same time kept him abreast of the developments in Christendom. Without soliciting the office, he found himself gradually becoming the spiritual director as well as the moral and intellectual conscience of half the West. More even than Augustine, Jerome, from his cell in Bethlehem, raised his voice, and became the "oracle of the Christian world."

Thus, among the monasteries sought out by the tourists and by the people who came in ever greater numbers to view the places where Christ had lived, suffered and died, Jerome's monastery in Bethlehem, so close to the grotto of the Nativity, naturally evoked the greatest attention. Jerome's own world-wide reputation was an added attraction for the curiosity of the pilgrims. There were also numerous occasions when charity was demanded of the monks, and when other burdens of hospitality crowded in upon this already fully occupied ascetic. Such an occasion was afforded by the sack of Rome under Alaric, in A.D. 410. The evacuees arrived in the East in groups, ruined and penniless, seeking from Jerome, along with bread for sustenance, a word of consolation and hope.

Those who had remained behind in Rome looked with increasing impatience for answers to their letters. Jerome obliged them with long, careful documents, such as they could exhibit with pride to their friends, and which were worthy of the reputation of this great scholar. He had even to make provision that from time to time letters he received from the West should be accompanied by large alms whereby he was enabled to provide for the sustenance of his monasteries, and to undertake expenses necessitated by his own personal labors.

Jerome retained an extensive contact with the Christian world at large, and it can be said without shade of paradox that there was no one better informed of the Christian life in the West and of its vicissitudes than this irascible but kindly monk, who refused to go outside the walls of his own monastery. For visitors and letters reached him from all sides: from Africa, Spain, Gaul, Italy, Pannonia, and even from the lands of the Goths. It was this that enabled him to intervene with competence and even with authority in situations where orthodox doctrine was threatened, or to give assistance to deserving champions of the faith, though not always without exposing himself to danger of grave error. Usually when he felt himself insufficiently informed, he did take the precaution of forwarding mere provisory answers while awaiting better information. It was thus that he was able successively to

curb Helvidius, Jovinian, Vigilantius, and that much more redoubtable adversary, Pelagius. The latter he battled with in Palestine, thus exposing his own household to the possibility of reprisal.
As a result of his anti-Pelagian writings, his monastery was set on
fire and his work threatened with complete ruin. But this, of
course, did not affect his courage or his zeal, despite his already
advanced age. As a matter of fact, it increased his determination.
Not content with taking an energetic and combative position himself, he hurried encouraging missives to other parts of the world
then in danger—to Rome, to Italy, to Africa, summoning the
cooperation of all the orthodox forces, the while stimulating the
activity of his younger auxiliaries, such as Augustine, whom he
recognized with evident satisfaction as an outstanding defender
of the faith.

There is a certain emotional satisfaction in reading through
these final letters of Jerome's, both those already well known and
those recently published by Dom de Bruyne, wherein there is not
the least indication of waning physical powers. To the end, this
energetic defender of the faith fulfilled his self-assumed obligations. He remained the *vir ecclesiasticus*, ever pledged to the protection of the Church.

It would be most satisfying had we greater detail about the
everyday life of Jerome and the routine of his monastery. Postumianus, a friend of Sulpicius Severus, who lived there for a period
of six months, tells us that Jerome never ceased day or night from
his labors, reading and composing. He is eloquent in his admiration of Jerome's virtue and industry. We know that Jerome took
a paternal interest in the well-being of his monks, procuring for
them their daily bread as well as nourishment for their souls. One
of the greatest services which Dom Morin rendered the world
was his publication of the "Monuments of the preaching of
St. Jerome"—those familiar homilies which Jerome addressed to
his charges, without other concern than to fashion them in their
religious obligations and in the practice of the virtues becoming
their state in life. There is here no preoccupation with style; only
a simple language, interspersed with even minor inaccuracies and

colloquial negligences, that appealed vividly to the souls of even the least educated of his monks. It is a manner of speech that was direct and concrete, allowing these souls to profit from his wide experience and his profound knowledge of the Scriptures.

The exhortations that he addressed to outsiders are of a more studied nature. These include his letters on virginity and on widowhood, as well as those touching treatises wherein he tried to convey in Christian terminology the precepts of classical pedagogy for the use of his friends' children at Rome. The little ones, Paula and Pacatula, had been early consecrated to Christ, and Jerome set himself to instruct them, keeping in mind the Christian vocation they had already accepted. Nepotian, Rusticus, Salvina and Demetriada were among those who received admonitions given with an authority begotten of long reflection on the austerities of the Christian way of life. Jerome wrote as one who felt that his age was, more than any other, a most difficult period in which to be bound to live in preparation for eternity.

But this was not his sole occupation. From his own writings, as well as from the *Dialogues of Sulpicius Severus* and the *Lausiac History,* we know that Jerome was involved in personal difficulties in Bethlehem itself and in his own monastery. Too poorly informed to be able to pass judgment, we still cannot but be astonished that Jerome made no apparent effort to soften his intransigeance, and to clothe the demands of Christian life in a more acceptable form. He seems rather to have exaggerated them and to have employed a provocative tone, and formulas that in themselves called forth contradictions. His irascible nature did not soften with the years; and unfortunately, he was not treating with angelic spirits. Even the best of souls do not disguise differences of viewpoint. Community life has just as many difficulties as the life of the solitary. However, such troubles are but trifles in a life dedicated to a great ideal and pursued with vigor in its proper sphere.

Amid these considerations it should be kept in mind that Jerome, despite the multiplicity of his interests, never lost sight of the essential goal to which he was dedicated, and which the Church itself, before all else, had entrusted to him. Jerome gave himself more and more concentratedly to the study of the divine Scriptures through three particular mediums, which differed in value, but gave his work a very realistic turn: his translations, his commentaries, and what one might call his "works of introduction," which were destined to encourage the study of the Sacred Scriptures by minimizing difficulties and rendering various aids in keeping with the taste of the time. Alongside Origen, he is definitely one writer who did everything possible to make the sacred writings accessible. For this he deserves the gratitude of the ages.

We know, however, that in so frequently referring to the criticism which his Scriptural works provoked, Jerome was inventing or at least exaggerating rather strongly. The same is true of the lack of interest which he says from time to time greeted his pursuit of the *veritas hebraica*. In the course of his long years, it became a rhetorical figure which he employed to give added value to his work, and to attract the sympathy of his readers. Unfortunately, however, it was not entirely imagined. Accustomed as we are to his exaggerations, we must frequently check his veracity. The polemics with Rufinus, and those with Augustine, serve as a counter-gauge, and show clearly that, on some points, Jerome saw himself the target of misunderstandings and of attacks which can be easily pointed out as fancied. This also explains in part his attitude toward the Septuagint, which is, to say the least, astonishing. Jerome pursued that work with an increasing virulence which has its counterpart only in the extraordinary credit given it by others, and particularly by Augustine—a credulity on the latter's part out of all proportion to his usual insight.

In Augustine, Jerome had to oppose a strongly rooted prejudice. Occupied with practical problems, Augustine developed a singular and disconcerting theory in favor of the Septuagint. It is here that one can vividly appreciate the difference in intellectual temperament between the two men. Jerome is empirical, attending to the least nuance of data, constantly impelled by his translations to pore over the texts and compare them with other versions, to take into account and to underline the multitude of differences, however small, in which the Septuagint is opposed to that Hebrew version which commanded his confidence. Augustine's approach, on the other hand, is primarily speculative, dilating on the possible rather than on the actual. It takes him a long time to renounce belief in the "ancient city of the cells," where the seventy translators were supposed to have found themselves immured. Even then, the Septuagint did not lose his confidence altogether. To safeguard its position, Augustine constructed that disconcerting theory of a double Scriptural truth: that contained in the original text, and that complementary, inspired and designed by the Divine author specially for those passages wherein the Septuagint runs divergent to the original. His endeavor to cast doubt upon the utility of Jerome's work had its equivalent only in Jerome's determination to continue that same work. It demonstrates the power of Jerome's determination in pursuing so tenaciously an objective which, he judged correctly, would succeed as an accomplishment of the highest importance.

It is but proper to remark that in this arduous but eventually victorious endeavor, Jerome was sustained by numerous friends. They manifested their encouragement, not the least in the contribution of necessary financial resources—for both stenographers and supplies—without which he would not have been able to bring his project to a close. Thanks to his perseverance in this exhausting labor, Jerome was able to enrich his contemporaries with a Latin translation made from the original Hebrew which left them nothing to envy in the countries of the East, where there already existed good vernacular versions. On the contrary, his translation was not only a faithful one—in spite of certain peculiarities and of a few passages where Jerome, principally because of apologetic endeavors, renders *un coup de pouce*—but it was elegant and easy to read. This gave it an incontestable advantage over the older Vulgate, which was crude, and often obscure. This is the service then—both considerable and enduring—that the *Doctor Maximus in interpretandis Scripturis* has rendered the Christian people of all times.

As a commentator Jerome need not be looked upon very

favorably. He would, I believe, have fared much more admirably, had he confined himself to the terrain of the literal sense. His commentaries on St. Matthew, and on Isaias in the books dedicated to Bishop Amabilis, as well as on Daniel, are good instances of this. In these works Jerome shows himself fully at ease, explaining the true sense of a word or of a phrase, giving proper value to a passage, making things clear by means of a simile or of a comparison, and offering explanations with the aid of other sciences, both sacred and profane. But Jerome was a man of his age. In all domains, in philosophy as well as in religion, allegory was the mode. No truth was considered fully expressed unless it had been presented under some form which would oblige the reader to search out its symbol from behind a great display of effort and erudition.

Jerome had not wasted the time he spent reading Origen, or listening to his disciples, Gregory Nazianzen, Gregory of Nyssa, and Didymus. If he was convinced, as they were, that the beginning of all real exegesis is in the literal sense, he was equally persuaded, along with them, that thence one should hasten to abandon the *vilitas litterae* for a contemplation of the spiritual meaning, which alone was worthy of arresting one's thought. Like these scholars, and perhaps even a bit more artificially than many of them, he took great pride in the complicated ensemble of symbols and metaphors with which he fathomed the spiritual meaning. His interest in the Hebrew peoples as a study of history was only secondary. It absorbed him only insofar as he was there able to discover, recounted in advance with more or less verisimilitude, the history of the Church in its warfare with the devil, or with heretics, as symbolized by the hereditary enemies of Israel. He found little in his dealings with Bishop Amabilis or with Eusebius of Cremona that would lead him to a different way of doing things. The commentary he had composed on the Book of Daniel, written as a plain, brief essay, was so badly received, he informs us, that he hastened to return to the other type of commentary, so tiring and so diffuse for us, but so characteristic, for example, of his studies of the great and minor Prophets.

I have remarked that Jerome was particularly interested in the Old Testament. He had, however, actually begun his mature Scriptural works with a commentary on four of the Epistles of St. Paul. But he never returned to them. This was due perhaps to a growing penchant for the Hebrew Bible. Perhaps it was because he felt himself less at ease with the thought of St. Paul, and little prone to search out the profound meaning behind the doctrines which the great Apostle of the Gentiles propounds.

Rufinus, at almost the very start of their quarrels, pointed out another characteristic. Despite Jerome's vigorous denial, his former friend's judgment must be sustained. Jerome's first Scriptural commentary is much more influenced by the writings of Origen than its author ever dreamed. In fact, in this treatise the *vir ecclesiasticus* suffered an unbelievable eclipse, with Jerome expressing dogmatic opinions he simply could not sustain.

Of all his works the most useful is his adaptation of a *Geography of Palestine* composed by Eusebius, which Jerome enriched with worthwhile annotations that are still consulted for reference. But his *Onomastica*—or *Book of Hebrew Names*—is above all a proof of the then immature state of the science of etymology and the errors into which false or badly applied principles can lead. In transcribing and translating lists of proper names in the Bible, arranged alphabetically according to the Registers and interpreted by means of Hebrew roots, even where it is a question of Greek or Latin words, Jerome, who from the first manifested an inclination for this type of interpretation, as the conclusion of his Commentary on the Epistle to Philemon testifies, cannot clear himself of his own charge: *videndum satis absurde*. Nonetheless, he continued to indulge this *jeu d'esprit*, assuring its transmission to posterity. Even down to recent date, Bible editors took delight in this type of etymology, as is attested by the lists that regularly accompanied Latin editions of the Bible.

Such is the work of Jerome, and such is the man with his virtues and his defects, his weaknesses and his greatness. Nothing remains now but to gather the evidence of his last days. His health had been in decline for a number of years. He suffered the infirmities of old age. But what affected him most were the deaths he encountered on all sides: Paula the elder had long since died and Eustochium had recently joined her. Thus to Jerome was left the care of young Paula, who would constantly remind him of her aunt and her grandmother—a rather heavy charge for a young girl of twenty years.

Instead of the peace and quiet Jerome had looked forward to, he was weighed down with material cares.

Jerome's bodily powers gradually weakened, but his spirit seemed to grow in vigor. Until he breathed his last, he desired to bring to the Church the testimony of his devotion and of his fidelity. He died leaving to all the example of a life consecrated exclusively to God, sanctified by detachment from the world, by prayer and austerity, by persevering travail and by charity—magnificent qualities, and great virtues—merits made greater by the very obstacles which Jerome had to overcome in his own violent and difficult temperament. He thus appears a great benefactor of the Church and of the Christian people—a model for whoever desires to serve the cause of God and to bring to mankind the benediction of the Son of God.

St. Jerome as an Exegete

LOUIS N. HARTMANN, C.SS.R.

St. Jerome as an Exegete

FOR MANY REASONS the writings of St. Jerome have won just fame for their author. He is renowned as a master of Latin prose, a vigorous controversialist, an ardent advocate of Christian asceticism, and as a source of much useful historical information. But it is especially as a Scripture scholar that Jerome has won immortal laurels, and earned for himself not only the title of "Doctor of the Church" but that of *Doctor Maximus sacris Scripturis explanandis*—its greatest doctor in interpreting Sacred Scripture. This honor has been conferred upon him primarily because of his great masterpiece, his *monumentum aere perennius,* the translation of the Hebrew Bible into Latin, which not only became the "commonly accepted," or *Vulgate,* Bible in the Western Church, but was solemnly proclaimed by the Council of Trent as the "authentic" Bible of the Latin Church, "because it was approved by centuries of use in the Church itself." [1]

Dealing with Jerome as an exegete, as we are in this essay, we are not directly concerned with the Latin Vulgate. Yet after all, we cannot do full justice to St. Jerome as an exegete if we ignore his translation of the Sacred Scriptures. For every translation, unless it is a merely mechanical word-for-word rendering of the original, must be based on and include an interpretation of the mind of the original author. A translation is essentially a condensed form of exegesis. It sets forth the result of a process of reasoning about the mind of the author, without discussing the critical reasons for this conclusion. Jerome himself, as an expert translator, was fully aware of this truth. Thus in the preface to his translation of the Book of Job from the Hebrew, he tells us

37

that he hired a Jewish rabbi to give him an exegesis of this difficult Book, and adds, "I do not know if I gained anything from his
instruction. I only know that I cannot translate anything unless
I first understand it." [2]

I. Jerome's Exegetical Works

Before undertaking a critical judgment of the nature and value
of Jerome's achievements as an exegete, it seems well to enumerate
his principal works in the field of Biblical studies. By treating them
in the chronological order of their production we can note a certain progress in his aims and methods.

It is hard to say what external influences may have first led
the young Roman scholar into this particular field of ecclesiastical
studies, for which he was so eminently qualified by natural talents
and disposition.[3] At any rate, shortly after he finished his course
in the profane classics at Rome, he set out to apply his newly
acquired literary skill to the composition of an exegesis of Abdias,
the shortest Book of the Old Testament. Published surreptitiously
by one of his friends, this juvenile production, which indulged in
the then very popular allegorical style of interpretation, won for
its youthful author no little notoriety. But no trace of it now
remains, except perhaps inasmuch as parts of it may be incorporated in the saint's later commentary on this Prophet. In fact,
it is only from the prologue of this much more mature work,
written about a quarter of a century later, that we learn of the
opuscule of his early years. "In my youth," he there confesses to
his shame, "led by an ardent love for the study of the Scriptures,
I made an allegorical interpretation of the Prophet Abdias, the
historical sense of which I did not then understand." [4]

Only after several years of preparatory study in the East did
Jerome again produce a work on Sacred Scripture. But this time
he followed the safer course of confining himself to translating
the works of others. At Constantinople in 380–381, while attending the lectures of St. Gregory of Nazianzus, and no doubt under
the influence of this great admirer of the Alexandrian school of

exegesis, Jerome translated several homilies of Origen into Latin: fourteen on Jeremias and fourteen on Ezechiel,[5] nine on Isaias,[6] and two on the Canticle of Canticles.[7]

Apparently not fully satisfied with Origen's explanation of Isaias's vision of the Seraphim (Is. 6:1-8), Jerome published his own treatise on this passage.[8] This is his earliest Biblical work, apart from translations, that has come down to us, and it already shows the exegetical method that he was to follow more or less closely in all his subsequent work: a large dependence on previous commentators combined with a certain independent judgment of his own. Here, for instance, he borrowed freely from Origen; yet, at least in one important point (the interpretation of the two Seraphim as signifying God the Son and the Holy Ghost), he rejected the exegesis of the Alexandrian sage. This rejection was to prove very useful to him when, some years later, he was accused of being a blind follower of Origen (cfr. *Ep.* 84, 3). It is also to be noted that, although Jerome already possessed a good working knowledge of Hebrew, and used it occasionally in discussing the meaning of certain words, still his interpretation in this as well as in his other writings of the next few years is based not on the Hebrew text but on the Greek Septuagint, in the form of the Old Latin Version. To this he often adds a Latin translation of the later Greek versions—of Aquila, Theodotion and Symmachus.

During his stay in Rome from 382 to 385 Jerome produced no major work on the Scriptures. Yet several interesting little treatises, in the form of letters, show that during this time he was not occupied solely with the spiritual direction of pious ladies or with secretarial work for his good friend Pope St. Damasus. These minor works treat of the meaning of certain foreign words that had been left untranslated in the Latin Version, such as *Hosanna* (*Ep.* 20), *Alleluja, Amen, Maran Atha* (*Ep.* 26), *Diapsalma* (*Ep.* 28), *Ephod, Theraphim* (*Ep.* 28), and of the letters of the Hebrew alphabet in connection with the Alphabetic Psalms (*Ep.* 30). To this period also belongs his interpretation of the Parable of the Prodigal Son (Luke 15:11-32; *Ep.* 21), of Psalm 126 (*Ep.* 36), as well as his adverse criticism of the commentary of

St. Reticius of Autun on the Canticle of Canticles (*Ep.* 37). This last-mentioned epistle is noteworthy as one of the earliest examples, in the field of Biblical studies, of a "book review" (in quite a modern sense) by an eminently qualified critic. Here Jerome likewise states his own views on what constitutes good exegesis. After giving some examples of the absurd interpretations contained in this book under review, Jerome concludes with this remark: "Innumerable are such defects, which, it seems to me, make his commentary worthless. It is indeed written in an ornate style, fluent with Gallic pomposity. But what has this to do with exegesis? The prime concern of an exegete is not to show off his own eloquence but to help the reader understand the sense of the original author." [9]

It was also during this period that Jerome undertook, at the request of Pope Damasus, a work which was destined to have a profound influence upon all the following generations in the Western Church and, at the same time, no small influence upon the type of his own subsequent work. This was his revision of the Old Latin Version of the New Testament, which he made in accordance with the best Greek manuscripts at his disposal. Even though his zeal in correcting the *Vetus Latina* seems to have gradually slackened, so much so that it is uncertain whether his revision reached beyond the four Gospels, still this work—our present Vulgate New Testament—is on the whole based on an excellent critical text of the original Greek Gospels and is rightly considered one of the glories of the Latin Church. His first revision of the Old Latin Psalter, made at this time, following a few Septuagint manuscripts, proved less successful and never gained much popularity outside the Eternal City. It is now used only at St. Peter's, Rome, and in a few odd texts of the Roman Missal and Breviary. Hence it is usually referred to as "the Roman Psalter." [9a]

These labors on the text of the Bible gave Jerome a deeper realization of the value of textual criticism and the importance of getting back to the original texts. Therefore, when he left Rome shortly after the death of Damasus and became a voluntary exile in Palestine for the rest of his life, he spent his first years there in perfecting his knowledge of Hebrew and in preparing a better Latin edition of the Old Testament. Apparently because he did not yet feel competent to make an original Latin translation direct from the Hebrew, or at least because he did not yet wish to run the risk of meeting with opposition to so novel a translation, he at first undertook only a revision of the Old Latin Version of the Old Testament, made in accordance with Origen's Hexaplar Text. This latter he thought to be superior to the common Septuagint text from which the Old Latin had been made. How far he proceeded in this work it is difficult to say, but he seems to have published the revised text of only Paralipomenon (lost, except the Preface [10]), the so-called Books of Solomon—Proverbs, Ecclesiastes, Canticle of Canticles (the Preface [11] and a few fragments preserved), Job [12] and the Psalms. This second revision of the Psalms, now usually called "the Gallican Psalter" from its early popularity in Gaul, is still the Psalter of the official Latin Vulgate.[13] Despite its many defects, it has been used in the Roman Breviary up to the present, although now the new, much better Latin Psalter, recently made directly from the original texts and issued by the Holy See in 1945, may be used in its place.

During these first years in Palestine, 386–390, Jerome was still so faithful a follower of Origen that he interrupted his Hebrew studies in order to translate, at the request of Paula and Eustochium, thirty-nine Homilies of Origen on certain passages in St. Luke's Gospel.[14] Shortly before doing this work, and likewise as a favor for these same ladies, he composed his only commentaries on the Pauline Epistles, in the order of Philemon, Galatians, Ephesians and Titus.[15] These commentaries also depend to a large extent on Origen's work and, except for the one on Philemon, abound in allegorical interpretations.

A much more original work is the *Commentary on Ecclesiastes*,[16] which Jerome published about the year 389. It marks an important milestone in the history of exegesis, inasmuch as it is the first original Latin commentary to take cognizance of the Hebrew text. The text which Jerome here comments on is not indeed his definitive translation of Ecclesiastes that is now found

in our Vulgate. This final rendering of the text he had not yet
made at this date. The text of this commentary is basically that
of the Old Latin Version (an early translation made by an unknown author from the Greek Septuagint) but corrected according to the Hebrew text. "I must briefly note," says the exegete
in his Preface, "that here I am not following any authority [*i.e.*,
any standard text] but, while making use of the Hebrew, I am
accommodating myself rather to the customary readings of the
Septuagint [*i.e.*, the Old Latin], at least in those passages which
do not differ too much from the Hebrew. Sometimes I also record
the readings of Aquila, of Symmachus and of Theodotion, in
order not to scare away the reader's interest by too novel a text of
my own, although on the other hand I would not want to go
against my conscience by following up these rivulets of conjectures
at the cost of thereby abandoning the source of truth [*i.e.*, the
Hebrew text]."

About this time, probably in 390, Jerome published his very
interesting *Liber Hebraicarum Quaestionum in Genesim.*[17] The
title "Hebrew Questions" hardly gives an adequate idea of the
nature of this valuable work. We might describe it as a series of
notes made on various short passages of the Book of Genesis while
the author was studying the Hebrew text of this Book in preparation for his new Latin version direct from the original. These
notes, therefore, are intended partly to show where and why the
Old Latin needed correction, and partly to explain the meaning
of those proper names which could not well be translated, but
whose etymology is alluded to in the text. But besides this, these
"Hebrew Questions" also record the current Jewish exegesis of
various passages of this Book. This work therefore forms a veritable treasure-house of curious Rabbinical interpretations. Many
of these were later on preserved in the Talmud, but others are
not recorded elsewhere. It is a pity that Jerome did not complete
and publish his "Hebrew Questions" on the other Books of the
Old Testament.[18]

While engaged on this task, he issued two other works which
he hoped would prove useful to Latin readers of the Bible: his

Book on Hebrew Names and his *Book on the Sites and Names of Hebrew Places*.[18a] The former, which was the main source whence the Latin writers of the Middle Ages drew their knowledge of the meaning of Hebrew proper names, has now not much more value than a museum curio. It attempts to give the meaning of almost all the proper names occurring in the Old and the New Testament, but, based largely on the works of Philo and Origen, it offers in most cases mere fanciful and popular etymologies devoid of scientific exactness.

On the other hand, his work on Biblical place-names will always retain a certain scientific value. Many of the identifications with modern sites are indeed somewhat inexact, and a few are far from correct. But they represent the traditions of the fourth-century Christians and Jews who lived in Palestine, and as such they must be taken into consideration by any modern author who would write on the topography of ancient Palestine. This work is, of course, essentially a translation of the Greek *Onomastikon* of Eusebius of Caesarea. But Jerome, who was well acquainted with Palestinian geography from his long sojourn and many journeys in the Holy Land, added his own corrections, additions and observations to a fairly appreciable degree.[19]

The next fifteen years, from 391 to 406, formed the most productive period in the industrious life of Jerome. During these years he published his new Latin translation of all the Books of the Hebrew Bible, besides writing numerous commentaries and shorter treatises.

This is not the place to treat either of the great merits or the small defects of this justly famous version of the Sacred Scriptures, which had such a profound influence on all later ages in the Latin Church. It is sufficient to point out here, in passing, that this work won its subsequent popularity not merely because of the illustrious name of its author, but more particularly because of its own intrinsic value. We must not forget that it was undertaken without any official authorization on the part of the Church, and even in the face of no slight opposition from high-standing ecclesiastics who, like St. Augustine,[20] feared that it would undermine the value of the Septuagint—which, after all, had the approval of the Apostles. Augustine felt that it would, at the same time, disturb the simple faith of ordinary Christians, whose Old Latin Version seemed to them the *ipsissima verba Dei*. Others, from less sincere motives, even accused Jerome of wanting to Judaize the Church of Christ.[21] Yet within a few centuries his new translation gradually succeeded in supplanting all the Protocanonical Books of the *Vetus Latina* Old Testament, with the sole exception of the Psalms. The "Gallican Psalter" still remains the Psalter of the Vulgate, while the superior translation of the Psalms which Jerome made directly from the Hebrew has come down to us in only a few manuscripts.[22] Of the seven Deuterocanonical Books —those not found in the Hebrew Canon of the Sacred Scriptures —he translated only two; the other five have been carried over into our Vulgate just as they were in the Old Latin Version. Even the translation of the two, Tobias and Judith, which Jerome made from the Aramaic merely to satisfy the request of his friends, was done in a halfhearted and hasty manner.

While Jerome was engaged in the publication of this new translation of the Scriptures, he also composed commentaries on each of the twelve minor Prophets.[23] These commentaries, in which his new Latin Version is used as the basic text to be explained, are rightly reckoned among the most valuable of his exegetical works. The numerous difficulties in these short but often very obscure Prophetical Books offered the exegete of Bethlehem a broad field on which to display his vast erudition. Of much less worth is his *Commentary on St. Matthew's Gospel*.[24] It is rather a series of brief notes on the Gospel than a commentary in the strict sense. According to its prologue, this work was written at the urgent entreaty of his friend Eusebius of Cremona, in the short space of two weeks while Jerome was recuperating from a three-months illness.

Of a similar nature of brief notes, or *scholia,* are his *Commentarioli in Psalmos,* which he wrote sometime before 402.[25] This long-lost work was discovered by Dom G. Morin and published by him in 1895.[26] To the same learned Benedictine we owe our knowledge of St. Jerome as a homilist; he published seventy-four of his homilies on the Psalms, ten on St. Mark's Gospel, and ten on other passages of the Bible.[27] These homilies were preached to the monks at Bethlehem in the years 392–401.

During these same fifteen years Jerome wrote, in the form of epistles, many smaller treatises on Biblical subjects, such as "On the Study of Sacred Scripture" (*Ep.* 53), in which he not only exhorts Paulinus to devote himself to a deeper knowledge of the Bible but also rejects with no little vehemence the pretensions of rank amateurs and dilettantes to usurp the authority of specialists in Scripture. Another valuable opuscule of his is his essay "On the Right Way to Make a Translation" (*Ep.* 57), in which he justifies the sane use of free translation as long as it is faithful to the thoughts of the original author. Of less value, because of the excessive use of allegorical interpretations, are his treatises "On the Vestments of the High Priest" (*Ep.* 64), "On the Judgment Rendered by Solomon" (*Ep.* 74), and "On the Forty-two Stations of the Israelites in the Desert" (*Ep.* 78). Some of the questions he treats sound very odd: "How could Solomon and Achaz beget children while still mere boys themselves?" (*Ep.* 72), and "Was Melchisedech an ordinary mortal or was he an apparition of the Holy Ghost?" (*Ep.* 73).

To several of his friends Jerome sent interpretations of various passages of Scripture which they had asked him to explain. Thus, for Amandus (*Ep.* 55) and for Marcella (*Ep.* 59) he explains certain difficulties in the New Testament. Even two Goths, Sunnia and Fretela, send him their Scripture doubts, and for their benefit he writes a long and interesting discussion of the textual differences between the Septuagint-Old Latin and the Hexaplar-"Gallican Psalter" in 178 places of the Psalms (*Ep.* 106).[27a]

We are all the more astonished that Jerome could produce so much in the field of Scripture studies during these fifteen years (391–406), when we recall that most of his controversial writings on other subjects likewise fall in this same period. Thus, his well-known dispute with Rufinus over the accusation of Origenism, which began in 393, covers roughly this same time.

It is sometimes asserted that, on account of this controversy, the year 393 forms an important turning-point in Jerome's attitude toward the great Alexandrian theologian. It is true that his ardent admiration for Origen's exegetical writings did cool off considerably during this period of his life. No doubt the anti-Origenist controversy had something to do with this. But this point can be easily exaggerated.[28] Even before 393 Jerome was not an entirely uncritical follower of Origen's exegesis, and at least on one fundamental principle of interpretation he never followed him at all: on the Alexandrian's strange notion that certain passages of Scripture are devoid of any literal meaning, having only an allegorical or spiritual sense.[29] On the other hand, Jerome continued to employ Origen's allegorical method of interpretation to the very end of his life, albeit with ever decreasing frequency.

During the last fifteen years of his life (406–420) Jerome's Biblical works are much less numerous. This is only in part due to the aged scholar's failing health and to the disturbed circumstances of the time, when his monastery at Bethlehem fell victim to the fury of the Pelagians and the ravages of several waves of barbarian invasions. The main reason why his published works are comparatively few during these years is that they are mostly of much greater length and more carefully written. It was at this time that he crowned his exegetical masterpiece, the *Opus Prophetale,* as he himself calls it, with his great commentaries on the four major Prophets: Daniel [30] in 407, Isaias [31] in 408–410, Ezechiel [32] in 410–415, and Jeremias [33] in 415–420. This last commentary had covered only the first thirty-two of the fifty-two chapters of Jeremias when the hand of death wrote "Finis."

Likewise, relatively few of Jerome's minor works date from this last period of his life. We have only his discussion of the textually disputed passage in I Corinthians 15:51, on the resurrection of the body (*Ep.* 119), his answers to various questions on the New Testament proposed by Hedibia (*Ep.* 120) and Algasia (*Ep.* 121), his allegorical interpretation of "The Promised Land" (*Ep.* 129), and his eloquent exposition of Psalm 89 (*Ep.* 140). This last opuscule, written about a year before his death, forms a fitting close to his long laborious life, for this magnificent Psalm contemplates the brevity and misery of human life, and when our septuagenarian exegete writes here so touchingly of the sorrows and troubles of "decrepit old age," he may well be speaking from personal experience.

II. Influences that Affected Jerome's Exegesis

That the writings of St. Jerome exercised a far-reaching influence on all subsequent generations in the Church is generally recognized and need not be elaborated here. But it is perhaps not so well known how deeply he himself was affected by the Biblical scholars of the preceding ages as well as of his own age. It is sometimes said that Jerome was a self-educated man.[34] This is no doubt true enough in the sense that he received his Biblical education more from private reading than from oral instruction. But he also attended the lectures of various experts in the Scriptures, and he himself insists that he was not a "self-taught" man. In *Ep.* 84, 3 he gives us such a detailed account of his schooling in the Biblical sciences that this passage is well worth quoting here in its entirety.

When Rufinus and others, who "loved him so much that they could not even be heretics without him," accused him of having had teachers who were themselves of dubious orthodoxy, Jerome (about the year 400) wrote this *apologia* of his education:

As a young man, I was carried away with a wonderful zeal for learning, but I did not teach myself, as certain ones presume to do. At Antioch I frequented the lectures of Apollinaris of Laodicea and I was much devoted to him. But, even though he instructed me in the Holy Scriptures, I never accepted his contentious doctrine about the mind. Later on, though my hair was already becoming gray, which is more becoming in a professor than in a pupil, I nevertheless journeyed to Alexandria and attended the lectures of Didymus. In many respects I gratefully acknowledge my debt to him. What I did not know I learnt; what I already knew I did not lose under his instruction. Then, when people thought I would finally call a halt to my schooling, I came back again to Jerusalem and Bethlehem, and there had Bar-anina teach me at night. With what trouble, too, and at what a cost! For he was afraid of the Jews and used to come to me like another Nicodemus.

All of these men I frequently refer to in my works. The tenets of Apollinaris are, of course, opposed to those of Didymus. Should each faction, therefore, pull me to their own opposing side because I admit that both of these men were my teachers? Moreover, if it is right to hate any men and despise any race, I am certainly a bitter enemy of the circumcised. For even to the present day they persecute our Lord Jesus Christ in their synagogues of Satan. Why then should any one throw it up to me, that I had a Jew as my teacher? Or will this certain someone be bold enough to quote the letter I addressed to Didymus as to a master? What a great crime for a pupil to call a learned old man "Master"!

Jerome had other instructors besides these whom he mentions in this letter, particularly "the very eloquent" St. Gregory of Nazianzus, of whom he says, "He was my teacher, and I learnt from his explanations of the Scriptures." [35] But the Nazianzene, like the two other great Cappadocians, Basil and Gregory of Nyssa, was more of an orator and theologian than an exegete. The chief lesson that Jerome learnt from him was probably that Origen's allegorical interpretations were indeed to be used and imitated, but with prudence and sobriety.

However, the other three teachers mentioned above were representatives of the three great exegetical schools of that time: Apollinaris (c. 390) of the Antiochian school, Didymus (c. 398) of the Alexandrian school, and Bar-anina of the Rabbinical school of the Palestinian Jews. Almost every page of Jerome's commentaries shows the influence of these three schools on his own type of exegesis. Hence, in order to have a full appreciation of his commentaries, it is necessary to know something of the aims and methods of these masters who taught him both by their words and by their writings. We will, therefore, first give a brief account of the main tenets of the two famous Patristic schools of exegesis, the Alexandrian and the Antiochian, and show the extent of Jerome's indebtedness to each of them; then we will treat of the part which the Palestinian rabbis played in molding his attitude towards the Scriptures.

Influence of the Alexandrian and Antiochian Exegetes.

All the ancient writers on the Bible, whether orthodox or heretical, Christian or Jewish, considered the Sacred Scriptures to be the word of God. The only exceptions were a few pagan adversaries, such as Celsus and Porphyry. This is, of course, an incontrovertible fact. But in our own age of rationalism it is often overlooked. Only within the last century or two have men who are otherwise not hostile to the Bible and its teachings treated this Book as if it were a merely human document. Modern rationalistic exegesis, therefore, is concerned solely with the investigation of what the human authors of the Bible meant by their words. It denies any Divine influence on them. Even the practice of some modern exegetes who still believe in the inspiration of the Scriptures has at times been tainted by this viewpoint.

On the contrary, all ancient exegetes laid great stress on the Divine message contained in the Sacred Scriptures. They held that God employed the human authors as His instruments, for the purpose of revealing to men His will and the knowledge of supernatural truths. Therefore, since God, as well as man, is the author of this Book, the concern of the exegete is to search out beneath the more or less obvious sense of the human author's words the deeper meaning intended by the divine author. Following the example of St. Paul, who often distinguished between the "letter" and the "spirit" of Holy Writ, Christian exegetes commonly called these two senses of Scripture the "literal" and the "spiritual." It is only in regard to the relationship between these two senses and in the method of deducing the spiritual from the literal sense that exegetes differed among themselves. This difference forms the chief distinction between the two famous schools of exegesis that had their headquarters respectively at Alexandria in Egypt and at Antioch in Syria.[36]

At the risk of oversimplification, we may sum up this difference by means of modern terminology by saying that, according to the Antiochians, whatever God wished to reveal to us in the Scriptures was also understood in some way or other by the inspired authors, and therefore any higher meaning given to a passage must be solidly based on the direct, literal meaning of this passage. According to the Alexandrians, on the other hand, God's message to us in the inspired Books often surpassed the understanding of the human author of these Books; and therefore, since God's meaning need not be tied down too rigorously to the direct sense as intended by the human authors, a passage may often be interpreted in a figurative way ("tropologically" or "allegorically" they called it), so that we may arrive at the fuller, higher meaning intended by God. Hence, while the Alexandrians did not entirely neglect the literal sense and in fact often made useful contributions to Biblical philology, grammar, etc., their special emphasis was on the elaboration of the allegorical or mystical interpretations. This art they developed to an astounding degree of ingenuity and beauty.

The Antiochians also admitted in many passages a meaning deeper than that contained in the superficial sense of the words. But they protested that this higher or "typical" sense, as they called it, must either be derived from the primary, obvious sense by a strict process of reasoning, or must be proved through the testimony of some other passage of Scripture to have this higher meaning. Even here, where, for instance, the New Testament interprets some event in the Old Testament as a "type" or prefiguration of something in the New Testament, they held that the Old Testament author himself foresaw this deeper meaning in his words through a certain vision, or *theoria,* granted him by God.[37] Thus, the typical sense was for them just as much the literal sense as was the direct, obvious meaning of the words. The latter, as distinct from the typical sense, they usually called *historia,* or the historical sense. But both senses they considered as the "literal" or true sense of Scripture, inasmuch as both are founded on the *words* of the inspired author *in the meaning intended by him.* Hence, they were opposed to the Alexandrian practice of reading into an earlier Book of the Bible ideas explicitly stated only in a later Book. They thus laid the base for the doctrine of the Development of Revelation, and so distinguished the Old Testament from the New, and older Books of the Old Testament from more recent Books.

Both schools had certain advantages as well as disadvantages. The Alexandrian method served admirably the purpose of edification, for it gave spiritual import to many parts of the Bible, especially of the Old Testament, which otherwise could hardly be distinguished from profane literature. But it also gave too much room to the free play of the imagination, and where a brilliant genius like Origen was deceived by some erroneous opinion of Neo-Platonic philosophy, he could too easily be misled into drawing certain heretical conclusions from what he believed to be the allegorical sense of the Scriptures.

The Antiochian method, on the other hand, was much more scientific. It was really based on the solid principles of sound reason. But here too, where there is question of the super-rational truths of a Divine revelation, mere unaided reason can be as dangerous as free imagination. Overemphasis on rational arguments can make a man a rationalist. Of course, none of the Antiochian exegetes, not even Theodore of Mopsuestia, the most erratic of them all, was a rationalist in the modern sense of one who denies the supernatural. But several of them did go astray. The excessive rationalism of Antioch begot the Nestorians, just as the exaggerated piety of Alexandria produced the Monophysites.

St. Jerome, as we have seen, came in contact with both methods of exegesis and was influenced by both. As a wise eclectic, he endeavored to draw the best from each school while avoiding the excesses of both.

To the Antiochians he owed, at least in part, his theoretic principle that the direct, literal sense of Scripture is first to be investigated and explained, and only then, with this clear, literal sense serving as a basis, is the higher, spiritual interpretation to be developed. His dependence in this regard is shown by his employment of the terminology of Antioch, since he usually speaks of the literal sense as that which is *secundum historiam,* or the *historiae veritas*—or, most often, simply *historia*. But actually, in practice, he often forgets to carry out this principle.

For, on the whole, his exegetical method is much closer to that of the Alexandrians. After explaining the literal sense, or even without this explanation, when he judges the obvious sense to be clear enough, he hastens to expound the spiritual message of the passage, and this he does almost always in the style of the Alexandrian exegetes, in fact, frequently in their very words, even where he does not explicitly state the source of his quotation. Only rarely does he develop the deeper meaning of Scripture according to the more exact method of the Antiochians. He leaves no doubt where his own preferences lie: his citations from the works of the allegorical interpreters of Alexandria are far more numerous than are those from the more cautious exegetes of Antioch. However, this preponderance is in part due to the fact that the latter school was still in its youth during Jerome's lifetime and had as yet produced only a comparatively small collection of commentaries to quote from, whereas the exegete of Bethlehem had at his disposal a much more voluminous library from the older school at Alexandria.

An examination of almost any of Jerome's commentaries will show this eclectic method, whereby he combined the literal interpretation, as favored by the Antiochians, with the spiritual interpretation of the Alexandrians, so that the former served, at least in theory, as the basis of the latter. But we also have several statements of his own to prove that this was his avowed purpose. The quotation of a few of these may not be out of place.

In his earliest extant exegetical work, on Isaias's vision of the Seraphim,[38] Jerome begins as usual by quoting the passage to be explained ("In the year that king Ozias died, I saw" etc.), followed by this comment: "Before we speak of the vision itself, it seems well to consider who Ozias was, how many years he reigned, and who were his contemporaries in the other countries." Then, after answering these questions, he continues, "Having thus first treated of this matter of history [*praemissa historia,* which might also be translated, "Having prefixed this literal interpretation"], it remains to give the spiritual interpretation, for the sake of which the history itself [or, the "literal interpretation"] has been unfolded (*spiritalis sequitur intellectus, cujus causa historia ipsa replicata est*)." The exegete then goes on to show, by a rather fanciful comparison with other similar temporal clauses, that the prophet could not have had a vision as long as the leprous king was alive.

Again, in his Commentary on Ezechiel 42:13f.,[39] a passage about the north and south Temple-chambers reserved for the priests, Jerome says: "The north and south chambers are, I think, either what they merely were in history [*i.e.*, the literal sense], or they symbolize the secrets of spiritual understanding (*quae vel historiae continent simplicitatem, vel spiritualis intelligentiae sacramenta*), so that through the *Aquilonem* [the dark clouds of the north] we should come to the *Meridiem* [the high point of the south]. For the *littera* [the literal sense] is not so to be read, nor the foundations of the *historia* [the historical sense, the explanation of passed events] so to be laid, that we may not come to the *culmina* [the top of the building, the highest sense of Scripture]. Yet neither is a most beautiful edifice to be built up to the roof, when the foundations beneath it are by no means solid."

Finally, we may quote Jerome's "Eulogy on Paula," for what is here [40] approved in the disciple is clearly the master's ideal also. "The Holy Scriptures she knew by heart. Although she loved their literal meaning (*historia*) and used to say that this was the basis of truth, she was still more concerned with their spiritual understanding, and with this high roof (*culmen*) she protected the edifice of her soul."

Influence of the Jewish Exegetes.

While it is generally admitted that Jerome owed much to the Christian exegetes who preceded him, it is not so widely known that he was likewise profoundly influenced by the Jewish scholars whom he eagerly sought as his teachers. We have already referred to Bar-anina, his *nocturnus praeceptor* at Jerusalem and Bethlehem. But there were several other erudite Jews, usually left unnamed in his works, whom he hired as his teachers—"for a goodly sum of money," as he complains in more than one place. He studied under these rabbis primarily for the purpose of being able to translate the Hebrew Bible into Latin, but their explanations were not limited to a merely grammatical exposition of the text. Jerome would have unconsciously absorbed a certain amount of rabbinical exegesis from them, even if he had not intentionally set out, as he really had, to find out what their traditional interpretations were.

In several of the Prefaces to his revisions or translations of the Old Testament Books he speaks of the help he received from these Hebrew scholars in preparing his Latin version. A quotation from one of these Prefaces—that prefixed to his lost revision of the Old Latin Paralipomenon [41]—will let him show in his own words, how and why he enlisted the aid of these Jewish scholars. At the same time this will give a fair sample of his interesting style, as far as it can be reproduced in another language.

This Preface, written about the year 389, begins as follows:

Just as those understand Greek history better who have visited Athens, and appreciate better the Third Book of Virgil who have sailed from Troy, passed Leucates and Acroceraunia, to Sicily, and from there to the mouth of the Tiber, so also will he have a clearer perception of the sense of Holy Writ who has gazed on Judea with his own eyes, and recalled at their own sites the stories of its ancient cities, whose names are either still the same or have been changed. For this reason we also took special care to undertake this labor in company with the most learned men of the Hebrews,[42] and likewise to travel all over this province, whose name resounds throughout the whole Church of Christ.

For I must admit, to you my dearest Domnion and Rogatian, that, in regard to the divine volumes, I have never trusted in my own ability, nor have I let my own opinion be my teacher. Even in those things which I thought I already knew, my custom has been to make inquiries, and I have done so all the more in those matters about which I was uncertain. Hence, when you recently wrote to me and begged me to translate the Book of Paralipomenon into Latin, I procured a former teacher of the Law from Tiberias, who was held in high esteem among the Hebrews, and I conferred with him "from top to toe," as they say. Only thus fortified, have I been bold enough to do what you asked of me.

In a similar way, he speaks of the assistance he received in preparing his translation of the difficult Hebrew text of Job: [43] "In order to understand this Book, I hired, for no small sum of money, a certain teacher of the city of Lydda who had the reputation of being 'A 1' (*primus*) among the Hebrews." He tells us likewise how he made his Latin version of the Aramaic Book of Tobias: [44] "Since Chaldaic (i.e., Aramaic) is related to Hebrew, I found a man who could speak both of these languages very well. So, devoting one day's work to it, I dictated in Latin to my secretary whatever he translated for me into Hebrew." Apparently the Hebrew translation was oral, not written. This interesting little scene, then, of Jerome acting as interpreter between his Hebrew-Aramaic friend and his Latin secretary shows us that he possessed a good *speaking* knowledge of Hebrew, something which is lacking in most of the modern philologists who presume to criticize him.[45] If he had wished, Jerome could have translated this Book directly from Aramaic himself, although he never fully mastered this language as well as he had Hebrew.

The first one, however, to teach him Hebrew was not a rabbi but a converted Jew. It was clearly an act of Divine Providence that led the young ascetic, who was destined to provide the Church with its authentic version of the Bible, to come in contact with this Hebrew-speaking monk in the desert of Chalcis. To this settlement of anchorites in eastern Syria, Jerome had retired in 376, after spending several months at Antioch, and here he stayed until 380. No doubt the principal motive that made him welcome this opportunity to learn the sacred language of Moses and the Prophets was his ambition to be an expert in the Biblical sciences. But, writing to the monk Rusticus in 411, he attributes a more pious motive to his initiation into the secrets of Hebrew grammar. His purpose was, of all things, to rid himself of impure temptations! This precious autobiographical notice (*Ep.* 125, 12) deserves to be quoted in full.

As a youth, even while I was hemmed in by the solitude of the desert, I could not bear the stimulation of the passions and nature's ardor. Though I tried to overcome it by frequent fasts, my imagination was still aflame with impure thoughts. So, in order to bring my mind into control, I made myself the pupil of a certain fellow monk who had been converted from Judaism to Christianity. And thus, after studying the acumen of Quintilian, the eloquence of Cicero, the majesty of Fronto, and the suavity of Pliny, I learnt the Hebrew alphabet and exercised myself in its hissing and aspirate words. What labor I then underwent! What difficulties I had to bear! How often I quit in despair, and how often I began again through my ambition to learn! This can be vouched for not only by the memory that I myself have of what I then suffered, but also by the memory of those who lived that life with me. But I thank the Lord that from this bitter seed of study I can now gather the sweet fruits.

We are told here of the almost superhuman efforts that Jerome made to master this Semitic tongue which was so different from the type of languages he already knew. We learn also how he, who began so many other scientific projects with great enthusiasm and yet failed to bring them to completion, stuck to this dry and discouraging task until he carried it to a successful end, because he realized far more than did any other Christian scholar of antiquity, how useful, or even necessary, a knowledge of Hebrew was for a thorough understanding of the Bible. But he does not tell us what methods he used in learning Hebrew. Certainly he had none of our modern aids in grammars and dictionaries. His only textbook was the sacred text itself. By reading the text with his Hebrew teacher, he learnt the meaning of the words together with the rules of inflection and syntax. Naturally, as he made progress in this, he could check for himself the correctness of the explanation that his teachers gave him, by comparing one passage with another, or by consulting the various translations of the Hebrew Bible that had already been published. But in many cases he had to rely solely on the traditional meaning that the Jews attached to difficult words or passages.

It is obvious, therefore, that Jerome depended on the authority of his Hebrew teachers to a considerable extent, first of all in his translation of their Bible. When his critics objected to some novel interpretation in his new Latin version, he would retort by saying, "Ask any Hebrew and he will tell you." [46] In his commentaries, too, he would at times justify his translation by saying, "The Hebrew who gave me instructions in the Sacred Scripture told me this." [47] But even where we have no direct testimony to this fact, we may rightly presume that, wherever his version departs from all or most of the older versions, especially in the meaning of Hebrew words which occur only once or twice in the Bible, such as the names of rare animals, birds, plants, etc., he is simply following the current interpretations among the Jews. A comparison between his translation and the Targums (the Aramaic translations made by the Jews of that period) will show a surprising number of striking resemblances.

One of the other examples will suffice to show how our Latin Vulgate still bears the effect of this tradition, even in passages where there is nothing rare or obscure about the Hebrew words in question. Thus, our Douay Version, which was made from the Vulgate, reads in Genesis 2:8: "And the Lord God planted a paradise of pleasure from the beginning." The Septuagint-Old Latin has: ". . . a paradise in Eden towards the east." Jerome's comment on this in his *Hebrew Questions on Genesis* [48] is as follows: "Instead of 'paradise' the Hebrew has *gan,* that is, 'garden.' Moreover, the Hebrew word *eden* means 'pleasure.' Likewise, the following, 'towards the east' is written in Hebrew, *mekedem,* which Aquila translated ἀπὸ ἀρχῆς, or as we would say, 'from the start'; Symmachus has ἐκ πρώτης, and Theodotion, ἐν πρώτοις, which also means not 'the east,' but 'the beginning.' From this it is perfectly clear that before God made heaven and earth, He first founded paradise." In confirmation of this current Jewish interpretation Jerome could also have cited 4 Esdras 3:6. The Targums likewise understand the phrase in the same way, and the equivalent of Jerome's conclusion is found in this statement of the Talmud: [49] "Seven things were created before the world was created; among these, the garden of Eden, of which it is written: 'And the Lord God planted the garden of Eden from the beginning.' " Yet almost all modern exegetes agree that the older Hebrew tradition, as represented by the Septuagint, is correct.[50]

Again, in Isaias 22:17 we have this strange comparison in the Vulgate: "Behold, the Lord will cause thee to be carried away, as a cock (*gallus gallinaceus*) is carried away." In his commentary on this passage (*PL,* 24, 273D) Jerome says simply, "All others have translated the word *geber* as 'man (*vir*)'; but the Hebrew who instructed us in the reading of the Old Testament translated it as *gallus gallinaceus.*" The word *geber* is indeed used in Neo-Hebrew for "cock," but in all the dozens of places where it occurs in the Old Testament, it is used solely for the male of the human species, and it should be so understood in this passage also.

While the number of passages in the Vulgate that have been influenced by the rabbinical teachers of St. Jerome may not be so great, there are scores, or rather hundreds, of places in his commentaries where the exegete refers to the current Jewish interpretations of Scripture. Nor need we attribute all of these to the oral instruction received from the rabbis. We have a valuable statement of his about his acquiring copies of certain Hebrew books which were certainly not the Books of the Hebrew Bible, for these he already had. They were most probably certain commentaries, similar to the *midrashim* which have come down to us in the Talmud. This statement of his is contained in a letter written at Rome in 384 to Pope Damasus (*Ep.* 36).

Incidentally, this letter also gives us an insight into Jerome's enthusiastic love for Biblical learning, which caused him to postpone the answer to a letter from the Pope, who was his personal friend and benefactor. Damasus had written to him and asked him for the solution of certain Biblical difficulties. Failing to get a reply, the Pope then sent a deacon to see why Jerome "had fallen asleep." Finally this answer was written:

Jerome to the Most Blessed Pope Damasus. When I received the letter from your Holiness, I called at once for my secretary and told him to take my dictation. While he was getting ready for the task, I was figuring out ahead of time what I was about to dictate. But just

as I was beginning to move my tongue, and he his hand, there suddenly came in on us a certain Hebrew carrying not a few volumes
which he had borrowed from the synagogue under the pretext of
reading them himself. "Here is what you have been asking for," he
said; "take them right away." And while I was hesitating and won-
dering what to do, he so frightened me by insisting on haste in the
matter, that I laid everything else aside and flew to the transcription
of these volumes. In fact, I am still engaged on this work. But yester-
day you sent a deacon to me to say that you were still waiting for
what you call a "letter" from me, but which I think would be more
like a regular Commentary.

Jerome then goes on to say that for the time being he can give
only a short and "off-hand" reply to the Pope's difficulties. Later
on, when he has finished copying the Hebrew volumes, he will
send him a longer letter.

Besides this reference to the written traditions of the Jews, we
have several other statements of Jerome to show that he was acquainted with the opinions of the rabbis who lived long before his
time. Traditional exegesis among them was very conservative. It
consisted largely in repeating what earlier rabbis had said. Thus,
concerning a peculiar interpretation of Ecclesiastes 4:13–16,[51]
Jerome reports: "When my Hebrew friend, whom I often refer
to, was reading Ecclesiastes with me, he told me that Barakiba,
whom alone they hold in the very highest esteem, gave this interpretation of the present passage." This Bar-akiba is also mentioned
by Jerome's contemporary, St. Epiphanius, who says (Haer. 15)
that he was known both as Bar-akiba and just Akiba, and in
another place (Haer. 33) calls him "Rabbi Akiba." In fact,
Jerome himself calls him simply "Akiba" in his commentary on
Isaias 8:14, where he gives an impressive list of the names of the
leading rabbis of the first two centuries.[52] There can be no doubt,
therefore, that Jerome is referring here to the renowned Rabbi
'Aqība ben Joseph, who organized a very influential school of
Jews shortly before their last futile rebellion against Rome in A.D.
132–135, and is rightly regarded as one of the main founders of
Rabbinical Judaism. Jerome mentions him again in Ep. 121,

10: [53] "The Jews say, 'Barachiba and Simeon and Hellel, our masters, have handed down to us that we may walk two miles on the sabbath,' and other such things, preferring the teachings of men to God's teaching." A few lines further on he says, "Their teachers are called σοφοί, that is, 'wise men,' and, whenever they set forth their traditions, they have the custom of telling their disciples, οἱ σοφοί δευτερῶσιν, that is, 'the wise men teach these traditions'." The Greek phrase used here is the literal translation of the common Talmudic expression, in Hebrew, *shānū hāḥakāmīm,* or in Aramaic, *tᵉnū rabbānīn.* Shortly before this, in the same letter, Jerome informs us that the Jews call their tradition δευτέρωσις, which is the exact equivalent of the Hebrew word *mishnāh,* meaning "repetition." Similarly, in his commentary on Habacuc 2:15ff,[54] we read: "At Lydda I once heard a certain one of the Hebrews, who was called 'a wise man' and a δευτερωτής among them, tell this story." The story is too long and unbecoming to repeat, but it should be noted that the Greek title, given here to the teacher, corresponds precisely with the Aramaic word *tannā'* (plural, *tannā'īm*), which is the title given in the Talmud to the rabbis of the first couple of centuries of the Christian era.

These examples, many more of which could be given, are sufficient to show that St. Jerome was well acquainted with rabbinical writings and their oral traditions. But from this, one should not conclude that he accepted all their interpretations with blind docility. On the contrary, he has made it perfectly clear in his commentaries, which interpretations he found reasonable and useful, which ones he considered merely interesting and harmless, but of little or no value, and which ones he rejected vehemently, as opposed to the true, Christian interpretation of the word of God.

First of all, the rabbis laid great stress on the literal sense of Scripture. To establish this sense correctly, they had sound, rational principles. The so-called "Seven Rules of Hillel" are, on the whole, very sensible and still quite useful. Although Jerome does not mention all these rules as such, their general influence can often be discerned in his literal interpretation of the text.

Occasionally he seems to refer to one or the other of these rules themselves, *e.g.*, the "rule of context" in his commentary on Matthew 25:13. However, in this matter of the basic importance of the literal interpretation, it is often difficult to judge how much he owes to the Jewish exegetes and how much to the Fathers of the Antiochian school.

Besides this investigation of the direct sense of the text, the rabbis also sought for a deeper meaning hidden beneath the more obvious one. They did so, however, in a manner quite different from that of either the Antiochian or the Alexandrian Fathers. Their purpose was partly to find a Scriptural basis for their peculiar religious customs, and partly to draw moral lessons from the pious legends that they thus added to the Biblical stories. The former class of comments are known as *halaka,* "way, conduct," the latter, as *haggada,* "exposition," or *midrash,* "explanation." Although the bulk of the Talmud is devoted to the *halaka,* Jerome seems to have taken comparatively little interest in these minutiae of Jewish observances. But many of the stories told as *midrashim* struck his fancy, and he thought that these curious tales would likewise interest his readers. He merely gives them for what they are worth. After narrating one of these legends,[55] he adds, "Just as this has been told us by the Hebrews, so we also have repeated it for the men of our own tongue, but as far as the reliability of these stories is concerned, we can only refer to those who have told them to us. For the rest, we who are enrolled under Christ's name, leave the letter that kills, and follow the spirit that gives life." Whereupon he interprets the passage in a "deeper sense" from the Christian viewpoint.

However, he does not pass on to his readers all the Jewish traditions he has heard of, for he considers many of them worthless or even scandalous. Thus he writes to Algasia (*Ep.* 121, 10): "I could not recount all the traditions of the Pharisees, which they call δευτερώσεις, nor their old-womanish tales. For the size of this book would not permit it, and moreover, many of them are so improper that I would be ashamed to tell them."

Here, as in many other passages of his works, Jerome speaks

so harshly of the traditions of the Jews that, if he were alive today, he would surely be called "anti-Semitic," even though he could say that many of his best friends were Jews. This is especially the case whenever he treats of the Old Testament prophecies which foretell the happiness of the Messianic age. According to the Christian interpretation, which the Church received from the Apostles, these prophecies are usually to be understood in a figurative sense, that is, under the image of an astounding material prosperity the prophets were describing the spiritual blessings brought by the Messias. Hence, in these cases the metaphorical sense is really the literal sense. But the Jews interpreted these obvious metaphors in a grossly literal sense, and therefore refused to accept Jesus of Nazareth as the Messias, since he clearly failed to live up to their fantastic expectations. Likewise castigated by Jerome's stinging ridicule were those Christian heretics, known as "chiliasts" or "millenarians," who indeed acknowledged Jesus as the Christ but believed that He would reign on earth with His saints in wonderful terrestrial pleasures for a thousand years at the end of the world—at the "Millennium." For Jerome these heretics were just "semi-Jews" and "Judaizers," because they followed the Jewish custom of interpreting the Scriptures in this "carnal" way.

Dozens of such passages in Jerome's commentaries could be cited, but just one or the other sample must here suffice. Commenting [56] on the words of Isaias 60:1-3, our exegete says:

The Jews and our own semi-Jews, who expect a golden and be-jewelled Jerusalem from heaven, claim that these things will take place in the thousand-year reign, when all the Gentiles are to serve Israel, and when the camels of Madian and Epha and Saba come there, bearing gold and incense. . . . From the islands, too, and especially on the ships of Tharsis, her daughters will fly like doves, bringing wealth in gold and silver. The walls of Jerusalem will be built up by the foreigners, with the kings of the Gentiles acting as foremen. . . . This is what they say who long for earthly pleasures, who seek beautiful wives and numerous children, and whose god is their belly, as they glory in their shame. This error of theirs is also followed by those who under a Christian name admit they are like the Jews.

Or again, on the words of Jeremias 31:23f., he says, "This prophecy was only partially accomplished under Zorobabel and Ezra. Its complete fulfilment is reserved for the times of Christ—either in His first coming, when these things have taken place spiritually, or in His second coming, when, according to our idea, they are entirely fulfilled in a spiritual sense, but, according to the idea of the Jews and of our own Judaizers in a carnal sense." Jerome sums up this matter very well by saying: [57]

Following the authority of the Apostles and the Evangelists, and especially that of the Apostle Paul, we demonstrate that, that which for the Jews is carnally promised, has been and is now being fulfilled spiritually among us. Nor is there any other difference between Jews and Christians except this, that, while both they and we believe that the Christ, the Son of God, has been promised, we hold that the things foretold of the Messianic age have already been fulfilled, whereas they hold that these things are still to be fulfilled.

We cannot dwell longer on the individual interpretations that Jerome heard of from his Hebrew teachers.[58] We must still mention the most important influence that the Jews exercised on him, an influence which affected his whole attitude toward the text of the Bible. This is the exaggerated esteem that they instilled in him for their own current Hebrew text. One of the most striking expressions which occur over and over again in all his writings is *"Veritas Hebraica*—the Hebrew truth." If he had meant by this that the original documents, as they left the hands of the inspired Hebrew authors, were the very words of God, he would have been entirely right. But he seems hardly ever to have considered the possibility that during the long manuscript history of the text before his time, innumerable accidental and even intentional changes may have crept into it. That he got this idea from his Hebrew teachers seems certain, for even the ordinary Jews of today never doubt but that their present Hebrew Bible is an exact copy of the very words of Moses and the Prophets. Of course, Jerome's Hebrew text, like the present Massoretic text, was substantially the same as the original and was, on the whole, probably more like the original than was the Hebrew text which the Septuagint translators employed six hundred years before. But it had unquestionably suffered many corruptions in the course of the centuries, and in numerous places had a poorer reading than that preserved in the Septuagint.

The principal results of Jerome's excessively high regard for his particular variety of the "Hebrew truth" were these. First of all, he drew from it the conclusion that any Book or any part of a Book that was not in his Hebrew Bible was therefore not a part of the Sacred Scriptures. This question, however, of his views on the Canon is treated elsewhere in this volume and need not detain us here.

Secondly, although Jerome was eclectic in borrowing from other commentators, in his translation of the Old Testament he limited himself solely to the current Hebrew text, and this despite the fact that he shows himself elsewhere an expert in textual criticism.[59] Departures from this principle, that is, instances when he follows the Septuagint-Old Latin readings where these are at variance with the Hebrew text before him, are comparatively rare and can usually be explained either as an indeliberate lapse due to haste, or a misunderstanding of a difficult Hebrew passage. Hence, on the whole, his Latin version is a very faithful but by no means slavish reproduction of the current Hebrew text. He would be perfectly justified in saying of his whole translation what he said in his Preface to the Books of Samuel and Kings: [60] "I am not at all conscious of having changed anything from the Hebrew truth." We can therefore make use of his version to ascertain the nature of the Hebrew text at the end of the fourth century. As far as the consonants are concerned, his was almost identical with our present Hebrew text, but quite different from the one on which the Septuagint is based. In regard to the vowels, however, it is certain that Jerome used a purely consonantal text with no visual aids for the pronunciation of the vowels except the *matres lectionis*.[61] Moreover, the vowels which his teachers told him to join to the consonants, differed in some respects from the "vowel-points" that were added a few centuries later by the Massoretes, not merely in regard to inessential differences in sound (as far as this can be shown from his inadequate Latin transcriptions) but even at times in a variant sense which a change of vowels gives to a word.

Thirdly, Jerome's infatuation with the current Hebrew text brought about in him a change of attitude toward the Septuagint. At first, like the other Christian writers of his time, he also regarded this Greek version as a supernatural production. Its translators were considered as divinely guided in their work. Hence, when he first noticed the great difference in the spelling of personal names between the Septuagint and his Hebrew text, and at the same time presumed that both texts were originally the same in this regard, he concluded that all the variant readings in the current copies of the Septuagint-Old Latin version were due to the errors of copyists. (Actually, most of the differences were original, each text being partly right and partly wrong.) Thus, in his *Praef. in lib. Paral. juxta LXX*,[62] written in c. 389, he says, "In the Greek and Latin codices this Book of names is so corrupt, that one would think it was compiled less of Hebrew than of barbarian and Sarmatian names. This, however, is not to be ascribed to the Seventy (*Septuaginta*) Translators, who, *filled with the Holy Spirit,* transcribed the true text correctly, but to the fault of the copyists." In his essay, "On the Right Way to Make a Translation" (*Ep.* 57, 7–11), written in 395, he observes that the New Testament authors often quote the Old Testament according to readings which differ somewhat from those of the Septuagint. This difference he attributes chiefly to the "free translations" made by the Apostles and Evangelists, although by this time he is willing to admit that even the original Septuagint was often in error. Finally, in his *Praef. in Pent.*,[63] written between 398 and 406, he has lost all faith in the supernatural origin of the Septuagint, which, according to pious legend, had been the work of seventy men working separately in seventy cells, each one producing independently of the others, yet in perfect agreement with them, the whole Pentateuch.

I know not (he says) who was the first author to fabricate with his lie those seventy cells at Alexandria. For neither Aristeas, the *hyperaspistes* of Ptolemy, nor Josephus, who wrote a long time after, mentions any such thing. These, on the contrary, say that the Seventy met in one basilica and translated, not prophesied. It is one thing to be a prophet, and quite another thing to be a translator. In the former case the Spirit reveals future events, in the latter, by mere erudition and a good vocabulary, a man renders into another language what he understands the original to mean. Unless, of course, we should hold that Cicero translated Xenophon, Plato, and Demosthenes under the inspiration of the rhetoric spirit.

It is very seldom that Jerome doubted the truth of his *veritas Hebraica*. Thus, in his commentary on Galatians 3:10, he notes that St. Paul quotes Deuteronomy 27:26 according to Septuagint, with which, our erudite scholar observes, the Samaritan Pentateuch agrees, whereas the later Greek translators and his own Hebrew text have a slightly different reading. Here he is inclined to suspect the latter reading. Again, in Galatians 3:13 the Apostle quotes Deuteronomy 21:22 as "Cursed is everyone who is hung on a tree," although all the texts, including even the Septuagint, have, "Cursed by God. . . ." Jerome feels that the latter phrase is unbecoming to Christ. After trying vainly to give it a favorable interpretation,[64] he concludes that either the Apostle quoted the passage somewhat freely, "or, as seems more likely, after Christ's Passion someone added the words, 'by God,' not only in the Hebrew codices but also in ours, in order that we might be branded with infamy for believing in a Christ who was cursed by God." But surely, this latter hypothesis is absolutely untenable.

Therefore, even though he was not entirely justified in the almost unbounded trust he placed in his Hebrew text, still his new version is so much superior to the Old Latin that we must be grateful for his bold assurance, which caused others to have confidence in his new version and thus helped to win the acceptance of this better Latin text.

III. Jerome's Merits as an Exegete

The account of Jerome's works and of the influence of other scholars upon him, as described above, has already given a fairly good idea of his importance as an exegete. It only remains to sum up his chief merits, and to answer certain objections which have been raised in depreciation of his worth.

There can be no doubt about the judgment which the men of his own time passed on him. Long before his death he was held by all, both in the East and in the West, to be the greatest authority on the Sacred Scriptures. In this field where he was supreme, and in a certain sense unique, everyone listened to his words as to the utterances of an oracle. His contemporary, Sulpicius Severus, has one of the disputants in his *Dialogus* [65] (written in c. 405) say to the other two, "I would be surprised if he [Jerome] were not already known to you through his writings, since he is read throughout the whole world." Even the great Augustine seems to have stood in awe at Jerome's immense knowledge of things Biblical. Although the zealous Bishop of Hippo felt obliged in conscience to disagree with the learned monk of Bethlehem on one or the other point, still he always expresses himself in remarkably humble tones. Thus, he writes to him, not in false humility but in simple honesty, "I have not as great a knowledge of the divine Scriptures as you have, nor could I have such knowledge as I see in you." [66] In fact, it is precisely because Augustine realized the great authority Jerome enjoyed, that he feared the mischief which could be done by even one wrong interpretation made by him on an important point of doctrine.

During the following centuries Jerome was universally acknowledged as the prince of Christian Scripture scholars—not only during the Middle Ages, but also among the savants of the Renaissance and the great commentators of the Golden Age of Catholic Exegesis, the sixteenth and seventeenth centuries. The first doubts were cast on his reputation only in modern times, when Biblical science was divorced from theology and began to be studied merely for the sake of science, solely from the viewpoint of philology, archaeology, history, and the like.

In keeping with this well-merited popularity, the Church in her Oration on his feastday (September 30th), calls St. Jerome her "Greatest Teacher in setting forth the Sacred Scriptures—*Doctor Maximus in exponendis Sacris Scripturis.*" It is commonly agreed on that this title, which apparently goes back to the fifteenth century,[67] is meant by the Church in a truly comparative sense and not merely in the sense of "a very great Doctor." Indeed, in comparison with all the other Doctors and Fathers of the Church, not only of the West but also of the East. But, understood in this meaning, Jerome's title has given rise to some discussion. For, if we take "exegesis" in its strictest sense, as signifying that penetrating investigation of the mind of the inspired author which seeks to fathom the logical sequence of his thoughts, it can hardly be denied that in this regard Jerome was really surpassed by several other exegetes, especially those of the Antiochian school, including another Doctor of the Church, St. John Chrysostom.

Murillo would take the qualifying phrase "*in exponendis Sacris Scripturis,*" to mean, "in translating the Sacred Scriptures." [68] Certainly, Jerome is the greatest Doctor of the Church in this respect. But such a statement is so obviously true that it seems rather ridiculous to insist on it. Why should the Church call him who alone of the Fathers made any Bible translation at all, her "greatest translator of the Sacred Scriptures"? To us, therefore, it appears more probable that this phrase is to be taken in a broad and general sense, embracing all forms of Biblical science, such as philology, textual criticism, history and archaeology, as well as exegesis and interpretation (or translation). If we make the comparison on this wide basis, we can well affirm that there has been no other ancient writer in either the Eastern or the Western Church who was greater than St. Jerome as a "Biblical scholar."

The only writer of the Latin Church before the sixteenth century who could be brought forth as a possible rival of Jerome's exegetical laurels is St. Augustine. But a comparison between these two might be unfair to both. Each is a specialist in his own particular field. In philosophy and speculative theology Augustine, of course, far outstrips Jerome. Hence, when it comes to the subtle study of certain theological texts of Scripture, the former Doctor usually excels the latter. Yet the eminent theologian of Hippo was seriously handicapped in his use of the Sacred Scriptures. He had to take his Old Latin Version just as he found it, and ran the risk of drawing serious conclusions from what was merely a wrong translation of some passage. He had but little knowledge of the history that lay behind the text he used, and still less ability in having recourse to the original texts, at least of the Old Testament.

But here Jerome was right at home. What he lacked in speculative talents and philosophical training he made up in critical acumen and in a vast positive knowledge of the Bible and the allied Biblical sciences. He shows clearly where the preference of his own genius lay. When Sunnia and Fretela offer him the opportunity of discussing numerous textual questions on the Psalms, he responds with obvious satisfaction (*Ep.* 106, 2), "You ask of me a work . . . in which not the ingenuity but the erudition of the writer is put to the test." Therefore, these two contemporary Doctors of the Church were in no sense rivals, neither subjectively nor objectively. They complemented each other's great work in laying the solid foundations on which later scholars were to erect the magnificent edifice of Catholic theology. It is really a pity that Augustine never saw the realization of his oft-expressed wish that he and Jerome might meet and work together.

In comparing St. Jerome with other famous exegetes of the fourth and fifth centuries, there is a certain matter that is not to be overlooked. Each of these men had his own special field of preference. Augustine's commentaries on the words of our Lord or on St. John's Gospel, and Chrysostom's commentaries on the Epistles of St. Paul do indeed surpass anything that Jerome wrote on the New Testament Books. But this was not Jerome's special field. His unique knowledge of Hebrew and Aramaic induced him to devote his talents to the study of the Old Testament. In this part of the Bible he chose the most difficult Books, the writings of the Prophets. Here he is *facile princeps*. He is the only ancient writer who commented on *all* the Books of the major and minor Prophets. And he did this extremely well.

Jerome, no doubt, would have admitted that Christians are naturally and rightly more interested in the New than in the Old Testament. But he felt that there was a danger of their neglecting the divine revelation made before the time of Christ. Thus, to Algasia, who had sent him several New Testament difficulties for solution, he complains good-humoredly of her failure to ask him about the Old Testament. "I notice," he writes to her (*Ep.* 121, Praef.), "that your questions which are all on the Gospels and the Epistles, show that either you do not read the Old Testament enough or you do not understand it well enough, for it is involved in so many obscurities and types of future things that it all needs explanation."

St. Jerome's outstanding characteristic, wherein he easily surpassed all other Christian writers of antiquity, is his enormous erudition. He was very well informed. As Sulpicius Severus says,[69] "In universal knowledge no one would dare to compare himself with him." God may not have endowed him with an intellectual capacity for deep speculation, but He did give him two precious talents which Jerome invested at Evangelical usury: an insatiable thirst for learning, and a phenomenal memory for retaining all that he learnt. Augustine, who was himself well-read in Latin literature, both ecclesiastical and profane, testifies [70] that Jerome "had read all or almost all the authors of both parts of the world who had written anything before his time on the teaching of the Church."

In like manner, we must still marvel at the frequency with which he makes the most apt quotations from the classics as well as from the Patristic writings. His own works are often brilliant mosaics of skillfully employed references to and citations from other authors. But nowhere is his prodigious memory so much in evidence as in his use of the Bible itself. He must have known most of the Scriptures by heart. For in those days there was no such thing as a concordance to help a faulty memory locate a pertinent text. Yet Jerome can pile on one quotation after another from various parts of the Bible whenever such references have some connection with the passage under discussion.

His encyclopedic knowledge, however, was not a mere accumulation of other men's ideas. Despite the efforts of his humility to present the truth through another's words, he cannot conceal the fact that he has made no mean independent contribution to the general fund of knowledge. Many a statement of his, for instance, about the critical reading of a certain passage or about its meaning, is quite original. His powers of observation were finely developed. He viewed the world with a keen eye and knew the faults and foibles of his fellow men as well as their virtues. Well-travelled especially in Palestine, he took note of its natural history, its physical features, its flora and fauna. Remarks on these interesting topics, often combined with a peculiar droll humor, enliven many a page of his commentaries.[71]

In order to have as much time as possible for the acquisition of new knowledge, Jerome usually worked very fast on his commentaries and translations. No doubt, some of his works would have been better if he had spent more time on their production. But the accusation of undue haste is generally overstressed. Indeed, Jerome himself is partly to blame for this false impression. Much given to rhetorical language, he makes a generous use of the licit figure of speech known as hyperbole, or in ordinary language, exaggeration. But he presumes that sensible readers, unlike literal-minded moderns, would not take his statements too strictly. Thus, when he says that his translation from the Hebrew of the three "Solomonic" Books—Proverbs, Ecclesiastes and Canticles—was "the work of three days" [72] he is obviously speaking hyperbolically. The mere dictation of even the final draft of these Books in so short a time would have been almost a physical impossibility. Since we still have practically the same Hebrew text as that on which he worked, a comparison between this and his excellent translation of it shows that he must have spent weeks, if not months, on his preliminary drafts. Therefore, even though he calls his Latin Tobias the outcome of "one day's labor," [73] and his Latin Judith the result of "one short burning of the midnight oil," [74] we should not draw the conclusion, as is so often done, that these are careless productions, because here we no longer have the original with which to compare his version.

Nor are we justified in saying that "another defect of Jerome, possibly more blameworthy than the hurry of his work, is a lack of hermeneutical method, an uncertain and inconsistent attitude towards the fundamental principles of scriptural exegesis." [75] On the contrary, Jerome had a very definite method in all his commentaries, and he carried it out quite consistently. His method, as shown above, was essentially eclectic: to borrow what is good from all three schools of exegesis, the Alexandrian, the Antiochian, and the Rabbinical. When he quotes the divergent opinions of these different schools he may seem to be inconsistent. But he is not necessarily making all these opinions his own.

In several places he states explicitly what his method was. We can cite only a few examples here. Thus, in the Prologue to his *Commentary on Osee*,[76] after enumerating all the previous commentaries written on this Book, he says to Pammachius, "I mention these that you may know what predecessors I have had in the field of this Prophet. However, to you, who are sensible, I admit in all sincerity and not from pride (as certain friends of mine forever insinuate) that I have not followed these commentators in all their opinions. I am acting as a judge rather than as a mere translator of their work. I state what I think is probable in each, and what I have learnt from one or the other of the Hebrew masters." In the Prologue to his *Commentary on Zacharias* [77] he speaks of having studied the previous works of Origen, Hippolytus and Didymus on this Prophet, and adds, "All their exegesis, however, is allegorical. They hardly ever treat of the literal sense (*historia*). So, desiring to imitate the 'householder who brings forth from his storeroom things new and old,' and the bride of the Canticle of Canticles who says, 'The new and the old, my beloved, I have kept for thee,' I have combined the literal interpretation (*historia*) of the Hebrews with the figurative interpretation (*tropologia*) of our own scholars, in order that I might build upon the rock and not upon sand, and might thereby lay a firm foundation, such as Paul, the wise builder, wrote that he had laid." Jerome, therefore, could well say (*Ep.* 61, 1), "Since it is my earnest purpose to read many authors, in order to gather different flowers from as many fields as possible, with the intention not of approving of everything but of choosing what is good, I do indeed use many books, but only that from these many I may learn much."

The complaint that Jerome often fails to keep his promise of showing which of the many cited interpretations he approves of and which one he disapproves of, is quite common and is not limited to modern critics. Even his devoted friend Paula seems to have found this difficulty in his commentaries, as he himself admits in his Eulogy on her (*Ep.* 108, 26):

She persuaded me to give her a running commentary as she read through the Old and the New Testament together with her daughter [Eustochium]. Though from modesty I would have refused this, yet, on account of her repeated and persistent pleas, I consented to teach her what I myself had learnt, that is, not my own ideas, for such presumption is a bad teacher, but what I had learnt from the illustrious men of the Church. Whenever I was in doubt and frankly admitted my ignorance, she would never accept my excuses but would always force me by her unremitting questioning to tell her which of the many weighty opinions I considered the more probable.

Nevertheless, there is this to be said in defence of Jerome's habit of presenting various opinions without indicating which ones he makes his own. He generally does this only when he is quoting different *allegorical* interpretations. Now, although several such interpretations on one and the same passage may often seem to contradict one another, they can really be all more or less justified. For none of them pretends to give the genuine literal sense of the passage. Hence, when Jerome finds one Father making a spiritual application of a text in one way, and another Father accommodating the same text in quite a different way, there is no reason why he should feel himself obliged to praise the one and condemn the other. Instead, he rightly leaves it up to his readers to choose any of these ingenious interpretations that may seem the more appropriate.

At least one practical advantage that we have from his habit of making numerous citations in his commentaries is that he has thus preserved for us large parts of the writings of older exegetes whose works would otherwise have been completely lost. In fact, the writings of St. Jerome formed one of the main channels through which much of the erudition of the Greek Fathers reached the Latin-speaking Church. In the same way, his commentaries as well as his version of the Scriptures have enriched all Christendom with much of what was good in the Biblical lore of the Jewish scholars. "I have made it my resolve," he states expressly,[78] "to make available for Latin readers the hidden treasures of Hebrew erudition and the recondite teachings of the masters of the Synagogue, as long as these things are in keeping with the Holy Scriptures."

The last adverse criticism of Jerome's exegesis that we shall consider is the assertion that he indulges far too much in allegorical interpretations, either of his own concoction or borrowed from others. We readily grant that in this respect a great deal of his exegesis is not written in the manner of a modern commentary. But first of all, we must note that even in his own works there is a steady progress from his earliest commentaries, which abound in allegorical interpretations, to his mature works on the Prophetic Books, where much more restraint is shown in the use of such farfetched accommodations. "We do not at all deny," says Pope Benedict XV in his Encyclical on the occasion of the fifteenth centenary of the death of St. Jerome,[79] "that Jerome, in imitation of the Latin and Greek exegetes who preceded him, made use at first of allegorical interpretations to perhaps an excessive degree. But his love of the sacred Books and his unceasing toil in constantly reading them and in weighing their meaning, led him ever on to a right appreciation of their literal sense and to the formulation of sound principles regarding it."

Jerome, however, never completely abandoned the allegorical

method, not merely because it was in vogue in those days and was expected of him by his readers, but also because he himself was convinced of the utility or even necessity of such exegesis. For him the Bible was not meant to be the plaything of men's minds; it was a heaven-sent manna for men's hearts and spiritual nourishment for their souls. He never forgot the truth, always taught by the Church and recently again enunciated by Pope Pius XII,[80] that "the Sacred Books were not given by God to men to satisfy their curiosity or to provide them with material for study and research, but, as the Apostle observes, in order that these Divine Oracles might 'instruct us to salvation, by the faith which is in Christ Jesus' and 'that the man of God may be perfect, furnished to every good work.' " Therefore, in those passages where the literal sense would merely be of historical interest, Jerome never hesitated to add to his literal interpretation a spiritual or allegorical interpretation, more or less founded on the direct sense, and thus "interpret so that the Church might receive edification" (1 Cor. 14:5).

In all this, Jerome showed himself a true "Father and Doctor of the Church." Immeasurably far above his fame as a scientific exegete is his immortal glory as a Saint of God. He was, as Sulpicius Severus says,[81] "a man above all else Catholic—*vir maxime Catholicus.*" Except for his mistaken and quite understandable attitude on the Canon, his orthodoxy has never been questioned. The mind and sense of the Catholic Church he made his own. Before all else he was guided by tradition: "the men of old who have preceded us in the Faith." It is this spirit of his, inspiring every line he wrote, that makes his writings so dear to all true Catholics and so disliked by many outside the Church. He had no need to submit his works to the subsequent approval of the Church; he made sure that there would be nothing in them that could offend her. "I made it my resolve," he said (*Ep.* 119, 11), "to read all the men of old, to test their individual statements, to retain what was good in them, and never depart from the faith of the Catholic Church."

His love for the Church sprang from his love for Christ, whose

Mystical Body she is. And it was his love for the Incarnate Word of God that enkindled in him his ardent love for the written word of God. For him "every single page of both Testaments seems to center around Christ." [82] "Ignorance of the Bible means ignorance of Christ," he would say, [83] "for 'Christ is the power of God and the wisdom of God,' and he who does not know the Scriptures does not know God's power and wisdom." "What other life can there be without the knowledge of the Scriptures," he wrote (*Ep.* 30, 7), "for through these Christ Himself, who is the life of the faithful, becomes known!"

We, who in the midst of our modern pagan civilization still cherish the precious heritage bequeathed us by our Fathers in the Faith, have need to listen again to Jerome's message of enthusiastic love for God's word in the Sacred Scriptures. To us also he addresses the words that he wrote to Paula (*Ep.* 30, 13):

What, pray, can be more sacred than this sacred mystery [of the Scriptures]? What can be more delightful than the pleasure found therein? What food, what honey can be sweeter than to learn of God's wise plan, to enter into His sanctuary and gaze on the mind of the Creator, and to rehearse the words of your Lord, which, though derided by the wise of this world, are really full of spiritual wisdom! Let the others, if they will, have their wealth, and drink from jewelled cups, be clad in silk, and bask in popular applause, as if they could not exhaust their riches in all kinds of pleasures. Our delight shall be to meditate on the Law of the Lord day and night, to knock at His door when it is not open, to receive the bread of the Trinity, and, with our Lord going before us, to walk on the billows of the world.

Notes

[1] "Haec ipsa vetus et vulgata editio (sacrorum librorum), quae longo tot saeculorum usu in ipsa Ecclesia probata est . . . pro authentica habeatur" (*Enchiridion*, Denz.-Banw.-Umberg n. 785).

[2] "Cujus doctrina an aliquid profecerim nescio; hoc unum scio, non potuisse me interpretari nisi quod ante intellexeram" (*PL*, 28, 1081). It is to be noted that Jerome uses both the word *interpretari* and the word *exponere* somewhat interchangeably in both the sense of "to translate" and the sense of "to ex-

plain, to expound, to give an exegesis"; *e.g.*, in the Preface to his translation of Tobias (*PL*, 29, 26) *"exposui"* means simply "I translated."

[3] One might be tempted to attribute this to the example of Victorinus, who taught rhetoric at Rome while Jerome was studying there and who wrote certain commentaries (now lost) on the *Apostolum* (the Acts and Epistles). But two facts militate against this hypothesis: Jerome says, at least according to the better manuscripts, merely that "Victorinus taught rhetoric in Rome while I was a boy (*me puero*)," and not that he "taught me as a boy (*me puerum*)" and secondly, in his later life Jerome despised the commentaries of Victorinus, as containing more rhetoric than Biblical knowledge. Cfr. *Prolog. in Comment. in Gal.* (*PL*, 26, 308), *De vir illus.*, 101 (*PL*, 23, 701), and *Chronic. an. Dom.* 358 (*PL*, 27, 687).

[4] *PL*, 25, 1097. In this later work, written in 395, he seems to imply that the early work was composed some thirty years before: "Nec diffiteor per hosce triginta annos in ejus (= Domini) opere me ac labore sudasse." But the "thirty" is perhaps to be taken as a somewhat exaggerated round number. The first commentary was probably written not much before 370, that is, after rather than before his journey to "the semi-barbarous banks of the Rhine."

[5] *PL*, 25, 583–786.

[6] *PL*, 24, 901–936.

[7] *PL*, 23, 1117–1144.

[8] *Ep.* 18. (The more recent editions of St. Jerome's Epistles are in *PL*, 22 and in Vols. 54–55–56 of the Vienna *Corpus Scriptorum Ecclesiasticorum Latinorum*.) For the date of this composition, cfr. Jerome's statement in his Commentary on Isaias, written in 408–410 (*PL*, 24, 91): "I admit that about thirty years ago, while I was at Constantinople and was receiving instructions there in Scriptural studies from that very eloquent man, Gregory the Nazianzene, who was then bishop of that city, I wrote a short treatise on this vision (*i.e.*, Is. 6:1ff.) without adequate preparation." In *Ep.* 84, 3, written in 399 or 400, he says that this little treatise had been composed some twenty years before.

[9] *Ep.* 36, 3: ". . . sed quo eum, qui lecturus est, sic faciat intelligere, quomodo ipse intellexit qui scripsit."

[9a] This has been the traditionally accepted explanation of the fate of Jerome's first revision, and this opinion is still widely held. But D. DeBruyne (*Revue Bénéd.*, 1930, 101–126), has apparently proved that Jerome had nothing to do with the "Roman Psalter"; this would be merely one of the variant forms of the unrevised Old Latin Psalter; Jerome's first revision, accordingly, would now be completely lost except for some quotations from it preserved in Jerome's earlier works.

[10] *PL*, 29, 401.

[11] *PL*, 29, 403.

[12] *PL*, 29, 61–114; P. de Lagarde (Göttingen, 1887); C. P. Caspari (1893).

[13] Together with Origen's critical marks it is published in *PL*, 29, 117–398, where the "Roman Psalter" is given in a parallel column. According to D. De Bruyne (*Revue Bénéd.*, 1929, p. 299) the name "Gallican Psalter" is due originally not to its early use in Gaul but to the widespread use of manuscripts made in the monastery of St. Gall, Switzerland, bearing the title, *"Psalt. Gall."*

[14] *PL*, 26, 219–306. This work was probably issued in 389.

[15] *PL*, 26, 507–618. These works were written in 386–387.

[16] *PL*, 23, 1009–1116.

[17] *PL*, 23, 935–1010.

[18] In the Preface to this work he speaks of "the books of 'Hebrew Questions' which I have decided to write on *all* the Sacred Scriptures." Several times in his *Onomasticon* he refers the reader for further information to these books which he hoped soon to publish.

[18a] These two works are published in *PL*, 23, 771–928.

[19] Jerome himself says in his Preface that he "omitted some items that do not seem to merit recording and changed many other items." Actually his omissions are very few and his changes and additions are not too numerous; cfr. E. Klostermann, *Das Onomasticon von Eusebius* in the Berlin Corpus of the Greek Fathers (Leipzig, 1904), pp. xxiv f.

[20] *PL*, 22, 833, 952. Augustine, however, later on acknowledged the worth of Jerome's new translation, and in his later writings often cited it with praise; cfr. Vaccari, *Institutiones Biblicae* (Rome, 1929), 288.

[21] Rufinus, for instance, who maliciously changed the name of Jerome's Hebrew teacher, Baranina, into Barabbas (*PL*, 21, 611–616).

[22] Published in *PL*, 28, 1125–1240; and in a more critical edition by P. de LaGarde (Leipzig, 1874), and by J. M. Harden (London, 1922).

[23] *PL*, 25, 815–1578. These commentaries were not written in their present order, which is that of the Vulgate; but *Nah.*, *Mich.*, *Soph.*, *Ag.*, and *Hab.* appeared in 392; *Jon.* and *Abd.* in 396; *Zach.*, *Mal.*, *Osee*, *Joel* and *Amos* in 406.

[24] *PL*, 26, 15–218. This work was written shortly before Easter in 398. The only other commentary on the New Testament, besides the ones on the Pauline Epistles, mentioned above, in which Jerome had a hand is his revision of the Commentary on the Apocalypse by Victorinus of Pettau; ed. *CSEL*, 49.

[25] Cf. *Apol. adv. Ruf.*, I, 19 (*PL*, 23, 413).

[26] *Anecdota Maredsolana*, 3, 1. These *scholia* were used by the compiler of the *Breviarium in Psalmos* (*PL*, 26, 821–1378) which was once falsely attributed to St. Jerome.

[27] *Anecd. Mareds.*, 3, 2–3.

[27a] According to De Bruyne (*Zeitschr. f. d. neutest. Wiss.* 28 [1929], 1ff.), these two Goths and their learned letter is a mere fiction, invented by Jerome as a literary device whereby he could refute the common objections raised against his second revision of the Psalms. Cf. however, A. Zeiller, "La lettre de S. Jérôme aux Goths, Sunnia et Fretela," *Comptes rend. Acad. Inscript. et Bel.-Let.* (Paris, 1935), 238–250.

[28] As is done, for instance, by L. Schade in his "Inspirationslehre des hl. Hieronymus" (*Bibl. Stud.*, XV, 4–5 [1910], 119).

[29] Cfr. A. Vaccari, "I fattori della esegesi geronimiana," in *Biblica* I (1920), 466ff.

[30] *PL*, 25, 491–584.

[31] *PL*, 24, 17–678. The Fifth Book of this Commentary, explaining only the literal sense of the "Ten Visions" of Isaias (Is. 13:1–23, 18), was first published as a separate opuscule in 397.

[32] *PL*, 25, 15–490.

[33] *PL*, 24, 679–900; *CSEL*, 59.

[34] So L. Schade, who says simply, "Er war Autodidakt" (*Bibliotek der Kirchenväter: Hieronymus,* 1914, p. lxii).

[35] *De vir. illus.,* 117 (*PL,* 23, 707).

[36] Hence, we speak here of the "Alexandrian" and the "Antiochian" exegetes chiefly in the sense that the basic principles of their exegesis were derived from one or the other of these two schools, even though many of these men actually lived in various other parts of the Roman Empire. The Alexandrian school was the older. Among its outstanding exegetes were Pantaenus, its founder (+ c. 200), Clement (+ c. 215), Origen, the greatest of them all (+ 254), Dionysius (+ 265), Pierius (+ c. 300), Eusebius of Caesarea (+ 340), Athanasius (+ 373), Didymus (+ c. 398), and Cyril of Alex. (+ 444). The chief exponents of the Antiochian school were Lucian, its founder (+ 213), Theodore of Heraclea (+ 355), Eusebius of Emesa (+ c. 359), Apollinarius (or, Apollinaris) of Laodicea (+ c. 390), Diodorus of Tarsus (+ c. 393), John Chrysostom (+ 407), Theodore of Mopsuestia (+ 428), Polychronius of Apamea (+ c. 430), and Theodoret (+ 458).

[37] Cfr. A. Vaccari, "La θεωρία nella scuola esegetica di Antiochia," *Biblica* I (1920), 3–36.

[38] See footnote 8.

[39] *PL,* 25, 412.

[40] *Ep.* 108, 26.

[41] *PL,* 29, 401.

[42] In Jerome's writings, as in ancient Christian literature generally, "a Hebrew" (*Hebraeus*) is a respectful term which regards merely the man's race or language, whereas "a Jew" (*Judaeus*) is a term of reproach, emphasizing the man's religion, which from the Christian viewpoint is worthy of reprobation.

[43] *Praefatio in Job secundum Hebraeum* (*PL,* 28, 1081).

[44] *PL,* 29, 25f.

[45] Jerome admits, however, that the Jews used to laugh at his quaint accent and faulty pronunciation of the strange sibilants and gutturals of Hebrew; cfr. his *Comment. in Tit.* 3:9 (*PL,* 26, 594f.).

[46] This appeal to the authority of the Hebrews backfired on Jerome in the rather comical dispute with Augustine about the name of the ephemeral plant that sheltered Jonas (Jon. 4:6f.). When a certain North African bishop had Jerome's new version publicly read in church, the people raised such a hubbub at hearing the old "cucumber-vine" of Jonas now changed into "ivy," that the bishop had the choice of either restoring the old reading or finding himself without a congregation. The Jews of those parts, who were asked about it, said that the change was no improvement. Augustine admits that they might have said this from ignorance or malice, but they were really quite right. Cfr. *PL,* 22, 833f., 929ff. Actually, Jerome's description of this plant in his Commentary on Jonas (*PL,* 25, 1147f.) shows that his teachers correctly identified it with the castor-oil plant, but the Latin word for it, *ricinus,* had apparently slipped his memory.

[47] Cfr. his Commentary on Amos 3:11 (*PL,* 25, 1019C).

[48] *PL,* 23, 940.

[49] *Pessachim* 54a; *Nedarim* 39; *Jalkut* 20.

[50] The Hebrew phrase *miq-qedem* means literally, "from the front," but by usage it means either "of old" or "in the east." The Septuagint was also

correct in taking "Eden" for a proper name. Jerome, as usual, likes to show its popular Hebrew etymology.

[51] *PL*, 23, 1048f.

[52] *PL*, 24, 119. This passage mentions, among others, the well-known Scribes: Shammai, Hillel, Johannan ben Zakkai, and Meir. Unfortunately, the text here, as published by Migne, seems to be rather corrupt.

[53] *PL*, 22, 1033f.

[54] *PL*, 25, 1301B.

[55] *Comment. in Zach.* 11:11 (*PL*, 25, 1496).

[56] *PL*, 24, 587f.

[57] *PL*, 24, 865D; *CSEL*, 59, 367. This statement occurs in the introduction to the last part of the last Commentary that Jerome wrote.

[58] Many good studies have already been made on the relationship between Jerome's Commentaries and the Rabbinical literature. But this mine of research has not yet been exhausted. Among the more valuable studies are the following:

H. Grätz, *Monats. f. Gesch. u. Wiss. d. Jud.*, 1854, 1855.

M. Rahmer, *ibidem*, 1865, '67, '68, '97; also, *Die Commentarii zu d. 12 kl. Proph.* (1902).

M. J. Lagrange, *Rev. Bibl.*, 1898.

V. Aptowitzer, *Zeits. altt. Wiss.*, 1909.

A. Condamin, *Rech. de science relig.*, 1914.

F. M. Abel, *Rev. Bibl.*, 1916, '17.

[59] *E.g.*, in his revision of the Latin Gospels, and in his knowledge of the Septuagint MSS. Even modern textual critics still divide the Septuagint MSS into three main families according to Jerome's statement in his *"Praef. in lib. Paral. juxta Heb."* (*PL*, 28, 1324f.): "In regard to the recensions of the Septuagint, in Alexandria and Egypt they use the edition of Hesychius, from Constantinople to Antioch they approve of the copies edited by Lucian, the martyr, while in the regions between these two provinces they read the Palestinian codices prepared by Origen and published by Eusebius and Pamphilus. Thus the whole world is divided by this threefold form of the text."

[60] *PL*, 28, 557f.

[61] Several times he speaks of the ambiguity of Hebrew words because they were written with consonants only; *e.g.*, in his *Comm. in Jer.* 9:22 (*PL*, 24, 745B; *CSEL*, 59, 126—his last major work!), he says, "The Hebrew word which is written with the three letters, *daleth, beth,* and *res*—for it has no vowels between them—, if, according to the context and the judgment of the reader, it is read as *dabar*, it means 'word,' if as *deber*, it means 'death,' if as *dabber*, it means 'speak.'" However, even in his time the text already had the marks now known as "extraordinary points"; *e.g.*, in Gen. 19:33 (on Lot's daughter lying with him) the Massoretic text still has a seemingly meaningless dot over the phrase, "and in her rising"; Jerome says (*Quaest. in Gen., PL*, 23, 973), "They put a point over it, as if it were something unbelievable and beyond nature to have intercourse and not know it." So also the Talmud (*Rabba in Gen.* 51): "Why is there a point here? To show that he did not know it when he was asleep, but that he did know it when he got up."

[62] *PL*, 29, 402A.

[63] *PL*, 28, 150f.

[64] *PL*, 26, 361ff. One of his attempts to explain the phrase, "Cursed by God," is of special interest. "The Hebrew who gave me some instructions in the Scriptures used to say that it could also be read as, 'Because with reviling

God was hung up.'" Jerome rightly doubts the possibility of the Hebrew words having such a meaning. But it is to be noted that this *Hebraeus qui me in Scripturis aliqua ex parte instituit* was most probably the converted Jew who gave Jerome his first Hebrew lessons, for no other Jew would have tried to give such a Christian interpretation to the passage.

[65] *Dial.* 1, 8 (*PL*, 20, 189; *CSEL*, 1, 161).

[66] *PL*, 22, 912; 33, 247; *CSEL*, 34, II, 269.

[67] Cfr. L. Murillo, "S. Jerónimo, el 'Doctor Máximo,'" in *Biblica* 1 (1920), 434, n. 3; 442, n. 1.

[68] Murillo, *l.c.*, pp. 447ff.

[69] *Dial., l.c.*

[70] *Contra Julianum*, 1, 34 (*PL*, 44, 665).

[71] Cfr. Leop. Fonck, "Hieronymi Scientia naturalis exemplis illustratur," in *Biblica* 1 (1920), 481–499.

[72] "Tridui opus": *PL*, 28, 1241.

[73] "Unius diei laborem arripui": *PL*, 29, 26.

[74] "Huic unam lucubratiunculam dedi": *PL*, 29, 39.

[75] O. Bardenhewer, *Patrology* (T. J. Shahan's translation, 1908), 463. Essentially the same statement is repeated in Bardenhewer's last German edition, III (1912), 628.

[76] *PL*, 25, 820.

[77] *PL*, 25, 1418.

[78] *Comment. in Zach.* 6:9ff. (*PL*, 25, 1455D).

[79] *Encycl.* "Spiritus Paraclitus," Sept. 15, 1920, *Acta Apost. Sedis* 12, 410.

[80] *Encycl.* "Divino Afflante Spiritu," Sept. 30, 1943, par. 49; quoted here from the "English Translation Provided by the Vatican," N.C.W.C., 23.

[81] *Dial.* 1, 7 (*PL*, 20, 188; *CSEL*, 1, 160).

[82] *Encycl.* "Spir. Parac.," *Acta Apos. Sedis* 12, 418.

[83] *Prol. in Comment. in Is.* (*PL*, 24, 17B).

St. Jerome and Greek Thought

GUSTAV BARDY

St. Jerome and Greek Thought

S<small>T. JEROME WAS BORN</small> in 347 in Stridon, a small town in eastern Italy on the borders of Pannonia and Dalmatia, but he spent the greater part of his life in the East. As early as 374 he left Aquileia where, in the company of friends, he had been living the life of an ascetic, and betook himself to Antioch. For four or five years he lived either in that city or in the desert of Chalcis, not far distant from it. Between the years 379 and 382, we find him in Constantinople, where he became acquainted with the most illustrious Oriental bishops of the time. He returned to the West for a short sojourn in Rome—from the autumn of 382 to the month of August in 385—but even during that time he did not lose contact with the East, for Pope Damasus entrusted to him his correspondence with the Churches of the Greek world. The death of this protector of his forced Jerome to say a final adieu to Italy. Having visited Palestine and Egypt, he finally settled in Bethlehem in the spring of 386. Thereafter he would not leave the land sanctified by the birth of our Savior. It is here that he composed his great exegetical works. It is here that he breathed his last, in fullness of years and merit, on September 30, 419.[1]

There is a question, then, as to the measure in which St. Jerome was influenced by Greek theological thought during the long years spent in the Orient. A short time before him, St. Hilary of Poitiers had been forced into temporary exile, taking up residence in Phrygia. His grasp of affairs had been considerably widened by this experience. The bishop of Poitiers quickly learned to distinguish the subtle nuances which were the bases of controversy between the various Arian groups; he rapidly acquired an understanding of the use of expressions of Greek origin; grasping their exact meaning, he came to recognize the theologians of the East and their characteristic works. Hilary's great treatise *On the Trinity* and his book *On the Synods* testify abundantly to the vast extent and the reliability of his information, to his interest in Oriental controversies, and to the care he had taken to be informed in the minutest details. Can we detect a similar development in the thought of St. Jerome? Or did the mentality of the Solitary of Bethlehem remain exclusively Latin, fixed on Occidental problems, closed, in consequence, to the problems debated so violently in the East? This question is an interesting one, for it permits us to bring to light a whole aspect of the psychology of St. Jerome. It is intriguing from a more general point of view also, for it compels us to ask whether, at the end of the fourth and the beginning of the fifth century, the Christian East and West were still capable of taking an immediate interest in the same ideas and the same controversies.

We must remark first of all that the years of Jerome's sojourn in the East correspond to a period strikingly fruitful in theological thought. The controversies concerning the Trinity, instead of being settled at the Council of Alexandria in 361, broke out afresh, with unexpected reverberations, after this assembly. Two questions in particular come to the fore: the use of the term *hypostasis,* and the divinity of the Holy Ghost. With reference to the divine Trinity, is it correct to speak of three hypostases? and if the answer is in the affirmative, what are the characteristics of each divine *hypostasis*? How, in particular, does the γέννησις of the Son differ from the ἐκπόρευσις of the Holy Ghost? Likewise, can we apply the name of God to the Holy Ghost? Is the Holy Ghost consubstantial with the Father and Son? Is He entitled to the same adoration and to the same honors?

The great Cappadocian doctors examine these questions very closely. Each was led to study and solve them in accordance with the personal preoccupations which influenced his vocabulary. Saint Basil, conscious of his obligations as a man of authority, attempts to spare people's sensibilities in an effort to keep within the Catholic Church the weak and the hesitant. To the best of his abilities, therefore, he avoids naming the Holy Ghost, while, at the same time, maintaining that He is to be adored and glorified with the Father and the Son.

St. Gregory Nazianzen had other responsibilities. At Constantinople in particular, he found that he had to maintain the faith of the orthodox against the heretical Arians. Hence he used explicit formulas and declared categorically that the Holy Ghost was God.[2] St. Amphilochius of Iconium, in turn, found himself constrained to place in relief the special characteristics of the Holy Ghost. At Alexandria, Didymus the Blind systematized the words of the Cappadocians. He wrote a treatise on the Holy Ghost, several dialogues against the Macedonians, and, finally, three books on the Trinity which, at the time they were published, were for the East the most complete synthesis that theological thinking had accomplished.

Meanwhile, however, Christological problems were gradually coming to the fore. It had been hardly noticed, it would seem, that Arius had refused to admit the existence of a human soul in Christ. This strange doctrine suddenly gained attention when it was taken up again by Bishop Apollinaris of Laodicea, a man most interested in maintaining the unity of person in the Savior. Of course, Apollinaris quickly reversed himself by saying that Christ possessed an animal soul, and that what he lacked was the spirit, the νοῦς, the principle of spiritual life.[3] He was condemned, nevertheless, for his teachings, which were refuted by St. Athanasius; then he was personally censured by a Roman council in 377. All the doctors who had had anything to do with the Arians were led, by the course of these events, to develop their own ideas concerning the nature of Christ. St. Gregory Nazianzen, St. Basil, St. Gregory of Nyssa, St. Epiphanius; each played a decisive role in the refutation of the new heresy and in the exposition of the Catholic faith.

Upon his arrival in the East, therefore, Jerome had almost immediately found himself involved in controversy. Antioch, at that moment, was the scene of perfervid theological activity, its

controversies assuming, in a sense, the character of personal rival-
ries. Since 361, the officially recognized bishop had been Meletius,
who, though he had formerly belonged to the faction grouped
around Basil of Ancyra, had finally, in 363, subscribed to the
Nicean formularies. Nevertheless he had been exiled by the Emperor Valens. Although he was in communion with Basil of
Cappadocia and the whole Catholic episcopate of Asia Minor, he
had the misfortune of falling out with a small group of intransi-
geants who pretended to having preserved unbroken fidelity to the
terminology of Nicea. Under the leadership of Paulinus, unfortunately elevated to the episcopal dignity by Lucifer of Calaris, they
refused to admit the distinction then current in the Oriental vocabulary between the two words οὐσία and ὑπόστασις.

Naturally, St. Jerome was called upon to take sides. The monks
who dwelt with him in the desert of Chalcis were inflexible disciples of Meletius and rigorous exponents of the three *hypostases*.
They tried to compel the newcomer to adopt their view. Jerome
began by protesting: Paulinus was recognized as the only legiti-
mate bishop by Peter of Alexandria and Damasus of Rome, who
had not yet forgotten the dubious origins of Meletius, and who
were too badly informed concerning the affairs of the East to
understand the exact nature of the problems involved. Jerome
owed it to himself, he owed it to his traditional unequivocal orthodoxy and to his Western origin, to side with Paulinus. Moreover,
his knowledge of Greek was inadequate since, like all his Western
contemporaries, he had only learned it in school, and as yet had
had little opportunity to speak it.[4] Hence the doctrine of the three
hypostases at first seemed to him to be a monstrous heresy; in his
eyes it connoted the acceptance of tritheism. Nothing is more
revealing than a letter of Jerome's written at the time to Pope
Damasus, begging his advice:

Now, alas, after the faith of Nicea, after the decree of Alexandria
which the West accepts, the progeny of the Arians, these *peasants*
require of me, a Roman, this new formula of three *hypostases*. What
apostles, pray, have so written? Whose teaching is this? What new
apostle of the nations? What new St. Paul? We wonder what they

suppose one understands by three *hypostases*. Three subsisting persons, they affirm. We answer that we believe the same. The sense is not sufficient; they clamor for the word itself. And I do not know what venom may be lurking under these syllables. We proclaim: If any one refuses to admit the three *hypostases,* meaning three *enhypostata,* that is, three subsisting persons, let him be anathema. But because we do not use their terms, they declare us heretics. But if anyone, meaning by the word hypostasis *ousia,* does not believe in one sole hypostasis in three persons, he is a stranger to Christ. Because of such a confession, we are branded for being in union with you.[5]

Jerome's distrustful attitude is, in a way, understandable. He had not been long enough in the East to be master of a vocabulary entirely new to him. But soon one perceives something else, namely, that the theological problems discussed at Antioch or in Asia Minor interest him very little. Hardly had he left the desert on his way to Antioch, when he began to study under Apollinaris of Laodicea, of whose consummate knowledge of the Scriptures he availed himself in becoming acquainted with the art of exegesis.[6] Apollinaris, notwithstanding the services he had formerly rendered to the cause of orthodoxy in opposition to the Arians, had become himself a heretic. He had even consecrated one of his disciples, the priest Vitalis—a man unable to clear himself of accusations brought against his faith—and had placed him in the See of Antioch, in the very same position as Meletius and Paulinus. But Jerome did not concern himself about such things. He followed the lessons of the bishop of Laodicea without scruple The controversies concerning the nature of Christ seem to have had small interest for him.[7]

Some time later, in 379, he undertook a new voyage, travelling to Constantinople. Among the Catholics there, he found much talk concerning the eloquence and the holiness of Gregory Nazianzen, who had just arrived to take over the direction of the orthodox group. Jerome was naturally eager to make Gregory's acquaintance and to follow his exegetical lectures. But at Constantinople no more than at Antioch did he wish to become involved in doc-

trinal issues.[8] He kept himself aloof even in 381, when the whole
Eastern episcopate gathered in the capital for the great council at
which the Pneumatomachi were to be condemned.

Doubtless it is at this time that St. Jerome had the opportunity
of meeting St. Gregory of Nyssa, who read him a work against
Eunomius,[9] and St. Amphilochius of Iconium, who informed him
of his book on the Holy Ghost.[10] These great men interested him,
but their books did not. What is the purpose, he wondered, of
busying oneself with questions which Rome has already solved,
and which find no echo among the people of the West? Moreover,
he judged with surprising severity most of the Eastern bishops with
whom he had occasion to talk, including Meletius of Antioch, who
had lost the merit of his exile by betraying his faith; [11] Basil of
Caesarea, whose holiness had been endangered by his pride; [12]
Cyril of Jerusalem, a heretic,[13] Peter of Alexandria, a simo-
niac.[14]

It must be added that, since his departure from Aquileia,
Jerome had lived mainly with people from the West, or at least
with men long familiarized with Occidental culture. At Antioch
he received the generous hospitality of Evagrius, a man whose
family was of Roman origin and who had himself spent ten years
in Italy. In his home Jerome found a common friend of theirs, the
monk Innocent. He was visited many times by pilgrims who were
going to the Holy Land or coming from it: Niceas, subdeacon of
Aquileia, Heliodorus, the future bishop of Altinum, and many
others. He had kept up an active correspondence with the West,
and in this Evagrius had been his intermediary. Paul of Con-
cordia, Julian, Eusebius, Jovinus, Chromatius, all had written to
him, and he had answered them with joy. Others who had not
deigned to write—the sub-deacon Niceas, the monks Chrysoco-
mas and Anthony, the virgin Haemona, his aunt Castorina—had
nevertheless received long and numerous letters from him. Moreover, his correspondents in the East were pilgrims or monks, now
settled there, but of Latin origin: Rufinus of Aquileia, Florentinus
of Jerusalem. At Constantinople, he found a friend and confidant

in the priest Vincentius, who encouraged him in his work and received the dedication of his first translations.

Under these conditions, it is understandable that in returning to Rome after a six years' absence Jerome found himself at home. He had hardly changed his spiritual atmosphere. His experience had increased. He had studied Greek, learned Hebrew. He had seen many things and many men; but he had remained a Latin. At this very time Ambrose of Milan, by way of contrast, while remaining in Italy, still kept closely in touch with the Orient. He began by communication with St. Basil. He took an active part in the negotiations destined to put an end to the schism of Antioch. He opposed the election of St. Gregory of Nazianzus to the See of Constantinople, and that of Flavianus to the See of Antioch. As soon as an Oriental theologian wrote a book on a great theological problem, Ambrose hastened to read it and adapt it for his congregation in Milan.

Strictly speaking, Ambrose did not translate. But at times he followed his sources so closely that one is entitled to use the word translation. St. Basil, St. Gregory of Nazianzus, Didymus of Alexandria, St. Cyril of Jerusalem, St. Athanasius became so familiar to Ambrose that one can trace in his writings what he owed to each of them. His inspiration was entirely Greek and he made no secret of it. There is nothing similar in Jerome. The only recent work whose translation he undertook during his stay in Rome was the *De Spiritu Sancto* of Didymus. Even in this case he undertook the work in order to satisfy personal rancor rather than to inform his countrymen about the teachings of the Oriental doctors. Jerome's preface to Paulinus clearly reveals his intentions:

I have decided to translate another author's work. In imitation of a certain ugly Crow, I have clothed myself in strange colors. I have read recently a little work on the Holy Spirit—the *De Spiritu Sancto* of St. Ambrose—and, as the *scriptor comicus* would say, "from excellent Greek has come poor Latin." There is in it no dialectic, no virility, no clever logic which should convince the reader almost against his own will. Everything is spongy, soft, glossy and hewn, spotted here and there with smart colors. . . . Whoever, on the other hand, reads my Didymus will now recognize these Latin thefts, and will despise the rivulets after having once drunk at the source.[15]

The ugly bird mentioned above is none other than St. Ambrose, bishop of Milan. Jerome did not like him, and seldom missed an occasion to belabor him.[16] Yet in spite of Jerome's actual admiration of Didymus, he would not have thought of translating a theological treatise of his if he had not this very special reason for doing so.[17]

It is true that, at the same time, Jerome continued the work begun at Constantinople. Having there translated Origen's homilies on Jeremias, on Ezechiel and on Isaias, he now tackled two more homilies on the Canticle of Canticles. The letters he wrote from Rome were full of glowing praise for the "first Master of the Church after the Apostles," [18] for that incomparable person whose knowledge and eloquence have been envied all over the world.[19] But Jerome's admiration is not for the audacious and profound metaphysician who had written the *De principiis,* nor for the apologist who so resolutely refuted the calumnies of Celsus. It is rather for the erudite scholar who had compiled the *Hexapla,* for the exegete who had spent the greater part of life commenting on the books of the Bible, one after another. Jerome's ambition, indefinite still, was to imitate such a model.[20] Why not now devote his time to a study of the written works of the Alexandrian master?

However, Damasus entrusted him with a different mission. He chose Jerome to answer the innumerable questions which came to him from all parts of the world, and particularly from the Orient. Jerome seemed to possess all the qualities required for such a task, his now perfected knowledge of Greek giving him additional title to the office. One may well wonder whether he contributed all that his position demanded. The only incident recorded concerning his activities as "secretary for Greek correspondence" is not to his credit. Having been asked to draw up a formulary on the Incarnation, to be submitted for approval to the Apollinarists, he found means of inserting in the document the expression *Domini-*

cus homo, which was favored by the heretics but already questioned by the more rigid among the orthodox. Although certain details of this affair remain obscure, it is probable that Jerome acted imprudently, allowing himself to be deceived by a group of heretics more artful than he. Evidently he was not capable of following the Greeks on the slippery ground of theological jousts.[21]

Nor would he become more skillful when, after his departure from Rome, he settled permanently in Bethlehem. On his way he stopped at Salamis in Cyprus, where he met St. Epiphanius. He put up at Antioch, where he found his friends Paulinus and Evagrius; finally, in Egypt, he visited the monasteries of Nitria, afterwards spending a month in Alexandria with Didymus. He would boast, later on, of the lessons which he then received from his old master. He recalls with joy that Didymus composed for him and dedicated to him three books of Commentaries on Osee and five on Zacharias. As a matter of fact, Didymus' influence on him was most superficial. Like Origen, Didymus interested Jerome only as an exegete, and Jerome often availed himself of his works on the Scriptures. But his theology left Jerome indifferent, at least until he began to oppose Origenism and its supporters.

But in 386, this time had not yet come. The first years of Jerome's residence in Palestine were occupied in work and prayer. The monastery was filled with Latins, including the priest Vincentius, Jerome's younger brother Paulinianus, and a few other monks.[22] As the years rolled by, other Occidentals joined the group, such as Valerianus and Lupulus, who tried to persuade the master that he should write a book on the proper names contained in the Scriptures. Jerome acceded to their importunities and began to work on a new basis, instead of simply translating, as he had planned at first, the ancient *Onomastica* of Philo and Origen.[23] Other Westerners to join the group were Eusebius of Cremona, a restless blunderer, who did not know one word of Greek and yet was always on the alert for news to spread and calumnies to propagate; [24] Rufinus the Syrian, who, in spite of his origin, exercised his talents in the West, and, prior to Pelagius himself, scattered there the venom of heresy; [25] Firmus, who seems to have been the business man for Paula and Eustochium, and who, in the performance of his duties, was constantly on the roads, going from Bethlehem to Ravenna, and from there to Sicily and Africa [26]—he acted as messenger for Jerome and St. Augustine, carrying back and forth the letters which they exchanged [27]—and yet, withal a most devoted monk; Quintilianus, who constantly sought new vocations.[28] With little trouble, one could unearth other names. But the foregoing are sufficient to show that the milieu in which Jerome lived remained Latin.

When the monks left the place for some reason or other—and this happened often, for stability is not a dominant virtue among the monks of that time—it was to the West that they returned on personal business, or to visit their families.[29] When Jerome tried to draw his correspondents to an ascetical way of life, it was always with Occidentals that he pleaded. Desiderius of Rome,[30] the Spaniard Lucinus,[31] the Pannonian monk Castricianus,[32] the officer Exsuperantius,[33] Paulinus of Nola, with whom, in fact, he seemed to play hide-and-seek, advising him not to undertake the pilgrimage to Jerusalem when he wished to do so,[34] and then insisting on his coming when he became aware of his hesitations.[35] Many of these appeals are fruitless; neither Lucinus, nor Castricianus, nor Paulinus came to Bethlehem. Others produce no decisive results. Desiderius spent only a few months at Bethlehem; Exsuperantius was expelled without any reason that we know exactly.[36] The deacon Sabianus was expelled for bad morals.[37]

On the other hand numerous Latin pilgrims, without intending to remain permanently in Palestine, came there to visit the Holy Places,[38] and they never failed to stop for a time at Bethlehem, to enjoy the company of Jerome. Among them we can cite the priest Vigilantius, a man recommended by St. Paulinus of Nola, but one whose rusticity, ignorance and vanity did not escape Jerome's judgment.[39] Fabiola and Oceanus, lifelong friends, were welcomed with such cordiality that Fabiola dreamt for a time of settling there permanently, near a master so well-versed in the interpretation of Holy Scriptures.[40] Another is Postumianus, the friend of Septimus Severus, who, between two visits in Egypt,

spent six months in Bethlehem, leaving his family there so as to
be free to visit the solitaries of the Thebaid.[41] Finally there is the
priest Paul Orosus, whom St. Augustine had asked to follow the
development of the Pelagian controversy in Palestine.[42] These are
only a few names among many others.[43] It is difficult to realize
the extent of this ceaseless movement of travellers, back and forth
between the Latin West and the Holy Places of Palestine.

After the devastation of Italy by the barbarians and the capture
of Rome, the stream of Latin travellers increased to unimaginable
proportions. They came thereafter, no longer motivated by the
desire of making a pilgrimage, but driven by fear. "Who would
believe," writes Jerome, "that the shores of the Orient, of Egypt,
of Africa are crowded with slaves and servants, arrived from
the City which was formerly the queen of the world, that every
day, Holy Bethlehem shelters as beggars those who formerly were
nobles and who abounded in wealthy possessions of all kinds? We
cannot help everyone: but at least we sympathize with their sufferings, and we unite our tears with theirs." [44] Palestine became
for those poor exiles a kind of promised land, the more so since
they found compatriots who had been settled there for a long
time. In the midst of people speaking Greek or Aramaic, these
Latins constituted there a small agglomeration, isolated and almost
impervious to Hellenism in any form.

Under such circumstances Jerome ceased to consider himself a
complete stranger, as he had in the desert of Chalcis; hence he
did not bestir himself very much to take part in the spiritual life
of the East. In Bethlehem, there were other monasteries besides
his own; Cassian and Germanus spent the years of their youth
there without having had Jerome as a master of asceticism.[45]
Palladius did not dwell with Jerome during his residence there.
The same thing was true of Jerusalem. The Greeks did not live
with the Latins. To the latter, the double monastery on the Mount
of Olives, under the direction of Rufinus of Aquileia and his
pious friend Melania the Elder, offered a natural shelter. During
the first years of their stay in Palestine, Jerome and Paula had
preserved most cordial relations with Rufinus and Melania, who

were old friends of theirs. They had not exactly the same ideas on mortification and the practices of the monastic life; they disagreed on the utility of profane culture and the use of pagan poets and orators; but these divergences in details did not interfere with their friendly intercourse. Rufinus' monks copied manuscripts for St. Jerome—not only the Sacred Books and ecclesiastical writers, but profane authors as well; and Rufinus, to whom we owe this information, adds that Jerome paid much more generously for the work when it happened to be the *Dialogues* of Cicero.[46]

The reason for this generosity was that Jerome needed these books to accomplish the tasks which kept him occupied part of the day, at least during a certain period. He had become a self-appointed school teacher. In spite of the solemn promises which he had made after his famous dream, he did not hesitate, in order to help young minds, to open again the books which he had promised never to touch. Though we are poorly informed concerning Jerome's pedagogical activity, we do know that it was restricted to the Latin language and literature. We can hardly conceive that his pupils were from Greek families desirous of initiating their children into the language of administration and of the army. That desire rarely existed in the Oriental world. Most probably, the school of Bethlehem was filled with young Latins, sons of officials, children of parents living as exiles in Palestine. Once more we find the same Latin atmosphere enveloping Jerome and, as it were, dominating him.

There is only one domain in which Jerome was constrained to yield to the discipline of the Orient—that of liturgy and the sacramental life. The monastery of Bethlehem was situated in the diocese of Jerusalem and, in a certain measure at least, was under the jurisdiction of its bishop. Jerome had, it is true, an oratory to which the monks might go to pray, and even to sing the psalms at the canonical hours. But, properly speaking, he had no church, so that for the liturgical ceremonies on Sundays and feast days the inhabitants were compelled to go to the Sanctuary of the

Nativity, where, naturally, the offices were celebrated in Greek, and where the sermons also were given in Greek.[47] Between the monks and the priests of Bethlehem relations were excellent,[48] as they had been at first between Bishop John of Jerusalem and Jerome.[49] They remained such to the end. Nevertheless the monks regretted not having their own officials in their monastery, and having to depend almost completely on an alien clergy. Jerome himself and his friend Vincentius had been ordained priests—the one at Antioch, the other at Constantinople—but they refused to exercise their sacerdotal powers, particularly to baptize and to celebrate the Holy Eucharist, a refusal owing as much to their humility as to the fact that they wished to maintain their monastic freedom.[50]

In order to comply with the desires of the Latin monks, St. Epiphanius of Salamis did not hesitate to confer the diaconate and the priesthood on Jerome's own brother, Paulinianus, in 394. The bishop of Jerusalem, however, refused to confirm the validity of this irregular ordination. He even went so far as to put an interdict on the monastery, so that for a time the religious found themselves deprived of all spiritual help and were forced to send their catechumens to Diospolis to receive baptism there from the hands of the bishop of that city.[51]

On one point, however, Jerome did modify this rather negative priestly attitude. He did not hesitate to address his monks, to explain to them the Psalms and the Gospels. His sermons have a very simple tone. They are familiar talks addressed to a restricted and well-known audience. Frequently one finds in them allusions to incidents of monastic life, to the singing of the Psalms and the recitation of the hours, to the good example monks should give, to the proximity of the Manger of the Savior, et cetera. One finds there also criticism, more or less veiled, of the customs of the Greeks, who err in the interpretation of this or that passage of Scripture, who celebrate the feast of Christmas on January 6th and not on December 25th, as is done in Rome and among the Latin monks. Jerome does not let pass a single occasion of reminding his confreres that they are Occidentals, and that, at least in their monastery, they constitute one family with the same language and the same spirit.[52]

This does not mean that there were no Easterners among the disciples of Jerome. The contrary would have been surprising. But it does not appear that these recruits were as numerous as the pious women grouped around St. Paula. As far as the latter are concerned, we know that they came from all the provinces, and that they were divided into three groups, corresponding to their social rank, although subject to the same discipline.[53] Less numerous, the monks remained grouped together, and it is probable that occasionally Jerome took into account the needs of his Greek-speaking brethren and gave them sermons which they could understand. At least this is suggested by the beginning of a Homily on Psalm 143, as it is interpreted generally: *"Propter eos qui ignorant latinam linguam, licet multa de evangelio dixerimus, tamen debemus et de psalterio quaedam dicere ut aliis saturatis, alii ieiunii non redeant."* The meaning of this text is not completely clear,[54] but the hypothesis seems to be that a Latin homily, and then a Greek homily destined for Orientals, followed one another during the same ceremony.

This delicate charity of St. Jerome touches us here the more because it compelled him to abandon his accustomed medium. We have just seen him surrounded by Latins. The monastery of Bethlehem has appeared before our eyes as a kind of Roman oasis in the midst of a foreign people. Yet this is not satisfactorily expressed. The thought of the saint is concerned only with Occidental problems, couched in Occidental terms. Years pass, ancient friendships are broken, one after the other, by the exigencies of life or by death. Yet the learned exegetic scholar, the tireless translator does not stop for a moment in his looking to Rome, Italy, Gaul for approval and criticism. Until the end, his relations put him in contact with the Latin world, and it would appear that the Orient became more and more foreign to him.

Formerly, at Constantinople, he had occasion to see the principal representatives of the theological thought of this time—

Gregory of Nazianzus, Gregory of Nyssa, Amphilochius of Iconium. At Alexandria, he had been the disciple of Didymus. He did not think for one moment of writing to them or of reading their theological works, or even of citing them in his letters or his commentaries. Only Epiphanius of Cyprus, John of Jerusalem, Theophilus of Alexandria play a part in his intellectual life. He had not been able to avoid the first two, with whom he was in constant touch. He had been introduced to the third at the time of the Origenist controversy, and for a few years he interpreted and vouched for him in the Christian society of the West. The difficulty once settled, however, Theophilus in turn disappears from the horizon. He will not appear again.

Jerome's great work—that which gives his laborious life its true significance—is the translation of the Bible from the Hebrew text, with comments which were destined more or less to explain and justify it. The translation was done for the Latin Church— it is hardly necessary to remark—and was destined, in the mind of its author, to replace the ancient versions made from the Septuagint. A profound feeling for the importance of his task and the real value of his work made Jerome unjust towards the venerable Greek translation. While praising the Hebrew text, he seems to have forgotten that the Septuagint had had that as a starting point, and that, all things considered, the Septuagint was of the same order as his own translation. He liked to point to its weaknesses, and for that purpose he delighted in comparing it with the other Greek versions. He considered the Hebrew text to be a collection of documents unquestionably free of error, which time had left untouched, while he stressed the variety of interpretations that the Greek manuscripts offered, which were proof of their corruption.[55]

It is true that he had to put up a stiff fight, for in the Latin world for which it was destined, his new translation met more adversaries than supporters. People found fault with it at first because of its novelty, then because it contained interpretations which were contrary to long-standing tradition. The complaint had some foundation, but it must be admitted that Jerome's replies were not always pertinent. Does not contemporary criticism show that in many cases the Septuagint is based on a Hebrew text anterior and preferable to ours, and that it helps in making useful corrections? On the other hand, is it not evident that St. Jerome's translation, in spite of its merits, is not free of mistakes, of false interpretations even, and that, like all human works, it could be perfected? The contemporaries of St. Jerome's, however, did not judge his work from this angle. Neither did he.

We must admire the perseverance with which he pursued his task during several years, regardless of the objections which were constantly before him. The Latins for whom he worked without respite did not do him justice while he was still living. After his death at least he has been splendidly requited.

Jerome's Biblical commentaries were, at the same time, justifications of his new translation and explanations, more or less literal, of the text. Here again, it was the Western public that the great doctor wished to reach. One may well wonder whether he had planned to build an original work, or merely to bring to the attention of the Latins the interpretations offered by the Greek authors. His first Biblical works were avowed translations of Origen: fourteen homilies on the Books of Jeremias, fourteen homilies on Ezechiel; then, a little later, two homilies on the Canticle of Canticles. The commentary on Ecclesiasticus, begun in Rome but completed in Bethlehem, is a transitional work. It is full of quotations, for, although Jerome makes frequent use of the words of his Hebrew master, he continually quotes the opinions of Christian exegetical scholars who have preceded him, at times approving their ideas, at times repudiating them: Origen, Victorinus of Pettau, Apollinaris, St. Gregory Thaumaturgus. In the course of several beautifully lyrical passages Jerome cites such profane authors as Sallust, Cicero, Horace, Terence, and Virgil. But all this is still rather badly digested and insufficiently assimilated.

In his commentaries on the Epistles to Philemon, to the Galatians, to the Ephesians, to Titus he is, on the contrary, in full control of his method. He still copies his predecessors extensively, especially Origen. However, he does not feel obliged to cite them. Hence his own thought is not always easily distinguished from that of his masters. In succeeding commentaries, until the end of his career, he acted in the same way. Some, such as the commentary on St. Matthew, are little more than adaptations. But others, especially the commentaries on Jeremias and Isaias, are much more the product of his own personal approach. Never does the master consent to abandon the Greek models which have become so familiar to him. When people criticize him for it, he explains with much vigor that the proper role of the exegete is not to excuse the reader from the task of criticizing and approving by offering him, gratuitously, ready-made formulas, but to face him with opinions widely at variance so as to give him opportunity to choose the best.[56] Most probably the method did not displease his Western readers. For if Jerome had to defend himself against passionate adversaries, he found, even in far-distant Gaul, enough fervent admirers for him to continue, until the end of his long career, the exegetical work he had undertaken in his youth.[57]

Though important, this work was not sufficient to fill the active life of so tireless a worker. Catholic primarily, devoted to the cause of orthodoxy even unto sacrifice, St. Jerome hardly heard of an erroneous doctrine without coming forth to refute it and to defend the traditional teaching of the Church. But we must add immediately that the only errors which seemed to interest him were those which might perturb the souls of his compatriots. His attitude, from the beginning of his stay in the Orient, toward the controversies involving the *hypostases* is characteristic; he did not seek to understand, to explain, to justify the vocabulary used by the Greeks. Firmly attached to the Latin formulas, he threw himself on their side, heart and soul. As his intervention was in fact unwise, and did not receive the approval of St. Damasus, he would not return to the question. He let this Trinitarian theology develop without him, outside of him. He took no part in the principal doctrinal movements of the Orient.

On the contrary, Jerome took a passionate interest in the questions then being debated in Rome. He wrote against the Luciferians—not, however, without treading as lightly as he possibly could, for Bishop Lucifer of Calaris, though now fallen into schism, had once been noted for his indomitable attachment to the faith of Nicea.[58] Some while later on, Jerome launched into circulation his violent pamphlet *Against Jovinian*. Jovinian had caused considerable turmoil in Italy by his attack on the doctrine concerning the perpetual virginity of the Blessed Virgin, which had issued in an attack on the Christian ascetical ideal as a whole. His Roman friends had advised Jerome of the matter. He could hardly contain himself before the prospect of such an adversary. He crushed him so completely that the refutation, once it arrived in Rome, gave rise to a series of scandalous comments, to the extent that Pammachius, who had originally requested the document, felt obliged to do his utmost to withdraw it from circulation. Nor did the letters which Jerome wrote to Domnion and to Pammachius himself by way of explanation have much effect toward calming spirits troubled by his original work.

Several years pass. Then, in faraway Gaul, a priest named Vigilantius, who had once been a guest at the monastery in Bethlehem, and who had made a fine impression there, ill-advisedly decided to criticize the cult of relics, and at the same time to call Jerome's attention to the matter. One night was sufficient for Jerome to dictate a new piece of invective whose thrust all but annihilated the imprudent Vigilantius. Then finally, after the fall of Rome in 410, Pelagius began to draw people's attention and to spread abroad his heretical ideas. After bringing down a condemnation upon himself in Africa, he took refuge in Palestine, together with some of his chief partisans. Jerome found himself in a position, once again, where he felt called upon to defend the cause of orthodoxy. First in his *Letter to Ctesiphon* and then in his *Dialogue against the Pelagians*, he denounced the new error with considerable fervor, seeing in it, in particular, one of the many evidences of a re-arising Origenism.

As a matter of fact, at that moment, the Origenist controversy had been long dead. Yet in the Alexandrian master, Jerome chose to see everywhere reminders, as it were, of the father of all heresies.

He attacked Origen without respite; the more so, it would seem, by way of making amends for the praise with which he had loaded him in his youth, and for the use he was still making of the great man's exegetical methods in his own commentaries. We need not here recount the incidents, sufficiently involved, that make up this controversy. But we must point out its artificial character, showing how Jerome used his talents, and, for a time at least, succeeded in keeping Rome and the West passionately interested in a question which, in our eyes, has but small importance.

Even during his lifetime, Origen had been a sign of contradiction among men. He remained such in death. But people hardly spoke of him at the end of the fourth century. It was for this reason that Jerome had been able to translate a number of his homilies into Latin without let or hindrance, and to incorporate others into his own commentaries. Only the theologians and heresy hunters immersed in the study of the past interested themselves sufficiently in his doctrine to find error there, and to refute it to the best of their ability. St. Epiphanius of Salamis had attacked him relentlessly. But no one, either in his entourage or elsewhere, found it necessary to take him very seriously.

But it happened that in 393 a certain monk of unknown origin, named Atarbius, took a notion, without particular authorization, to make a demand on all sides for a condemnation of Origen. Jerome, in his passion for orthodoxy, was weak enough to yield to this solicitation. The incident would have passed without consequence, had not Bishop John of Jerusalem been brought into the affair, and had he not found it necessary, for the preservation of his episcopal rights, to cut off from communion with his church both the monks of Bethlehem and their chief, St. Jerome.

For the moment, the trouble was localized strictly in Palestine —as a matter of fact, in Jerusalem. It was Jerome who poured oil on the flame by translating into Latin a letter of Bishop Epiphanius in which he attacked Bishop John of Jerusalem. Jerome, of course, maintained that the translation had been done in haste, at the explicit request of Eusebius of Cremona, and that it had not been intended for publication. But he was not naive enough to believe that a letter from his pen would long remain unknown to his friends in Rome. As a matter of fact, this translation was not slow in being circulated throughout the capital, where it caused an immediate tumult. A violent pamphlet, the *Contra Joannem Hierosolymitanum*, followed it to the West, as an explanation and justification of Jerome's part in the affair. With matters coming to a climax, it was at this very moment, in 398, that Rufinus of Aquileia had the almost inconceivable audacity to publish a Latin translation of Origen's *De principiis* —that is, of the very work wherein the Alexandrian's principal theological opinions—and, as a consequence, his most notable errors—were developed most precisely.[59] Thereupon, the center of the battle shifted from Palestine to Rome, as all the world soon came to realize.

In truth, even the most learned of the Christians in Rome were hard put to explain the content of Origenism. They had never heard much talk of Origen until the appearance of the exegetical works of Jerome; and even Rufinus' translation of the *Peri-archon* was not intended to enlighten them to any large extent. For Rufinus, as a wise man, felt himself authorized to tone down certain audacious opinions of his author, and to eliminate those passages which he rightfully considered interpolations. Hence, when the people at Rome first became acquainted with Jerome's translation, they gave way to no little astonishment. Why make such a stir over a work so harmless—as a matter of fact, so orthodox? Why should Jerome, the counsellor of the Christian aristocracy of the capital, betray such great emotion when speaking of the errors of Origen? And why, indeed, as Rufinus had pointed out so carefully in his preface, had Jerome never heretofore hesitated to take inspiration from Origen in his own Biblical commentaries? It was Pammachius and Oceanus who undertook to forward these queries to Bethlehem, pointing out how universally they were being made. Their letter, as one might imagine, provoked a tempest. Jerome's answer consisted in three documents: An apology to Pammachius;[60] a letter to Rufinus; and, of prime interest, a new translation of the *De principiis*.

This translation was placed before the Latin public as a strictly literal version. As a matter of fact, it is no more so, though done from a completely opposite viewpoint, than that of Rufinus. For the hypotheses of Origen, Jerome substitutes affirmations; for delicate nuances shaded by formulas of doubt, Jerome supplies vivid and striking colors, punctuated by expressions both trenchant and categorical. We possess only fragments of the work, but they suffice to inform us of the state of mind in which Jerome found himself when setting out to do the translation. If he had really set out to provoke wonder and scandal thereby, he certainly should have been satisfied. Even though, in the beginning, his translation was carefully guarded, the public was not slow to get copies of it; and, as if to increase the danger, it got about at first in extracts which seemed carefully selected to provoke the immediate reaction of all the orthodox consciences at Rome, and then in the whole of Italy.

It was in the wake of these happenings that Theophilus, the bishop of Alexandria, took occasion to make a pronouncement against Origen. One would like to be able to say that, in so doing, he was indulging his zeal for orthodoxy; but, as a matter of fact, it was the pursuit of a personal matter, his own tendentious difficulties with several influential monks, that occasioned his action. Jerome, happy to find in the bishop a powerful auxiliary, did not take time to inform himself of the latter's real sentiments. He made himself the willing translator of the bishop's letters against Origen; thanks to which, the West was, for a number of years, kept up-to-date on Theophilus' literary productions. He even went so far as to pass on into Latin a violent pamphlet, at once unjust and odious, which Theophilus had composed against St. John Chrysostom. But Jerome was poorly compensated for his pains. For the Alexandrian bishop wound up by becoming reconciled to the monks in question, and from then on, failed to find anything further of an heretical nature in the works of Origen, which he began to read without scruple.

The scholar of Bethlehem was at least more loyal. Until the end of his long career, he pursued Origen with a tenacious rancor, and all those, as well, who had either sustained or appeared to sustain Origen in doctrinal matters. Among these, Rufinus was, in Jerome's eyes, the most guilty. Even after he had died, Jerome did not spare him, nor did he ever forgive him the translation of the *De principiis*.

The aspect of the controversy that is most remarkable, as far as we are concerned, is that which, by the will of St. Jerome, it took on in the West. Until the end of the fourth century, the Latin world had simply not been interested in the Alexandrian doctor. Most Latins hardly knew his name, and those who did saw in him an intrepid commentator on the Scriptures. Whether or not he was a heretic made very little difference. It required a *coup de force* on Jerome's part to change the situation. For several years thereafter, Rome and Italy at least were passionately concerned with the subject. After the death of Pope Siricius, who sympathized but little with Jerome, Pope Anastasius, his successor in the apostolic see, took a more favorable attitude. He condemned all that Origen had written against the Catholic faith, without even taking the trouble to verify the exactness of the propositions thus rejected. He writes to Simplicianus of Milan,[61] and to his successor, Venerius,[62] to spark their zeal in favor of the cause. He refused to accept the defense of Rufinus, whom he leaves, he says, to the judgment of God.[63] Jerome fans this fire as much as he can. The important thing is to prevent it from dying out. He writes to his friends, he composes at one sitting his *Apologia,* as an answer to that of Rufinus, and when Chromatius of Aquileia advises him to put an end to the quarrel, he refuses to do so. The third book of his *Apologia* is still more violent than the first two. Peaceful minds are finally saddened, even scandalized at such relentlessness.

"I do not know," writes St. Augustine to Jerome, "what the slanderous writings are that are supposed to have come to Africa about you. I have received, however, what you have deigned to send me in answer to these libels. After having read it, I confess that I have felt much sorrow that there should have arisen the evil of discord between persons so dear and so intimate, and whom all the Churches knew to have been united by the closest bonds—Woe to him by whom scandal cometh! What hearts can now be sure of fidelity? In whose bosom will sincere affection find a place? What friend will not fear to become some day an enemy, realizing the lamentable case of Jerome and Rufinus?" [64]

In reality, however, the excitement proved to be of minor consequence, for the controversy died out as unexpectedly as it had begun. Yet, as we have seen, St. Jerome continued until his death to heap insults and railleries upon Rufinus' memory; and though continuing to use Origen in his *Commentaries,* he was careful to distinguish between the intelligent exegetical scholar and the dangerous theologian. Jerome was simply one of those who find it impossible to forgive. But his friends thought rightly that it was better for them to turn their minds to other things. A solitary instance of continued interest in the question is supplied in 409, when the Spanish priest Avitus asked St. Jerome for a correct copy of his translation of the *De principiis,* complaining that he had only one poor copy, full of mistakes.

At this time, the Romans had enough worries without bothering about Origenism. The Barbarians occupied Italy, and the inhabitants of the capital felt far from secure behind its Aurelian wall. The fall of Rome in 410 drew their minds away from theological quarrels. The Origenist affair as such had had no repercussion in the East, for it was only superficially and arbitrarily that some had tried to link the name of the old Alexandrian exegete with that of St. John Chrysostom. In the West, the influence of St. Jerome alone had caused the explosion. As soon as he ceased his agitations, calm returned, and one does not find in letters written after 405 any evidence of a fresh disturbance.

All things considered, nothing is more significant than this story in making us realize the influence exercised by St. Jerome in the West, along with the indifference with which he is met in the East. Jerome is certainly the most learned man of his time.[65] He dedicates his whole life to theology and exegesis. He resides in Bethlehem without interruption from 385 to 419. Around him are discussed important questions. The Orientals pay as little attention to him as he himself pays to them; and if he translates a few letters of St. Epiphanius and of Theophilus of Alexandria into Latin, it is not because of their real value, but because their subject is somehow related to the quarrels in which he is personally involved.

On the other hand, he is the oracle of the West. Messages go back and forth without interruption between Italy, Africa, Gaul, Spain and Palestine. Everybody seeks his advice: pious women, desirous of making progress along the arduous path of perfection; laymen interested in exegetical matters; priests concerned with theology; even the bishops solicit the help of his learning. Many come to visit him, from Bishop Alypius of Thagaste to Senator Oceanus. Several Popes entertain cordial relations with him. As soon as he raises his voice, everybody listens to him respectfully. The least important works that come from his pen stir universal attention. His private letters even are copied, so that sometimes the general public is informed concerning them before they can reach the person to whom they were directed.[66]

Facts apparently so strange throw a striking light on the situation of the Christian Church at the end of the fourth century and at the beginning of the fifth. Unquestionably, the unity of the Church is maintained in theory. There is no schism between the Christian East and West. Rome is the center to which all questions are eventually referred, and it is from Rome that all the answers come. But actually the Orientals concern themselves with their own affairs and the Occidentals with theirs, and rarely does it happen that the same questions solicit the attention of both groups. Even men of Jerome's stature do not succeed as mediators between the two, despite their favorable position. Hence, in the over-all picture, should we not be justified in feeling that the separation of two sections of the Christian Church contains real dangers?

NOTES

[1] Cf. the chronology worked out by F. Cavallera, *Saint Jérôme, sa vie et son oeuvre* (Louvain, 1922), II, 3–63.

[2] Cf. F. Cavallera, *Le schisme d'Antioche* (Paris, 1905); R. de Regnon,

Etudes de théologie positive sur la Sainte Trinité (Paris, 1892); K. Holl,
Amphilochius von Ikonium und sein Verhältnis zu der grossen Kappadoziern
(Tübingen, 1904).

[3] Cf. G. Voison, *L'Apollinarisme* (Louvain, 1901); H. Lietzmann, *Apollinaris von Laodicea und seine Schule* (Tübingen, 1904).

[4] Cf. P. Courcelle, *Les lettres grecques en Occident, de Macrobe à Cassiodore* (Paris, 1943), 37–47; G. Bardy, "La culture grecque dans l'Occident chrétien au IVe siècle," *Rech. de Sci. relig.*, 29 (1939), 32. There is question as to whether it was in Rome or at Antioch that Jerome became acquainted with Aristotelian dialectics and read Porphyry's *Isagoge*, Aristotle's *Categoriae*, and the *De interpretatione*, *Analytica* and *Topica*, along with the Commentaries of Alexander of Aphrodisias. See Jer., *Ep.* 50 (*Ad Domnion: PL*, 22, 513). Rome appears the more logical place. It is quite possible, however, that Jerome is doing a bit of boasting, and has only read these books in Latin translations.

[5] Jer., *Ep.* 15.

[6] Cf. F. Cavallera, *Saint Jérôme*, II, 19. P. Courcelle (*Les lettres grecques*, 38, n. 4) thinks Jerome may have met Apollinaris during his first sojourn in Antioch. But even before 375, Apollinaris' doctrine, if not his person, had been condemned explicitly.

[7] Jerome, later on, tries to exonerate himself by saying that he never discussed doctrinal questions with Apollinaris (cf. *Ep.* 84, 3): "Dum essem iuvenis, miro discendi ferebar ardore nec iuxta quondam praesumptionem ipse me docui. Apollinarium Laodiceum audivi Antiochiae frequenter et colui; et cum me in sanctis Scripturis erudiret, nunquam illius contentiosum super sensu dogma suscepi."

[8] Jer., *De vir. ill.*, 117; *Ep.* 50, 4; 52, 8; *Adv. Jov.*, I, 13; *Apol. in Ruf.*, I, 13, 30; *Comm. in Eph.*, V, 32; *Comm. in Is.*, III, iv, 1. Jerome's phrase *praeceptor meus*, in reference to Gregory Nazianzen, does not necessarily mean that they were on intimate terms at this time. Jerome likes the phrase; cf. on Donatus, Jer., *Chron. can.* ad annum 354.

[9] Jer., *De vir.*, 128: "ante paucos annos mihi et Gregorio Nazianzeno contra Eunomium legit libros."

[10] Jer., *ibid.*, 133: "Nuper mihi librum legit de Spiritu Sancto . . ."

[11] Jer., *Chron. can.* ad annum 360.

[12] Jer., *ibid.*, 376.

[13] *Id.*, 348.

[14] *Id.*, 375.

[15] Jer., *Didymi de Spiritu Sancto liber*, praef. (*PL*, 23, 103–4).

[16] Cf. Jer., *De vir.*, 124: "Ambrose of Milan continues to write; as he is still alive, I refrain from formulating any judgment, to avoid being accused of flattery or of truth." The allusion to St. Ambrose in the preface to Paulinian is made certain by the witness of Rufinus (*Apol. adv. Jer.*, II, 24–5: *PL*, 21, 603). Likewise in Jerome's preface to the translation of Origen's homilies on St. Luke, he writes to Paula and Eustochium: "You tell me you have read certain commentaries on St. Matthew and St. Luke. The first is as dull from its matter as from its style; the second wrestles with words, but it limps as far as ideas are concerned. . . . I have thus put my own book on *Hebraic Questions* aside for a while, to comply with your wishes; and in my free moments I have taken to dictating the work of another [Didymus] author rather than my own, principally because I hear an oracular crow [Ambrose] croaking on the left, who clothes himself quite

strangely in the plumage of other birds, when he himself is really very dark." (*PL*, 24, 219–20.)

[17] Cf. Jer., *Ep.* 61, addressed to Pope Damasus: "I have in my hands Didymus' *Book on the Holy Ghost*. I desire to dedicate it to you, now that I have translated it."

[18] Jer., *Orig. hom. in Ezech.*, praef. (*PL*, 25, 583–6).

[19] Jer., *Ep.* 33.

[20] Jer., *Quaest. Heb.*, praef. (*PL*, 23, 938): "Hoc unum dico, quod vellem cum invidia nominis eius habere etiam scientiam scripturarum, flocci pendens imagines umbrasque larvarum quarum natura esse dicitur terrere parvulos et in angulis garrire tenebrosis."

[21] This incident is mentioned by Rufinus (*De adult. lib. Orig.*, I: *PG*, 17–629–30). Cf. F. Cavallera, *St. Jérôme*, I, 96.

[22] Jer., *Apol. adv. Ruf.*, III, 22.

[23] Jer., *Onomast.*, praef. (*PL*, 23, 771).

[24] For Jerome's own notice of Eusebius, who plays a rather sad role in this whole controversy, see Jer., *Ep.* 57, 2.

[25] Marius Mercator, *Comm. adv. haer. Pelagii* (*PL*, 48, 3); cf. Jer., *Apol. adv. Ruf.*, III, 24; F. Cavallera, *St. Jérôme*, I, 96–7.

[26] Jer., *Ep.* 134.

[27] Jer., *Ep.* 115 (in 404 or 405); *Ep.* 116. He seems to be the same person who also brings Jerome the Letter of Sunnia and Fretela (*Ep.* 106).

[28] Jer., *Ep.* 145.

[29] In 397 or 398, four monks left Jerome's monastery to return to the West. Cf. Jer., *Apol. adv. Ruf.*, III, 24.

[30] Jer., *Ep.* 47.

[31] *Id.*, *Ep.* 71, dated as of 398.

[32] Jer., *Ep.* 68, of about the same time. Heraclius, its bearer, seems to have been a monk from Jerome's monastery.

[33] Jer., *Ep.* 145, apparently before 400.

[34] Jer., *Ep.* 58, of 395; cf. Cavallera, "Hieronymiana II," *Bull. de lit. eccl.* (1924), 148–150.

[35] Jer., *Ep.* 53, of 395.

[36] Cf. Pallad., *Hist. Laus.*, 36, 7: "In this environ, there lived the priest Jerome, a man distinguished by his competence in Latin letters and by his natural gifts. But he was afflicted with such umbrage that his literary work was eclipsed thereby." Posidonius, who had also lived with Jerome, says of him: "On account of this man, there will never be another saint in these parts, for his enviousness reached even unto his own brother." There is no need to go into the question of Palladius here. It is sufficient to recall that Jerome returned his antipathy. Cf. Jer., *Dial. contra Pelag.*, prol. (*PL*, 23, 497): "Palladius servilis nequitiae eandem haeresim [Pelagianism] instaurare conatus est, et novam translationis hebraicae mihi calumniam struere."

[37] Jer., *Ep.* 147. Cf. Tillemont, *Mém. pour Hist. eccl.*, 12, 399. Cavallera, *St. Jérôme*, I, 172.

[38] Cf. Baumstark, *Abendl. Palästinpilger des erst. Jahrt. und ihre Berichte* (Cologne, 1906); Vincent-Abel, *Jerusalem* (Paris, 1926), II, 396, 907, 921; *DACL*, 14 (1938), 65ff.

[39] Jer., *Ep.* 58, 1 (to Paulinus). Jerome here admits that Vigilantius was well received in Bethlehem, at first. But he describes their arguments, and admits he thought Vigilantius rather stupid.

[40] Jer., *Ep.* 77; *Apol. adv. Ruf.*, III, 4.

[41] Sulp. Sev., *Dialog.*, i, 9.

[42] Jer., *Ep.* 131 (inter *Ep.* Aug. 146); cf. Orosius, *Apolog.* 4 (*PL*, 31, 1177 B).

[43] Among these messengers were Ambrose, coming from Nola (Jer., *Ep.* 53), the sub-deacon Austerius (*Ep.* 103, 103); the deacon Cyprian (*Ep.* 104); the deacon Presidius (*Ep.* 103); and those from Africa; as well as Sisinnius and Apodemius, who bring letters from St. Euxuperius of Toulouse, and his compatriots Riparius, Desiderius, Minervius, Alexander, etc.

[44] Cf. Jer., *Comm. in Ezech.*, praef. in lib. III (*PL*, 25, 75); in lib. VIII (199).

[45] Cf. Cassian, *Collat.* 17, 7; Tillemont, *Mémoires* 12, 126.

[46] Ruf., *Apol.*, II, 8; Jerome fails to answer this accusation of Rufinus, thus depriving us of its full meaning.

[47] The information supplied by the *Peregrinatio Aetheriae* on the liturgy of Jerusalem is applicable to Bethlehem as well.

[48] Jer., *Ep.* 12, 2: "In viculo Bethlehem presbyteris eius quantum in nobis est, communione sociamur."

[49] Jer., *Ep.* 83, 11: "Sit talis qualis ante fuit, quando nos suo arbitrio diligebat." Given the theological school to which John belonged, however, it would be hard to see how Jerome could have had much affection for him.

[50] Jer., *Ep.* 51, 1; *Contra Joan. Hier.*, 41 (*PL*, 23, 395).

[51] Jer., *ibid.*, 41. It is not extraordinary to find monks not yet baptized. Rufinus himself received baptism in the monastery of Bishop Chromatius at Aquileia.

[52] Jer., *Ep.* 108, 20.

[53] Cf. G. Morin, *Etudes, textes, découvertes, contribution à la litterature et à l'histoire des douze premiers siècles* (Maredsous, 1913), 220–93: Les monuments de la prédication de Saint Jérôme.

[54] The simplest meaning seems to be as follows: "I have just spoken in Latin on the Gospel; and I am now going to speak in Greek on the Psalter for those who do not know Latin." However, the sermon on the Psalter is in Latin, and it is difficult to look upon it as a translation. Our text may also be interpreted: "After having spoken (in Greek) on the Gospel, on account of those who do not know Latin, I am going now to speak in Latin on the Psalter."

[55] Cf. Jer., *In Eccles. comm.* (*PL*, 23, 1050); *In Ep. ad. Gal.*, praef. (*PL*, 26, 309); *Ep.*, 61, 1; 85, 1; *In Matt. comm.*, praef. (*PL*, 26, 15–18).

[56] Jer., *Apol. adv. Ruf.*, I, 16 (*PL*, 23, 409–10); "Commentarii quid operis habent? Alterius dicta edisserunt, quae obscure scripta sunt plano sermone manifestant, multorum sententias replicant et dicunt: 'Hunc locum quidam sic edisserunt, alii sic interpretantur, illi sensum suum et intelligentiam his testimoniis et hac nituntur ratione firmare, ut prudens lectorum diversas explanationes legerit et multorum vel probanda vel improbanda didicerit, iudicet quid verius sit et quasi bonus trapezita adulterinae moretae pecuniam reprobet.' "

[57] On the criticisms passed on Jerome's commentaries, see F. Cavallera, *op. cit.*, II, 110–13. There is question as to whether Jerome's Scriptural writings were not appreciated in the East. His Psalter was translated, first of all, upon the request of Sophronius, a Greek by birth who lived in Palestine, probably at Bethlehem. (Cf. *In transl. Psalt.*, praef.: *PL*, 28, 1113.) According to the *De vir.* (134), the same Sophronius seems to have translated into Greek a few of the minor works of St. Jerome, along with the Latin version

of the Psalter and the Prophets: "Opuscula mea in graecum sermonem ele-
gantissime transtulit, psalterium quoque et prophetas, quos nos de hebraeo in
latinum vertimus." See also Jerome's Preface to *Esdras* (*PL*, 28, 1404):
". . . aliud est si, clausis quod dicitur oculis, mihi volunt maledicere et non
imitantur graecorum studium ac benevolentiam, qui post septuaginta translatores, iam Christi evangelico coruscante Iudaeos et Ebionitas, legis veteris
interpretos, Aquilam videlicet et Symmachium et Theodotionem, et curiose
legunt et per Origenis laborem in ἐξαπλοῖς ecclesiis dedicarunt. Quanto
magis Latini grati esse deberint, quod exsultantem cernerent graeciam a se
aliquid mutuari!" Sophronius seems to have promised this translation of the
Latin Psalter even before it was finished.

As for the commentaries, Père Abel wonders if St. Cyril of Alexandria had
not known and used them. Given the almost intimate relation which joined
the Solitary of Bethlehem and Theophilus, the patriarch of Alexandria, uncle
of St. Cyril, during the Origenist controversy and until 406, it would not be
surprising that Jerome had sent him a copy of his writings, and that this copy
had been deposited with care in the episcopal library. At Alexandria one
could hardly help knowing about the literary activity of St. Jerome, especially
as his friends and acquaintances came there to embark for Europe. They
must have spoken about the books they were carrying with their luggage. It
is not certain that St. Cyril knew Latin, but he had in his chancery interpreters capable of reading and translating it in his stead. The parallels noted
by Père Abel are not conclusive; they are, however, numerous and suggestive
enough to attract our attention. Cf. F. Abel, "La géographie sacrée chez St.
Cyrille d'Alexandrie," *Rev. Bibl.*, 21 (1922), 407–27; "Parallélisme exégé-
tique entre Saint Jérôme et Saint Cyrille d'Alexandrie," *Vivre et Penser*, I
(1941), 94, 119, 212, 233.

[58] The date of the *Altercatio Luciferiani et Orthodoxi* is controverted. Cf.
F. Cavallera, *Saint Jérôme*, II, 18–19. He holds that the years involved are
from 377 to 379, during Jerome's second stay at Antioch, a contention he
bases on Jerome's autobiography in the *De vir.*, 135.

[59] Cf. F. Murphy, *Rufinus of Aquileia (345–411), His Life and Works*
(Washington, 1945), 59–110.

[60] Jer., *Ep.* 84.

[61] Anast., *Ep ad. Simplic.* (*PL*, 20, 74).

[62] *Id., Ep. ad Vener.* (ed J. Van den Gehyn, "La lettre du pape Anastase
Ier a Saint Vénérius, évêque de Milan," *Rev. d'hist. et de litt. relig.*, IV,
1899, 1–12).

[63] Anast., *Ep. ad Ioan. Hier.* (*PL*, 20, 68–73).

[64] Aug., *Ep.* 73, 6.

[65] In a matter of erudition, one can hardly find a name to couple with his,
except that of St. Epiphanius, whose panegyrists are pleased to write that he
knew five languages. But that knowledge, at least as far as Latin was concerned, was very superficial. As a writer, the Bishop of Salamis had a style
without elegance and without gracefulness, a fact which does not argue in
favor of a large culture. Jerome's case is absolutely different; he is a Latin
author who preaches in Greek, and for whom Hebrew has no secret.

[66] This was the case particularly with letters written by St. Augustine to
Jerome. There were also letters of Jerome's that went astray: the letter to
Rufinus, for example, sent him after the translation of the *De principiis*.

St. Jerome as an Historian

FRANCIS X. MURPHY, C.SS.R.

St. Jerome as an Historian

T HE SEVENTY-ODD years that form the Age of St. Jerome—
from 347 to 420—were hardly an era of great historical writing. As F. Lot and Professor Laistner have pointed out, but for
the productions of the pagan Ammianus Marcellinus and the
Christian Sulpicius Severus, the fifth century finds the West bereft
of any true historian. But the situation might easily have been
different. For, several times in the course of his long, eventful
career, the most erudite man of the age, Jerome of Stridon, had
promised himself and posterity that he would get round to writing
a first-class history of the Christian era. Thus, in the opening
chapter of his *Life of Malchus,* written in 390 or 391, Jerome
says:

I have purposed—if the Lord gives me life and my detractors
cease to persecute me, who am now a fugitive and shut off from the
world—to write a history from the coming of the Savior down to our
own times, from the Apostles to the dregs of this age, and to describe
how and through whom Christ's Church came into being; how,
growing up, it waxed by persecutions and was crowned with martyr-
doms; and how, after reaching the Christian Emperors, it became
yet greater in power and wealth, but declined in virtue.[1]

A decade earlier, when finishing his translation of the *Chronicle*
of Eusebius of Caesarea (381), he had also promised:

I have been content to reserve for a much broader history (*latiori
historiae*) the remainder of the reigns of Gratian and Theodosius,
not because I hesitate to write freely and truthfully about the living
—for the fear of the Lord dispels the fear of men—but because, with
the barbarians roving about wildly on our very own soil, all things
are uncertain.[2]

Jerome was actually haunted by an historical sense. It permeates his Scriptural commentaries. It is continually betraying itself in his letters and controversies. It was due unquestionably to the classical training to which he had been subjected as a boy—to his familiarity with Tacitus and Livy, with Suetonius, Herodotus and Xenophon. But it was just as certainly due to the influences of Christianity thrust upon him in Rome, as an impressionable youth coming into contact with the recently recognized ecclesiastical authorities, as well as wandering through the catacombs, and meditating upon this new spiritual force that "in the fulness of time" was found gradually growing upon Imperial Rome.

An early indication of such historical awareness is given in his preoccupation with the work of Hilary of Poitiers, *On the Synods,* when he arrived in Treves in 367, having completed his classical studies in Rome.[3] It is equally evident in his appeal to the Pope in Rome a few years later, when in the desert of Chalcis he is called upon by the contentious monks there to take a stand with regard to the Antiochian schism and the Trinitarian controversy then raging: "Now indeed, *proh dolor!* After the faith of Nicea, after the decree of Alexandria joined in by the West, a new expression for the three hypostases is demanded by the Arian offspring, by these peasants, of me, a man of Rome!"[4] It is fully apparent, once he has been through the "postgraduate" Scripture course at Constantinople under (among others) St. Gregory Nazianzen. For almost immediately thereafter, Jerome set about the translation and revision of Eusebius' *Chronicle* of world history.

But even before turning his hand to the *Chronicle,* Jerome had betrayed a considerable historical interest and insight in his *Dialogue against the Luciferians*[5]—disciples of Bishop Lucifer of Calaris, who had gone into schism over the question of receiving back into the Church the bishops guilty of defection at the Council of Rimini. Writing the *Dialogue* at Antioch in 378, Jerome utilizes the conversation between an orthodox Catholic and a Luciferian named Helladius to refute, one after another, the objections brought against granting pardon to the bishops who had already been admitted to penance at the Council of Alexandria in 362. He displays at once a complete mastery of the historical narratives of the Gospels, and in particular of the Acts of the Apostles. He manifests a thorough familiarity with the Acts of the councils of Nicea and of Rimini, as well as with the writings of Cyprian, Hilary and Tertullian.

Though this dialogue is an early work of St. Jerome's, it demonstrates at once his clear-cut appreciation of the role of tradition in explaining and supporting the Scriptures. In it he witnesses to the ecclesiastical patterns that go back to the very origins, concerning the sacraments, the role of the Church and of the episcopate, as well as to numerous liturgical practices.[6] He likewise displays a concern for the history of heresy, from the days of the Jewish religion down through the earliest Christian heretics to his own day—a preoccupation that will be characteristic of all his future writings. And everywhere he points to historical sources, to trustworthy evidence, in support of his contentions. Thus he advises:

If anyone desires to learn further about these matters, let him consult the Acts of the Synod of Rimini, whence we ourselves have drawn these facts. . . . Should anyone think these things to have been made up by us, let him consult the public records. The archives of the Church are complete. And indeed, the memory of these things is still fresh. There are still men living who were present at this Synod [Rimini]. And, what decides the matter, the Arians themselves do not deny that these things happened as we report them. . . .[7]

It seems really as a result of his stay in Constantinople (c. 380–381) that, along with his Scriptural interests, Jerome caught sight of the real meaning and indispensability of historical studies for the Scripture scholar. It was as a result of his contact with men like Apollinaris of Laodicea and Gregory Nazianzen, as well as of his wide reading in Origen, Irenaeus, and above all in Eusebius of Caesarea.[8]

Jerome had been brought up in the West in an age when historical writing had reached a low ebb. The pagan productions of the day, with the already mentioned exception of Ammianus

Marcellinus, were a few epitomes and biographical surveys—the works of men like Eutropius, Aurelius Victor and Rufius Festus, along with the so-called *Historia Augusta*: mainly abridgements of Livy and conventional pictures of the Roman emperors, traceable to the imitation of Suetonius and Tacitus. For the most part, the age had lost the concept of the historian as a literary artist who gives a well-rounded picture of an epoch "in which the importance of individual persons and episodes are justly appraised as larger or smaller parts of a whole, and in which certain broad philosophic concepts serve as a guide through a maze of history and as an aid for the reader towards a true interpretation." [9]

In coming upon Eusebius' *Chronicle*, Jerome had been immediately struck by the vast sweep of its accomplishment. For Eusebius had published a résumé of universal history from Adam down to the reign of Constantine, complete with chronological tables and references. It was really part of his *Preparatio Evangelica*, a vast work of synthesis that was to form a complete apology for the Christian religion.[10] Jerome at once perceived the immensity and the utility of the résumé. Before him, Hilary of Poitiers, Eusebius of Vercelli and Chromatius of Aquileia had been exposed to this Greek ecclesiastical learning, but had apparently failed to appreciate its full significance. Jerome grasped its indispensability in permitting the Western Christian to orientate himself in the course of world history, and thus facilitate his study both of the Scriptures and of the milieu of profane knowledge. Hence his determination to translate the *Chronicle*, without, however, also doing into Latin the chronological tables which were really an adaptation from the chronographer, Julius Africanus (c. 240).

By way of preparation for his task, Jerome seems to have familiarized himself with his own Latin authors, in particular with Suetonius and Tacitus, and perhaps also with the epitome of Pompeius Trogus' *Philippic History* made by M. Junius Justinus in the third century. For the translation, while faithful to the original, contains numerous references introduced by Jerome as of interest to his Western readers. He begins his own preface to the translation by some remarkably sensible observations with regard to translation methods. He then set forth part of the difficulty of the task:

And to this difficulty [the unreality of a strictly literal rendition] which is common to all translation work, this further affects us, that this history is so complicated, having strange-sounding names, things not known to Latins, inexplicable numbers, critical marks intertwined with text and numerals, so that it is almost more difficult to explain the method of reading than it is to proceed to a notice of the reading.[11]

He then explains his critical apparatus in which, while following the pattern set by Eusebius, he makes use of several columns in recording contemporary reigns, but marks each with a different type of ink, so that the brief text of commentary on each particular event or personage may be lined up with the proper year to which it belongs. He concludes his preface with the remark:

I would rather have my readers satisfied, so that they may assign to its proper author the truth of the Greek [original], and may realize that those things which we have inserted on our own have been culled from the most reliable authors. It should be known that I have used in part both the assistance of a translator and of an amanuensis, so that I have given exact expression to the Greek, and have also injected into the story a good deal of Roman history, which Eusebius, the original author of this book, did not do, not so much because he was ignorant of the latter—for he was a most learned man—but because, writing for a Greek audience, he did not feel it necessary.

Thus, from Ninus and from Abraham down to the fall of Troy, it is a simple translation from the Greek. From Troy to the twentieth year of Constantine, many things have been added and changed round, which I have taken most carefully from Suetonius and from other illustrious historians. From the above-mentioned year of Constantine [325] down to the consulate of the august Caesars, Valentinian II and Valens [378], the whole is my own.[12]

In the beginning of his preface, Jerome makes some remark regarding the translation as an *"opus tumultuarium"* [13]—but he is certainly exaggerating. For the complexity and the ingenuity with which he has the various tables of parallel reigns worked out belie any such thing as haste. However, as Helm has remarked of the interpolations regarding the literary figures of Latin antiquity in particular, Jerome must have jotted down annotations from Suetonius and the other authors on the margin of his copy of Eusebius' text.[14] Then, under the confusion of his own revisions and rearrangement, a number of these additions tended to get misplaced. However, Jerome had no certain chronology regarding these ancient authors that he could follow without fear of error. There simply was no good Latin tradition dating these various writers. Thus are explained certain inconsistencies and apparent indecisions that Jerome is attempting to cover with his "*tumultuarium.*"

In translating the *Chronicle,* Jerome, as he says, added much new material for the period beginning with the Trojan war. It has been recently suggested that he was following, in his arrangement, Justinus' epitome of the *Philippic History* of Pompeius Trogus: [15] so that while Jerome appears to be definitely paralleling his history to fit in with a philosophy of the *Four Empires,* he is influenced much more particularly by the secular current of thought than by the Biblical commentaries of Hippolytus, Tertullian and Origen upon the Prophets of the Old Testament, and in particular upon the Book of Daniel. This presupposes a thorough familiarity upon Jerome's part with Trogus, and with the current of Latin thought he represents, which indeed goes all the way back to Ennius, and is reflected in the chronographers and in Claudian. But although Jerome does point with scorn to the evils inherent in the Roman Empire, there seems to be lacking in his observations the definitely anti-imperial spirit and condemnatory approach that is characteristic of Trogus. Likewise, there is serious question as to Jerome's familiarity with this particular historian. He does not mention him until he is writing his own *Commentary on the Prophet Daniel* in 407,[16] some twenty-seven years after his translation of the *Chronicle.* Then he is definitely influenced by the parade of authorities cited by Porphyry in his attack upon Daniel.

What seems to point to the influence of Trogus, however, is the fact that Jerome, departing from Eusebius' arrangement, outlines his history with the four great empires of Assyria, Persia, Greece and Rome succeeding each other in the second, or "guide," column of his manuscript. Like Trogus, he seems to have had considerable difficulty placing the Medes, whom, at this period, he did not consider one of the four principal imperial nations.[17] Eusebius, not following this pattern, had left one hundred and eleven years after the fall of Assyria free, before beginning an account of the Persians. Jerome fills in the gap with the names of eight kings of the Medes, only four of whom Eusebius had mentioned in his text, though he had named the other four in the chronological preface to the work. In his own preface, Jerome merely mentions Suetonius and "other illustrious historians" as the source of his additions.[18] Thus, though he is obviously conforming to a pattern other than that set by the original, it is still an open question as to whether he is being guided by his Biblical knowledge of Daniel and the commentators, or whether he is drawing from Trogus and the anti-imperial literature of the Augustan age.

The third section of Jerome's *Chronicle,* covering the period from A.D. 325 to 379, Jerome claims as his own, though here he leans heavily on Eutropius, the *magister memoriae* under Valens.[19] In general, he follows the previous pattern, and is thus little more than a recorder of the principal happenings in the political world, following up the detailed accounts of the Roman kings, the evolution of the Republic and Empire, the dealings of the Roman legions with various frontier tribes and legions, as well as anecdotal and geographic material, that had characterized Jerome's additions to Eusebius' original. Considerable attention is naturally paid to the series of bishops and important religious events, a listing of the main Christian and pagan authors of the age, and a recording of such phenomena as earthquakes, famines, battles, and monstrosities.

The whole work is thus a prodigious storehouse of historical lore, not well integrated nor properly proportioned, it is true.

Towards the end, Jerome indulges a number of personal judgments on men such as Basil, Cyril of Jerusalem, and Peter of Alexandria that are far from the spirit of impartiality. But it did furnish both Jerome and his readers in the West with a magnificent opportunity to locate themselves in regard to world history. And it is written with considerable verve and attention to style, no matter how short the item or notice being set down. As Père Cavallera remarks:

By relating the present to the past, it allowed for a continuous feeling of solidarity between generations. In linking sacred and profane history, it presented a double advantage. It confirmed the faithful in their conviction that their religion was the most noble, the most ancient and the most pure of all those creeds then cluttering the world; but, at the same time, in arousing, or in at least continuing, a sympathetic approach to profane history, it recalled for the reader the fact that, while a citizen of heaven, he was still a citizen of the Roman Empire, an heir to that ancient civilization of whose history the principal facts were here recalled for him. Hence it helped to prevent a loss of interest in the world, or a narrow isolationism from the things of the present.[20]

The popularity of Jerome's translation of the *Chronicle* is well attested by the number of manuscripts in which it was circulated, and in its numerous continuations down through the centuries, beginning with that of Prosper of Aquitaine. Along with Augustine's *City of God*—which, incidentally, owed much to Jerome's translation—the *Chronicle* was the staple of world history upon which the Middle Ages were nourished for over a thousand years.

Jerome had spoken of a "broader history" of the Christian age that he was contemplating, as he brought his translation of Eusebius to a close. But his Scriptural and controversial activities from now on would preclude any such strictly historical undertaking. His sojourn in Rome from 382 to 385 was the occasion for his applying himself to issuing a new Latin version of the four Gospels, collated from various Greek manuscripts, along with the older Latin versions. The evidence thus afforded of Jerome's interest in textual problems has been well set forth by K. Hulley in his study of the "Principles of textual criticism known to St. Jerome," [21] wherein he ranges up and down the avenues of both lower and higher criticism, and, by copious quotation from the prefaces and commentaries, demonstrates Jerome's genuine competence in these fields.

Jerome, of course, from his earliest days had been a great bibliophile. Particularly under the influence of his experiences at the great Christian library center of Caesarea, where he seems first to have actually examined Origen's *Hexapla,* his interest and his efforts in obtaining correct texts of the Scriptures, properly attributed and attested to, is paramount in all his endeavors. He became extremely aware of the necessity of coping with the original languages, and of using them properly—thus his own rather painful mastery of Hebrew, his excursions into Syriac, Coptic and Aramaic.

Jerome seems to have been particularly sensitive about the matter of knowing a language thoroughly, not only hiring, at considerable cost, a rabbi for lessons in Hebrew, but keeping an observant ear ever open to particularities and similarities in idiom and dialect, and between languages themselves, in the course of his travels and his association with peoples from all over the then known world. Thus, as a young man travelling through Gaul, he declares that he has paid close attention to the Celtic languages spoken by the several barbarian peoples settled round about Treves and Normandy. Years later, when writing his *Commentary on the Epistle to the Galatians,* he mentions how closely the tongues of the numerous tribes in the Near East resembled the speech of the Gauls:

Whence we infer that the Galatians . . . have their own language, which is practically the same as that of the peoples round Treves. Nor does it matter that they have corrupted it to a certain extent, for the Africans have changed the Phoenician language in good part, and Latin itself is modified in each age and clime. . . .[22]

It is possible, of course, that Jerome, knowing a good deal about the history of these tribes and their wanderings, claims a trifle too much for his own general experience—but at least he betrays a considerable interest in the subject.

Jerome too notes the wealth of historical detail afforded by monuments and other relics of the past, of various types and proveniences. Thus his early interest in the Roman catacombs; but likewise, his awareness of the "Pythagorean Monuments" scattered up and down the coast of Italy, witnessing to the prevalence of that particular philosophy and superstition in the pre-Christian ages, as Jerome points out for Rufinus.[23] In the matter of geographical detail, of place names, and of origins, he does not hesitate to correct his own opinions, garnered from his reading, by the actual state of affairs, as he came to see it in his travels.[24] Jerome was thus very well equipped as an historian, not only well-travelled, but supremely aware of the useful arts that contribute to the truth and accuracy of any attempt to capture and delimit what has taken place in the past. On the whole, he manifests a critical eye and an ability to evaluate data that are well beyond the stature of his age—with the sole exception, perhaps, of his contemporary chronicler, Sulpicius Severus.

In Jerome's controversial works, for example, historical references, appeals to tradition, citations of ancient authors abound, as well as the dramatic interest arising from story sources, and frequent attempts are made at clearing up involved problems and difficulties through the exercise of critical judgment. He exhibits great care in quoting his adversaries verbatim before smothering them under an avalanche of facts, figures and vituperation. In his *Adversus Helvidium*,[25] he devotes the main sections to the problems of the virginity of the Blessed Mother and the subsidiary questions of the "brothers of the Lord." In ferreting out parallel references and cases by way of proof, supplementary to his main argument, he roams all over the Old Testament, demonstrating at once his mastery of that great document and his recognition of its value as an historical source. He appeals then to profane literature and history. His final decision is rendered with reference to "the whole series of ancient writers: Ignatius, Polycarp, Irenaeus, Justin Martyr, and many another apostolic and eloquent man who wrote volumes full of wisdom on these same matters against Ebion, Theodotus, Byzantius and Valentine . . ." [26]

In his defense of virginity against the attacks of Jovinian, having exhausted his Scriptural references, Jerome turns to secular literature, exclaiming: "I will now run briefly through the Greek, Latin, and barbarian historians, and will prove that virginity has always been held to be the chief glory of chastity . . ." [27] And he reels off a host of fables, stories and anecdotes culled from Porphyry and Josephus, wherein he cites Herodotus, Strabo, Xenophon, Ovid, Virgil, etc., and reaches from Diana of the Ephesians and Dido of Carthage to the Milesians and the Gymnosophists of India (Ethiopia). He finishes with a catalogue of the evils of married life that is really staggering in its mounting vulgarity, but, as always, he calls upon Plutarch, Seneca, Plato, Aristotle and, in particular, the *De nuptiis* of Theophrastus— again via the *De abstinentia* of Porphyry—for the testimony and justification.[28]

In the second part of the *Adversus Jovinianum,* Jerome presents a myriad of parallels and contrasts between the customs, laws, eating habits and peculiarities of every nation and people then known to mankind, a feat that would bear comparison with the work of one of our modern sociological encyclopedists, though again, for the most part, Jerome is quoting from Porphyry without benefit of citation.[29]

Jerome was engaged in two other historical tasks during the course of his earlier career: the composition of several *Vitae patrum* and of the eulogies of a number of his friends. The former—the lives of Paul the Hermit, of Malchus and of Hilarion —are in the nature of edifying stories built in good part upon legend and hearsay that Jerome gathered from among the desert fathers, but having certain bases in fact. Jerome shows himself quite insistent as to the historical character of Paul, whom he nominates as the first hermit and the predecessor of St. Anthony, though he admits that Anthony is properly venerated as the Father of Monasticism as such.

In writing his preface to the Life of Hilarion, Jerome says explicitly:

In attempting this work, I contemn the words of my evil-wishers who, having once quarrelled with my Paul, will now try to detract from my Hilarion. To the former they objected on the score of his "solitary life"; against the latter, they will bring complaint that he was "too socially inclined"—maintaining that he who was never seen simply never existed; and he who was seen often did not amount to anything. . . .[30]

Despite the fact that Jerome follows closely the Quintilian-prescribed form of encomium, and that he refers to centaurs and other monsters in his *Vita Pauli*, he does place the "first hermit" in a strictly historical setting. Throughout the work he strives to give the impression that what he is relating is for the most part factual, though obviously intended as an edifying advertisement for the monastic state in which Jerome is so primarily concerned.[31] The same can be said for his *Vita Hilarionis*, based, as he maintains, upon conversations with St. Epiphanius, who knew the hermit intimately.[32]

In regard to the *Vita Malchi*, there is some appearance of verisimilitude, it being the story of an incident in the life of a monk captured by the Saracens, and finally saved through the instrumentality of a lion guarding the entrance to a cave in which he had taken refuge from pursuit—this latter incident, of course, being a most unfortunate circumstance as far as historical criticism is concerned. But it is really capable of being lived down.[33]

These *Vitae* are extremely well-written narratives. They pay close attention to geographical detail and give evidence of being linked to the history of the times. Shot through as they are with demons and monsters, they present a problem with which Weingarten and Winter, Dölger and Schiweitz have wrestled at considerable length. The outcome of their studies seems to be that there was a hyperconsciousness of demonology among the early desert fathers and, at the same time, a tendency towards over-credulity in regard to these and other such phenomena.[34] It gravely affected even such realists as Jerome and Augustine. But Jerome had set out to write true biographies in keeping with the standards of the times. From a literary viewpoint, from a monastic-propagandist viewpoint, and from an historical viewpoint, he succeeded, despite the rigidity of form imposed by convention and the distraction of bizarre episodes.

Of a more reliable historical character are Jerome's eulogies of a number of his friends, written by way of consolation to their loved ones, but also as a record and testimonial of their saintly lives. This is particularly true of his "Letters" concerning Blesilla and Paula, Eustochium, Fabiola and Marcella, Nepotianus and Nebridius. While outlining the main historical facts, and apparently eschewing the *loci communes,* Jerome lays great stress upon the practice of Christian virtue to which these heroes and heroines of his were wholly committed—in the case of Nepotianus, swinging into a characterization of the ideal young priest; and utilizing the life of Paula as a model for the Christian maiden. All is done very elegantly, and with sufficient detail to render posterity an exceptionally clear picture of the life of these well-to-do, ascetically inclined devotees and acquaintances of his.[35]

That Jerome was still thinking in terms of a full-scale historical work shortly after his permanent settlement in Bethlehem in 386 or 387 is evident from his preface to the *Vita Malchi,* wherein he spoke of the "larger history" he was then contemplating. Despite his good intentions, however, this projected history never saw the light of day. In its place, Jerome found himself more and more absorbed in Scriptural studies.

Writing to Paulinus in 395, Jerome expatiated at length upon the preparation necessary for a proper appreciation of the "word of God." He describes the pains taken by secular authors to obtain a proper understanding of the world about them:

We read in the older histories how men wandered over whole provinces, approached new peoples, crossed the seas, in order that they might see for themselves what they had read in books. . . . Thus Pythagoras, to see the sages of Memphis; thus Plato labori-

ously traversed Egypt . . . and, for the sake of Archytas of Taren-
tine, the coast of Italy formerly called Magna Graecia, that he who
was a master and a power in Athens . . . might become a foreigner
and disciple, preferring in a modest fashion to learn, rather than
impudently to pour forth his own. . . . We read that a man came
from the ends of the earth to see Titus Livy. . . . And Apollonius,
whether the magician, as it is commonly thought, or the philosopher,
as the Pythagoreans maintain, entered Persia, crossed the Caucasus,
the lands of the Scythians and Massagetes . . . penetrated India
. . . and came to the Brahmins, that he might listen to Hiarcas,
seated on a throne of gold, drinking the waters of the Tantalus and
expatiating upon nature, morals and the course of the stars. . . .
He travelled thence by way of Babylonia, Chaldea, the land of the
Medes, Assyrians, Parthians, Syrians, Phoenicians, Arabs and Palestine to return to Alexandria and enter Ethiopia, that he might there
see the Gymnosophists. . . .[36]

Thus making a vivid résumé of the *Life of Apollonius of Tyana*
written by Philostratus,[37] Jerome hurries on to discuss St. Paul
and the Christian heroes. He continues:

I have run through these things briefly, that you may understand
that one cannot embark upon the Sacred Scriptures without preparation and a guide pointing out the way. I will not pass over the
grammarians, rhetoricians, philosophers, geometricians, dialecticians,
musicians, astrologers and medical men, whose knowledge is most
useful for us mortals, and is divided into three disciplines: evidence,
method and practice.

I will take up the minor arts, which are controlled not so much
by "word" as by the hand. Farmers, bricklayers, builders, the hewers
of metals and wood, wool-makers, clothiers, etc., who put together
various furnishings and meaner products, just cannot become what
they desire to be without the aid of an instructor.

Quod medicorum est
promittunt medici, tractant fabrilia fabri.

Alone the art of the Scriptures is one that all indiscriminately claim
for themselves:

scribimus indocti doctique poemata passim.[38]

Then, pausing briefly to lacerate the fabricators of the centos of Homer and Virgil, Jerome proceeds to outline the nature and intent of the various books of the Old and New Testament.

For some time, then, Jerome had been determined to retranslate the Old Testament, at first by a revision of the Septuagint, but then directly from the Hebrew, and to provide commentaries and emendations for the whole body of the Scriptures. In so doing, his prefaces to the different books provide a course in lower and higher criticism, in paleography, diplomatic and heuristic, whereby he proves himself master of many of the disciplines ancillary to the competent historian.[39]

In the midst of this new Scripture work, Jerome paused once more for a strictly historical exercise. Ever since his translation of Eusebius' *Chronicle* he had felt the need of a good *nomenclator,* or handbook of Christian authors, that would at once parallel Suetonius' and the other secular manuals, and serve as an inspiration and justification of the Christian coming-of-age in the literary field.

For an Imperial official and friend of his, Flavius Dexter by name, Jerome drew up his *De viris illustribus,*[40] a list of 135 authors, from the Apostles down to himself, whose works or reputations had been preserved as part of the Christian tradition, including several pagans and heretics whose productions held a special interest for the Christian scholar: Philo, Josephus, Seneca and Justin of Tiberias.

There is nothing particularly original about the *De viris.* As both Sychowski and Bernouilli were at great pains to show, Jerome takes the first seventy-eight authors almost verbatim from Eusebius' *Ecclesiastical History,* filling in but a few minor details on his own.[41] As a matter of fact, he has read very few of these authors, though he gives the impression that he is familiar with most of them at first hand. But Jerome had to get the information from somewhere! And he is tremendously more self-reliant for the authors of his own times, including such contemporaries as Basil, Ambrose, Rufinus, and Hilary.[42] It is very easy to be over-critical of such apparent "plagiarizing," if the historian of today fails to realize that Jerome's procedure was not only in keeping with the temper of his age, but was also about the only thing he could do, lacking the tremendous facilities at the disposal of the critical historian of modern times. The copious use of footnotes today is, after all, hardly more than a mechanism to cover up a procedure that in its essentials differs from Jerome's but little.

The last of Jerome's 135 notices is given over to his own literary productions down to the year 392—and shows him off at the age of forty-five as a man who has already definitely made his way in the Christian literary world, and who felt considerably conscious of that fact.

Historically speaking, the book is most valuable for its effect upon the Christian consciousness of the day—the literary notices for the men of the fourth century are, of course, invaluable—but the main impact of the work was the fact that it demonstrated the coming of age of Christian scholarship. It was actually the first handbook of Christian literature, and served as a model throughout the ages from Gennadius and Isidore down to Trithemius, Cave and St. Robert Bellarmine—a guide and a reservoir for the current of literary awareness from the sixth to the sixteenth century.

The question as to what historians Jerome had actually read is a most interesting and complex one. Pierre Courcelle maintains that as far, at least, as the Greek authors are concerned, he had read only those that would be directly useful to him in the study of the Scriptures; and that, therefore, when Jerome lines up a list such as: Hermippius the Peripatetic, Antigonus of Carystos, Satyrus, Aristexenes the musician, Apollonius, etc., he is really citing them from the now lost preface to Suetonius. Even Thucydides and Polybius were hardly more than names to him. However, he had read a great deal of Herodotus. Xenophon he knew both in Cicero's translations and in the original, at least for the *Cyropedia*. He had first-hand knowledge of Philo. But his real picture of the world from an historical viewpoint comes from Josephus, whom he must have known in good part by heart. He was also well acquainted with the works of Porphyry, mainly, of course, through Origen and Methodius. But he makes such frequent and complete use of the *De abstinentia* of that great anti-Christian antagonist that he simply must have read it.[43] As far back as 1872, of course, Luebeck indicated most of this.[44] And Jerome's own contemporary friend and foe, Rufinus of Aquileia, had long previously blurted out a similar accusation: "Indeed he [Jerome] sprays Aristides and Chrysippus, Empedocles and other names of Greek authors like smoke or clouds before his readers' eyes, that he may appear learned and of wide reading. . . ."[45]

As for the Latin historians, it is quite certain that Jerome had first-hand acquaintance with most of them—*e.g.*, Sallust, Livy, Caesar, Suetonius, etc.—for they were used as school texts, along with the poets. He seems to have used Pompeius Trogus and his epitomist, Justinus; he certainly had an acquaintance with Eutropius, upon whom he bases most of his continuation of Eusebius' *Chronicle*. Hence he should also have known the lesser chronographers and court historians, such as Sextus Aurelius, Rufius Festus, and the "Epitomes" of the Caesars.[46] Jerome can be very frank with regard to his own testimony concerning these things, as he is in the prologue to the second book of his *Commentary on Galatians*:

Marcus Varro, a most diligent observer of all antiquity, and others who have imitated him, have handed down much about this people [the Galatians] that is worthy of being recalled. But because we have proposed not to introduce into the temple of God the uncircumcised —*and as I may simply confess, it is now many years since I have ceased to read these things*—I will merely quote the words of our own Lactantius. . . .[47]

In his preface to book three, he likewise assures Paula and Eustochium, for whose benefit he is writing:

You yourselves know that for more than fifteen years [*i.e.*, since the famous dream mentioned in his Letter to Eustochium #22] I have never had in my hands a copy of Cicero, Virgil, or of any other author of pagan letters. And if indeed while I talk, something of these authors slips out, it is due to a recalling as through a cloudy dream of the past. . . .[48]

Thus it becomes most difficult to decide when Jerome is really quoting from among his Latin authors—for his memory was really prodigious. "Dye the wool once purple," he had chided Rufinus, "and what waters will wash it clean?" [49]

It is, however, in his Scriptural works that Jerome gives clearest indication of his historical talents and critical tastes. Beginning with his *Hebraic Questions in Genesis* [50] he manifests a complete, fairly well-integrated, and comprehensive picture of the past. It is shot through with mistakes, of course, owing to the faulty state of historical knowledge and studies of the day. It stems from Josephus, Origen, Philo, Porphyry, and Eusebius, although Jerome not infrequently tries to give the impression that it is coming directly from Thucydides, Berosus, Plutarch, Dichaear-chus, Alexander Polyhistor, Callinicus, Suetonius, etc. But the fact is that, in itself it manifests what was evidently a rather clear picture in Jerome's mind. It begins with the origins of vari-ous peoples scattered over the farthest reaches of the then known world, and stretches from the outposts of the Caucasus and India to the fastnesses of Africa, and the northernmost outposts of Britain. Thus Jerome amplifies Josephus on Genesis:

To Japhet son of Noah, were born seven sons who possessed the land of Asia from Amanus and Taurus to Syria Coeli, and the moun-tains of Cilicia down to the river Tanain; in Europe, as far as Gadira, leaving their names upon both places and people. Of these latter, very many changed; yet many also remained as they were. The Galatians are of Gomer; the Scythians of Magog; the Medes of Madai; of Iavan are the Iones or Greeks, whence the Ionian sea. Of Thubal are the Iberians, also called Spaniards. . . . Of Mosoch, the Cappadocians: whence one of their cities is called Mazeca to this day. . . . Of Thiras, the Thracians. . . . I know that a certain man [St. Ambrose of Milan] has narrated the history of the Goths, who have been recently bacchanalizing in our lands, as of Gog and Magog, thus characterizing them by their present activities, and as they are referred to in Ezechiel. Whether this is a true interpretation or not will soon be seen by the finish of their war. But certainly the learned Goths themselves have in the past rather referred to themselves as of the Getes than of Gog and Magog. . . .[51]

The *Hebraic Questions in Genesis* is really part of a trilogy, made up of a translation of Eusebius' *Book of Place Names,*[52] together with his *Onomasticon,* or "Book of Hebrew Names," [53] originally attributed to Philo and Origen. Unfortunately, all three books are vitiated to a certain extent by the ancient pseudo-science of etymology, in which Jerome is an especially great offender. But, at the same time, they represent a considerable amount of personal erudition on his part, particularly in the elaborations on the geography of Palestine and its environs supplied by his own personal knowledge—information that is still useful, and that, incidentally, proved most timely for the pilgrims then beginning to resort to the Holy Land in such great numbers.

Jerome's commentaries, beginning with those on Abdias and Ecclesiastes, running through the attention he gives to St. Paul in Galatians, Philemon, Ephesians and Titus, as also his Matthew, along with the minor Prophets, and Ezechiel, Isaias, Jeremias and Daniel are a great amalgam of historical and Scriptural lore. He hesitates to begin a commentary unless he has Origen at his side— he was accused even in his own day, particularly in regard to the Twelve Minor Prophets, of having lifted from Origen bodily [54] —yet, to say there is little that is original in his work would be simply false. For Jerome paints vivid pictures, using his immense knowledge as a background. Frequently he is quoting verbatim, without mention of his source; but, as likely as not, having once made a passage completely his own, he could not then distinguish between his own thoughts and those of his reading. Yet you cannot read through these commentaries without being struck with the man's tremendous historical consciousness, no matter whence he may be garnering his material.

Thus in the *Commentary on Isaias,* Jerome insists over and over again, particularly in the first six chapters, that Isaias vividly foretold the tragic events that would come upon Judea under

Titus and Hadrian.[55] He maintains that he is not unaware that the city of Jerusalem had undergone other sieges in the course of the centuries. "But under the Romans, the whole of Judea was devastated, its cities put to the torch, and to this day the foreigner exploits the land." And he turns to Josephus to demonstrate that it is with this last spoliation that the prophecy has been carried out to the minutest detail. He is likewise insistent that all interpretation begin with history: "And we say this, not condemning the tropological sense, but because the spiritual interpretation must follow the order of history, which, many forgetting, they wander off into the most obvious errors against the Scriptures." [56] But as history is made up of many facets which succeed one another in the course of time, it belongs to the ingenuity of the commentator to discover the actual burden of events that carried out a particular prophecy.

When treating of a warning addressed to the king of Assyria, for example, Jerome insists upon remaining in the domain of ancient history: "From the context," he writes, "it is obvious that this applies to Sennacherib, king of the Assyrians." Several authors thought that Isaias 17:7, pertaining to the oracle uttered against Damascus, had received its realization in the time of Christ, when the Kingdom of the Savior replaced the already destroyed realm of Damascus. "A pious wish of the interpreters," is Jerome's comment, "but not in accordance with historical actuality." "We ourselves will follow the historical order, in the endeavor to cap off with historical fact an edifice begun on historical foundations." [57]

Jerome was really the first author of antiquity to question the story of the origin of the Septuagint, at least thrice expressing more than polite doubt and annoyance at the credulity of his contemporaries:

For I know not who was the first author to construct out of a falsehood the seventy cells at Alexandria, in which they [the translators] were supposed to have all written the same things, though separated from each other, since neither Aristeas, one of the coterie around Ptolemaus himself, nor, much later, Josephus makes mention of any such things. But rather, they tell us that these men, gathered in a large basilica, wrote down a translation, not a prophecy . . . unless perchance we are to believe that Cicero translated the *Oeconomicon* of Xenophon, the *Protagoras* of Plato, and the *Pro Ctesiphon* of Demosthenes under the influence of the "rhetorical spirit. . . ." Do we then condemn these older writers? Not at all. . . . For they translated before the coming of Christ; and what they did not understand, they translated in dubious phrases. But we are writing after His passion and resurrection . . . hence are handling not prophecy but history. It is one thing to describe what you have merely heard, and quite another what you have actually seen. . . .[58]

Jerome approaches the Scriptures as a strictly historical document, a fact which he makes clear in the following passage, where he is quoting almost verbatim from Origen:

Does anyone believe in God the Creator? He cannot believe unless he first believe that those things are true which are written about His saints, viz.: Adam was made of plasma by God; Eve, fabricated from a rib in his side; Enoch translated; Noah alone saved from amidst a shipwrecked world. . . . These and the rest that is written in Scriptures, unless one believe the whole of it, he cannot believe in the God of the saints. Nor can he be brought to the faith of the Old Testament unless he can prove to his own satisfaction all these facts which history records regarding the patriarchs, prophets, and other outstanding men. . . .[59]

He insists, again and again, that the Scriptures cannot be understood unless one start from an historical foundation. He knows, however, that

Many things are spoken of in the Scriptures in accordance with common opinion at the time when they took place, and not according to the real truth of the matter. Thus, Joseph is spoken of in the Gospel as the "father of the Lord," Mary herself, who knew she had conceived of the Holy Ghost, telling her Son, "Behold! Thy father and I have sought thee sorrowing." [60]

As has been seen, Professor Swain recently maintained that Jerome took at least part of his approach to the over-all picture of history from the anti-imperial literature represented by Pompeius

Trogus' *Philippic History*, rather than from the commentaries on the Apocalypse and on Daniel by Hippolytus, Irenaeus and Origen. But there is great difficulty in admitting that he was being so immediately influenced by an historian who was for Jerome but an obscure author. This is particularly true when one reflects that running through Jerome's thought there is a definite idea of progress in history that is bound up with a strictly Jewish concept of divine providence. For all the philosophical bent of Thucydides, Herodotus and Polybius, there was no real over-all plan to their idea of fate, certainly no integrated philosophy giving a spiritual as well as a cosmic meaning to the rise and fall of empires and kingdoms.[61] This latter was strictly the creation of the Jewish Scriptures, beginning with the story of the creation in Genesis, and being elaborated in set terms by the major and minor Prophets.[62] It is Eusebius who first appears to feel the tremendous swing of this trend of thought; and it is from Eusebius primarily that Jerome gathers his principal ideas, however much Trogus may have been on his mind.

Much of the burden of Jerome's *Commentary on Daniel* is in reality an attack upon Porphyry. The latter maintained that the book of Daniel was written not earlier than the time of the Machabees, about 165 B.C., and that, instead of being a prophecy, it was really a description of events up to the reign of Antiochus, of which there remained an historical record. Jerome makes use of all his predecessors—Origen, Methodius, Eusebius [63]—and hammers away at the position taken by the great pagan adversary of Christianity, not without some effect, though he finds the learning of Porphyry formidable. Thus, in his preface:

To understand the latter parts of Daniel, a multiple history of the Greeks is necessary, namely: Sutorius, Callinicus, Diodorus, Hieronymus, Polybius, Poseidonius, Claudius, Theonis and Adronicus called Alypius, whom Porphyry declares he is following; in like manner also, Josephus and those whom Josephus quotes, and particularly our own Livy and Pompeius Trogus and Justinus, who narrate the whole history of the final vision. . . .[64]

But he gives Porphyry fair play throughout the commentary, juxtaposing his interpretation to that of the general run of Christian commentators:

Thus far the historical order has been followed, and between Porphyry and ourselves there is no quarrel. The rest, continuing down to the end of the volume, he regards as of Antiochus. . . . Our commentators . . . refer all this to the anti-Christ. . . .[65]

But let this all be said of Antiochus. Wherein does that harm our religion? . . . Let them then say, Who is this "stone which is cut from the mountain without hands; which has grown into a great mountain and filled the earth, and assumed a fourfold form"? Who is this son of man, who is to come with the clouds, and to stand before the ancient of days, and to be given a kingdom to which there will be no end, while all the people, tribes and tongues shall serve him? Porphyry avoids these things which are quite obvious, and asserts that they are prophesied about the Jews, whom we know to be in servitude to this day. . . .[66]

Jerome himself, of course, refers this prophecy directly to Christ, the Light of the World.[67]

On the larger question of a pattern or direction in history, Jerome feels there is evidently a close connection between divine providence and the paths of human history, and that this is discernible through the fulfilment of events foretold by the prophets of old. But he seems to preserve a fairly open mind in his interpretations.[68] While his concept of the sweep of the historical process subsumes the rise and fall of the four great empires, there is not a deterministic nor an apocalyptic tinge to his thinking, least of all a millenarian twist. He maintains that the corruption and downfall of these great states has been due to pride and rapacity on the part of their rulers and people. Hence he is not surprised to see signs of disaster coming upon the Rome of his day.[69]

Yet in his *Commentary on Isaias*, speaking of the section where the prophet describes the "wolf lying down with the lamb, and the leopard with the goat" (11:16) Jerome says:

And this we see in our own day, in the Church, where the rich and the poor, the powerful and the humble, kings and private people, mingle together, and are governed by young men whom we call apostles, and apostolic men, unskilled in speech but not in wisdom.[70]

Again, in his comment on the famous sixtieth chapter of Isaias (10ff.), Jerome says:

This can be taken either in a material or in a spiritual sense. If in a material, we see the Roman Caesars bending their necks to the yoke of Christ, building churches at the public expense, and leveling the fiats of law against the persecutions of the gentiles and the attacks of heretics. . . . Although we now see these things coming to pass in the Church of today, they will be more fully carried out upon the consummation of the world, in the second coming of the Savior.[71]

As an historian, then, Jerome did have well in mind the necessity of possessing a vast sweep of the knowledge of antiquity. Insofar as his main interests were governed by the Sacred Scriptures, he confined his immediate endeavors to keeping himself abreast of works needful in that field—not, however, without at least making pretense of being well acquainted with all the literature of antiquity. In the long run he makes fairly critical use of most of his material, and he is as honest as any man of the deep past in acknowledging his borrowings—or failing to do so. But he did have a magnificent grasp of the history of civilizations as known to his day. He had even figured out for himself an entire *Weltanschauung,* completed by a chronological analysis of his world. Thus he ends his supplement to Eusebius' *Chronicle*:

Up to the consulate of Valentinian and Valens II [A.D. 378], all the years:

　a) From the 15th year of Tiberias and the preaching of our Lord Jesus Christ amount to 351;

　b) From the second year of Darius, King of the Persians, at the time when the temple of Jerusalem was rebuilt, equal 899;

　c) From the first Olympiad, the time when Isaias was preaching among the Jews, amount to 1,155;

d) From Solomon and the first building of the Temple, amount to 1,411;

e) From the capture of Troy, at which time Samson was alive among the Jews, amount to 1,161;

f) From the time of Moyses and of Cecrops, first king of Attica, equal 1,890;

g) From Abraham and the reign of Ninus and Semiramidis, equal 2,395.

Thus the whole course of time, from Abraham to the above-mentioned date, contains 2,395 years; and from the Flood until the time of Abraham, there are thought to have been 942 years; and from Adam to the Flood, 2,242 years. Thus from Adam down to the fourteenth year of the reign of Valens . . . the whole course of years amounts to 5,579.[72]

NOTES

[1] *PL*, 22, 53.

[2] *Chronici canones* (ed. J. Fotheringham, London, 1923), 5.

[3] Jer., *Ep.* 5, 2.

[4] Jer., *Ep.* 15, 3.

[5] *PL*, 23, 155–82.

[6] Cf. P. Batiffol, "Les sources de l'Altercatio Luciferiani et Orthodoxi," *Miscel. Geronimiana* (Rome, 1921), 97ff.

[7] *PL*, 23, 172.

[8] F. Cavallera, *Saint Jérôme, sa vie et son oeuvre* (Paris, 1922), I, 55–62; cf. P. Courcelle, *Les lettres grecques en Occident* (Paris, 1943), 84–86 (Irenaeus), 88–100 (Origen), 103–105 (Eusebius), 38 and 104 (Gregory Nazianzen).

[9] Cf. M. Laistner, "Some Reflections on Latin Historical Writing in the V Century," *Class. Phil.* 35 (1941), 241–58.

[10] *Ibid.*, 243.

[11] Cf. F. Foakes-Jackson, *Eusebius Pamphili* (Cambridge, 1933), 142ff.

[12] *Chronici canones*, 2.

[13] *Ibid.*, 4–5.

[14] R. Helm, *Hieronymus Zusätze in Eusebius Chronik* [*Philologus*, Supplemb. 21, Heft II] 92, 95.

[15] J. Swain, "Theory of the Four Monarchies: Opposition History under the Roman Empire," *Class. Phil.* 35 (1940), 1–21.

[16] Jer., *Comm. in Dan.*, Prologus (*PL*, 25, 494).

[17] Cf. Swain, *op. cit.*, 19.

[18] *Chron. canon.*, 5.

[19] Cf. R. Helm, "Hieronymus und Eutrop," *Rhein. Museum* 76 (1927), 138.

[20] F. Cavallera, *Saint Jérôme*, I, 66.

[21] *Harv. Stud. in Class. Phil.* 55 (1944), 87–109; *id.*, "Light cast by St. Jerome on certain paleological problems," *ibid.*, 54 (1943), 83–92.

[22] *PL*, 26, 357; cf. V. Sofer, "Das Hieronymus Zeugnis über die Sprachen der Galater und Trevirer," *Zeit. f. Klas. Phil.* 55 (1937), 148–158.

[23] Jer., *Adv. Ruf.*, III (*PL*, 23, 485).

[24] Cf. F. Stummer, "Corvallis, Mambre und Verwandtes," *Jour. Pal. Or. Soc.*, 1932, 6–21; *id.*, "Die Berwertung Palästinas bei Hier.," *Oriens Christ.*, 1935, 60–74.

[25] *PL*, 23, 183–206.

[26] *Ibid.*, 17 (*PL*, 23, 202); cf. P. Courcelle, *op. cit.*, 79–81.

[27] *Adv. Jov.*, I, 41 (*PL*, 23, 270).

[28] P. Courcelle, *op. cit.*, 60–62, where he points out the studies proving Jerome's main sources to be the *De matrimonio* of Seneca, the *Gamika Paraggelmata* of Plutarch, and a lost tract of Porphyry whence Jerome drew his citations of Aristotle, and the *De nuptiis* of Theophrastus.

[29] *Adv. Jov.*, II (*PL*, 23, 307–10); Courcelle, *op. cit.*, 62–3; E. Bickel, *Diatribe in Senecae philos. fragm.*, I (Leipzig, 1915), 395–420.

[30] *Vita Hilarionis*, I (*PL*, 23, 29).

[31] *Vita Pauli* (*PL*, 23, 17–28).

[32] *Vita Hil.* (*PL*, 23, 29–54).

[33] *Vita Malchi* (*PL*, 23, 53–60).

[34] Cf. O. Bardenhewer, *Gesch. d. altk. Lit.* 3 (Fri.-in. B., 1912), 638–639; S. Schiweitz, *Das morgenländische Mönchtum* 3 (Mainz, 1938), 214–20.

[35] O. Bardenhewer, *op. cit.*, 639–40.

[36] Jer., *Ep.* 53 (*Ad. Paulin.*).

[37] Cf. Courcelle, *op. cit.*, 65–6.

[38] *Ibid.*

[39] Cf. W. Stade, *Hieronymus in proemiis* (Rost., 1925); F. Stummer, *Einführung in die Latein. Bibel* (Paderborn, 1928).

[40] Jer., *De vir. illus.* (ed. E. Richardson, Leipzig, 1896).

[41] C. Bernoulli, *Die Schriftstellerkatalog des Hier.* (Fri.-in B., 1895); St. von Sychowski, *Hieronymus als Litterarhistoriker* (Münster, 1894); A. Feder, *Studien z. Schriftstellerkatalog des hl. Hier.* (Leipzig, 1927).

[42] P. Courcelle, *op. cit.*, 78–111.

[43] *Ibid.*, 66–78; on Josephus, 71ff.

[44] E. Luebeck, *Hieronymus quos noverit scriptores* . . . (Leipzig, 1872).

[45] Ruf., *Apol.*, II, 7 (*PL*, 21, 588).

[46] Cf. notes 17 and 19.

[47] *Comm. in Gal.*, II, prol. (*PL*, 26, 353).

[48] *Ibid.*, III, prol. (399).

[49] Jer., *Apol.*, I, 30 (*PL*, 23, 422).

[50] *Quaest. Hebr. in Gen.* (*PL*, 23, 935–1010). Cf. Courcelle, *op. cit.*, 67, n. 3; F. Cavallera, "Les quaestiones in Gen. de S. Jérôme et de S. Augustin," *Misc. Agost.*, II (Rome, 1931), 360–72.

[51] *Quaest. Hebr. in Gen.*, 10, 2 (*PL*, 23, 950–1).

[52] *Lib. de Nomen. Hebr.* (*PL*, 23, 771–858).

[53] *Onomastica Sacra* (ed. f. Wutz, *Texte und Untersuchungen* ii [41]).

[54] *In Mich.*, II (*PL*, 25, 1189); Courcelle, *op. cit.*, 95–6.

[55] *Comm. in Isaiam* (*PL*, 24, 9–687); cf. 30–31.

[56] *Ibid.*, 5:13 (158–9).

[57] *Ibid.*, 17:12 (177).

[58] *Praef. in Pentat.* (*PL*, 28, 151); cf. also *Adv. Ruf.*, II, 25 (*PL*, 23, 470); *Comm. in Ezech.* 6:12 (*PL*, 25, 55).

[59] *Comm. in Ep. ad Philem.* 4ff. (*PL*, 26, 609); the passage is taken almost verbatim from Origen, cf. E. Dorsch, "Aug. und Hier. über die Wahrheit der bibl. Geschichte," *Zeit. f. kat. Theol.* 35 (1911) 641 and 646.

[60] *Comm. in Jerem.* 28:10–11 (*PL*, 24, 855).

[61] Cf. C. Dawson, "St. Augustine and His Age," *A Monument to St. Augustine* (New York, 1930), 44–5.

[62] Cf. W. Irwin, "The Hebrews," *The Adventures of Ancient Man* (Chicago, 1946), 322–3.

[63] P. Courcelle, *op. cit.*, 63–4; J. Lataix, "Le commentaire de saint Jérôme sur Daniel," *Rev. d'hist. et de litt. relig.*, II (1897), 164–173.

[64] *Comm. in Dan.*, praef. (*PL*, 25, 494).

[65] *Ibid.*, 11:21 (565).

[66] *Ibid.*, 11:44–5 (573–4).

[67] *Ibid.*, (574); cf. *Comm. in Jerem.* 19:10–11 (*PL*, 24, 801–2).

[68] *Comm. in Isaiam* 24:17 (*PL*, 24, 258–86).

[69] *Comm. in Dan.* 3:40 (*PL*, 25, 504): "Sicut enim in principio nihil Romano imperio fortius et durius fuit, ita in fine rerum nihil imbecillius; quando et in bellis civilibus, et adversum diversas nationes, aliarum gentium indegimus auxilio . . ."; cf. *ibid.*, 7:8; (551).

[70] *Comm. in Is.* 11:6ff. (*PL*, 24, 148); *Ibid.*, 5:23–25 (*PL*, 24, 187–8).

[71] *Ibid.*, 60:10ff. (593).

[72] *Chronici canones*, 332.

St. Jerome as a Spiritual Director

EUGENE P. BURKE, C.S.P.

St. Jerome as a Spiritual Director

IN A VERY real sense, each individual creates his own world. He takes his talents, virtues, interests, enthusiasms, convictions and experience, and fashions them into a living whole which is his life and work. The greater the man, the more distinctive the axis upon which that world turns. It may be ambition, power, humanitarianism or idealism. With the saints it will be one or another of the manifold aspects of sanctity. Whatever it is, it either infects or informs all that the individual does. Occasionally, though, the scope of the man's work is so extensive or so influential that it tends to obscure the central reality of the man himself. Such would sometimes seem to be the case with St. Jerome. The enormous diffusion of his Latin translation of the Bible has made his name practically synonymous with the Vulgate. As a result, it is only infrequently realized that the axis upon which his life turned was Christian asceticism, and that its two poles were Scriptural study and spiritual direction. In fact, it is his spiritual direction that is uppermost in the minds of his contemporaries. It is his apostolate for asceticism, reinforced by his own rigorous life, that makes him an object of reverence and a subject of controversy in his own day. Hence it is, that any complete study of St. Jerome calls for an analysis of him as a spiritual director, and thus of his spiritual doctrine itself.

To understand St. Jerome's spiritual direction, account must be taken of the man himself. Neither the antagonism he aroused nor the devotion he inspired is understandable without an appreciation of his temperament and character. Decisive and enthusiastic, once he had committed himself to an enterprise it was a full dedication. All his ability, time, and energy were at the service of such a commitment. Having dedicated himself to the way of Christian perfection, temporizing was unthinkable for him. In his eyes, spiritual mediocrity deserved nothing but severity and condemnation. Those who would follow his lead must forgo any compromise, or be none of his. The wholehearted intensity of his personal convictions easily transformed a personal attack into an attack upon the movement that he had espoused. And it is this very ardor that causes him to strike out ruthlessly at his antagonists, and to direct his followers with warm affection. Cultured and facile of mind, master of rhetorical device, he is able to charm his spiritual subjects and flay his opponents. Moreover, to this full acceptance of the counsels of perfection he joined a first-hand experience of the atmosphere of moral laxity in Roman society. This knowledge, in turn, gives to his denunciations the tone of an Old Testament prophet. And it is this whole background of character and experience that often betrays him into exaggeration. Yet, informing the whole is the Christian enthusiasm for perfection whereby one takes up his cross and follows Christ. It is an enthusiasm which engenders a "love that cannot be measured, and an impatience that knows no bounds." [1]

Equally important in understanding the influence of St. Jerome as a spiritual director is some appreciation of the age in which he exercised that office. For his stature as a spiritual director does not rest on the fact that he taught a new doctrine or contributed to the development of the principles of the spiritual life. He takes his place as one of the Fathers of the ascetical tradition in the West mainly because of the impact of his own life, personality, and learning on minds already disgusted with the spirit of the age, and thence seeking spiritual leadership.

The essential spirit of this age is given voice in St. Augustine's *City of God*:

They do not trouble about the moral degradation of the empire; all they ask is that it should be prosperous and secure . . . [they say].

Let the poor serve the rich for the sake of their bellies and thus live in idleness under their protection. . . . Let there be plenty of public prostitutes for those who cannot afford to keep mistresses of their own. Let the noise of dancing be heard everywhere, and let the theatres resound with lewd merriment and every kind of cruel and vicious pleasure. Let the man who dislikes these pleasures be looked upon as a public enemy, and be hounded to death by the mob if he interferes.[2]

Granted some rhetorical exaggeration, this is substantially the picture painted by Jerome and Ambrose as well as by non-Christian writers. For though Christianity was the official religion, materialistic paganism was neither dead nor sleeping. Its hedonism was still the warp and woof of the social life of the leisure class. And like a fog it seeped into every level of society, clerical and lay, obscuring the hard facts and sharp edges of the full Christian life.

In such an atmosphere, not only Christians conscious of the depths of their religion, but the searchers after peace, the disillusioned, the decent but distressed patricians sought some release from the bondage and aridity of material pleasure and corporate selfishness. For the better part of a century the imaginations of such persons had been stirred by the promise of release found in the deserts of the Orient. Cultured men and women had brought back from Egypt and the Holy Land the stories of men and women who had cast off all material shackles and found peace in asceticism. Enthralled by such hopes, some had already begun to renounce luxury and ease even in the city of Rome. Still others, like Jerome himself, had been moved to join the desert recluses. Something of this fascination is portrayed for us by St. Augustine in his *Confessions.* He describes the stories that were told to him and Alypius by a fellow African, Pontianus, and the spell that they cast over them. Then he narrates the after-effects of these ascetical descriptions on his soul:

Disordered in look and mind by this desperate wrestling with my own soul in the secret chambers of my heart, I fell upon Alypius, crying out, "What has been brought to us? What means this tale thou hast heard? Simple men arise and take heaven by violence; and with all our heartless learning we are wallowing in flesh and blood. Shall we stand still because they have taken the lead? Shall we not follow because we did not lead?" I scarcely knew what I said, and fled away leaving him staring in mute astonishment; my face, eyes, color, tone expressed my meaning more clearly than my words.[3]

Admitting St. Augustine's extraordinary spiritual perception, this passage still gives a highly illuminating insight into the reaction of men of his time. For the incident took place before his conversion, and his reaction is that of a man who had drunk deeply of all that his age offered.

It is this combination of a pagan atmosphere and the consequent enkindling of some minds by the picture of asceticism that enables us to obtain a true perspective of the impression Jerome made in Rome. For he came to that city, not simply as another teller of tales, but as the living symbol of asceticism itself. Already familiar to them from the letters he had written, he appears now as the living embodiment of all that had been depicted, a desert recluse marked by a rigid and unrelenting ascetical life. To this he adds immense learning, and the fact that his very presence in Rome is accompanied by the friendship of Pope Damasus. All of this gives him a high moral authority and personal prestige that is the point of departure for the decisive influence he will exert in the apostolate of asceticism.

St. Jerome begins his apostolate almost immediately. He takes over the direction of a small group of women already leading a life of renunciation under the guidance of the noble and saintly Marcella. With her were her mother Albina and her sister Asella. Also in the group were Furia, Fabiola, Lea and Principia. To these must be added Paula, whose name is so closely connected with St. Jerome's work in Palestine, and her two daughters Blesilla and Eustochium. Cultured, intelligent, well-educated, already on the path of sanctity, these women are an ideal group for Jerome's work. Then, too, their very prominence makes his letters to them effective channels for propagandizing the ascetical life, a desire that was always with him.

The actual spiritual direction of this group was twofold: the development of heroic virtue through a rigorous asceticism; and the study of Sacred Scripture. The studies themselves called for a knowledge of Greek and Hebrew, along with considerable concentration and effort. How resolutely they carried through this part of the program is testified to by St. Jerome himself when writing of Marcella:

Whenever I picture to myself her ardor for study, her vivacity of mind and her application, I blame my idleness. I who retreated to this wilderness and have constantly before my mind the manger . . . am unable to accomplish what a noble woman accomplishes in the hour she snatches from the cares of a large circle and the government of her household.[4]

This is also borne out by the questions that they put to Jerome on the meaning of various texts of Scripture.[5]

Joined to this study was a detailed and exacting program that would lead to complete renunciation for the sake of Christ. It called for an unceasing watchfulness of every thought, fasting, the eschewing of worldly dress, manual work, and a regular schedule of prayer based on the Psalms. Through it all runs St. Jerome's basic conviction: It is not a question of denying that God created everything, or of pretending that God takes pleasure in the sufferings of His creatures or the cries of an empty stomach. The whole point is that virtue is not secure in soft living, or if severity to oneself is lacking.[6] And no one who reads his epistles to these women can accuse him of forgetting this fact.

As was to be expected, this rigor was publicly manifested in the lives of St. Jerome's spiritual children. As a consequence these lives became an affront to the spirit of the society in which they were led, and gradually the whole ascetical movement came under attack. Much of this opposition, however, can be attributed to St. Jerome's own letters, which portray with sardonic eloquence the foolish, selfish and immoral society of Rome. His rhetorical skill held up a mirror to the vanity, immorality, ambition, and greed of the city, wherein all too many recognized themselves, or worse yet were recognized by their friends. But the full fury of this attack surges over Jerome when death removes the protecting hand of Pope Damasus. His ascetical demands, his insistence on chastity, virginity, and celibacy, his strictures on Roman married life become, in turn, embarkation points for violent personal attacks. He is pictured as a magician and seducer.[7] His power over his followers is attributed to satanic wiles.[8] His relations with these women, and especially with Paula, are impugned and colored by calumny.[9] Disgusted with the whole thing, St. Jerome turns back to the peace of the desert and forsakes Rome. Before embarking, he sends a tender farewell to his spiritual family:

Greet Paula and Eustochium, who are my sisters in Christ, whether the world wills it or no. Greet Albina, my mother, and Marcella, my sister, as well as Marcellina and Felicity. Say to them that we shall all appear together at the judgment seat of Christ. Then shall be revealed the inner conscience and life of each. Keep me in your thoughts, model of virginal purity, and may your prayers subdue the angry waves on my journey.[10]

From this period on, St. Jerome's spiritual direction takes a much wider scope. By his letters to the West, through his controversies and Scriptural work, because of the pilgrimages to the Holy Land and, finally, through his work with the community of Paula and Eustochium in Bethlehem, St. Jerome assumes a position of spiritual arbiter and defender of ascetical practice throughout the West. Time will mellow him and moderate his language (as far as possible), but his singleness of purpose and wholehearted devotion to complete renunciation will remain the beacon light of the ascetical life during his day.

The Spiritual Doctrine of St. Jerome

Renunciation

The cornerstone of St. Jerome's spiritual direction is complete renunciation. Family ties, money, the good opinion of society must be cast aside. The true seeker after perfection, the perfect follower of Christ, must recognize these things for the hindrances that they are. Perfectly illustrative of this is his charge to Heliodorus:

Remember the day of your enlistement when you were buried with Christ and took your sacred oath to turn from mother and father. Consider what grief was caused the camp of the enemy by the gift you then received to carry on war against them. And now behold, the enemy strives to kill Christ in your heart. Hence, even if your nephew entwines his arms about your neck, and your mother, all disheveled and torn, shows you the breasts that nursed you, and your father throws himself across the threshold; trample him underfoot and fly, dry-eyed, to the banner of the cross. In this case the only filial love is cruelty.[11]

This renunciation of family ties looks even to the grief of a mother mourning her dead daughter. Yet, throughout this as always, St. Jerome has in mind one who has embraced the counsels of perfection. Thus, when writing to Paula on the death of her daughter Blesilla, he tells her that he is dealing with no ordinary Christian, but one whose renunciation of the world has been complete. Hence her tears and her grief are a betrayal and a denial of all that such a renunciation implies. Such grief but confirms the accusations made by the enemies of the perfect life. It is proof to them that she was deceived in the choice that she made. She is seeking the living among the dead. What her true attitude should be St. Jerome puts into the mouth of her dead daughter:

Do not grudge me my glory, nor act in such a way that we shall be separated eternally. . . . Do you pity me because I have left the world? Is it not rather I who should grieve for your lot? For the prison of the world still confines you. You must still struggle constantly with anger, covetousness, lust, and the whole variety of vicious incitements that drag one to ruin. If you wish to remain my mother, take care to please Christ, for I may not acknowledge a mother who displeases Him.[12]

Similarly, interest in or attachment to earthly possessions destroys all hope of an ascetical life. Renunciation is the only way. One must seek the riches of Christ. Money and possessions are the hawser preventing the ship from moving out to sea, and it must be cut, not loosed.[13] The weight of gold holds down the wings of virtue, since only when we are naked and unencumbered do we fly up to heaven.[14] Only the believer has wealth, only the miser is poor. If his property is in his own power, let him sell it; if he is poor, he is not to amass riches.[15] "Therefore do not seek what must be disposed of, but give up what you have. Thus Christ may know that His new recruit is resolute. So, while you are still afar off, His Father will run to meet you, clothe you in a robe, give you a ring, and kill the fatted calf." [16]

A true renunciation also scorns the mockery and ridicule of public opinion. Only the weak and the irresolute will allow it to bar the way to perfection. St. Jerome, however, realizes the power of public criticism and takes measures to show its futility. He notes that "a highly educated mind is more easily overcome by contumely than by fear; and that those whom no tortures would break down succumb to shame." [17] But as he states it, it is a primary principle for an ascetic to despise the judgments of men and to keep in his heart the words of the Apostle, "If I were still trying to please men, I should not be a servant of Christ" (Gal. 1:10). The honors that appeal to the public mind are transient, and bestowed more often on unworthy men than by merit. To renounce them is a small thing, but to possess Christ is a great thing.[18] There is no pleasing the crowd if one would follow Christ and walk in godliness:

Because we do not wear silken clothes we are called monks. Because we are sober and do not break down into raucous laughter we are held to be deliberately sour. If our garments are not shining, there is applied to us the vulgar epithet "Greek and impostor." But though their reviling be even more subtle, and we be surrounded by men whose paunches are stuffed with fat, our Blesilla will laugh at them, and will not lower herself to listen to the reproaches of these babbling frogs, since our Lord Himself was called Beelzebub.[19]

Such then, is Jerome's basic concept of renunciation. Its extreme severity, however, requires that it be viewed in the perspective of the man himself, and the Christian motivation he adduces in support of it. For, while recognizing the sacrifice and hardships, in his own mind he saw nothing impossible in such demands. After all, he and others had done it and were doing it, so it was not impossible. As he himself points out: "I am not unmindful that you may point to the fetters that shackle you at the moment. But my breast is not iron, nor is my heart stony. I am not sprung from the bare Macedonian rock nor bred of a tiger. And I have passed through troubles like yours." [20] He describes the interlocking bonds of affection that cause us to procrastinate, and concludes: "The love of God and the fear of hell easily break bonds such as these." [21]

Psychologically, though, the whole tone of these epistles leaves one with the impression that this rigid severity has some of its roots in St. Jerome's personal experience with the ascetical life. His first turning to the way of perfection, his life in the desert, and his personal struggle there, all play a part in shaping his conviction that renunciation must be absolute, or it is ineffective. The implicit reasoning would seem to be that, even after a complete renunciation, enormous and unceasing effort is still required. How can such a conflict be successful if the very first step is not complete? His letter to Eustochium is a graphic manifestation of this deep-seated conviction. He writes to her that, even after condemning himself to the desert and leading there the ordinary ascetical life, the pressure upon him did not cease. The fires of lust still glowed in an all but dead body. Even though his only company was the beasts and scorpions, his thoughts made present all the delights of Rome. Victory came only through weeks of special abstinence and continual prayer. And as he phrases it: "If such be the temptations of men who, emaciated in body, are attacked only by their thoughts, how shall a maiden enjoying a luxurious life withstand it?" [22]

To this personal ascetical experience must be added Jerome's own feeling about life in Rome. All through his epistles there breathes a spirit of detestation for all that the social life of Rome symbolized. Its luxury, decadence, and hedonism are painted in dark and unrelieved colors. The vanity of feminine adornment, its purposes and significance; the baths, the slaves, the eunuchs; the worldliness of the clergy, the nakedly material standards of the ruling class are all for him like so many axes laid at the root of the ascetical life. In his eyes no compromise is possible. A single chink in the armor, a small breach in the wall of the ascetical structure, and the whole dark flood will pour in. To profess a desire for the ascetical life and to tarry in that social milieu is to dally with it. To dally with it even transiently is to open the gates. If one would be perfect, the whole must be rejected. His experience with Rome as a young man, and then as an ascetic, make it evident to him that renunciation is an either-or decision.

Again, as is evidenced in the history of Christian spirituality, there is a difficulty that remains, no matter how sound the principles. It is a difficulty whose source is psychological rather than philosophical or theological. And the difficulty is this: To renounce God's goods so as to restore the divine order to life, and yet not denounce and hate them as evil in themselves. To detest the mass of deformity, disorder, and evil introduced into the world by man's sin, and yet not despise the things that God has made. To prefer the invisible and everlasting to the visible and transient, while realizing that the visible and transient have a place in the divine order. This always remains a problem for the ascetic. The line of demarcation is fine and easily obscured by enthusiasm, even when the conviction itself remains unchanged. Especially is this likely to be the case when the ascetic must stir up souls grown torpid in the enervating air of the purely transient and visible. If to this difficulty be added St. Jerome's rhetorical skill, ardent character, and bitter experience in Rome, much of what passes for exaggeration is easily understandable, and the sound substance of his teaching is readily distinguished from what is accidental and verbal.

Yet, granting this personal equation in St. Jerome's spiritual doctrine, the picture of it is neither complete nor accurate without the recognition of his fundamental and objective motivation. "If anyone wishes to come after me, let him deny himself, and take up his cross daily, and follow me" (Lk. 9:23). *"Abnegat seipsum"* and *"sequatur me,"* these are the two indivisible sides of the Christian coin of perfection. Deface one or the other side, and the coin is valueless; it cannot buy the kingdom of heaven. Isolate abnegation from imitation, and the end product is a Manichaean duality. Confine oneself to the following of Christ and reject renunciation, and the result is a chimera, or a "bloodless and insipid humanism." Christian perfection is no pursuit of a will-o'-the-wisp. It takes into full account the disorder wrought by original sin; disorders from within, "that which I would not that I do"; disorders from without, the world, the flesh, the devil. Unless these be controlled, perfection is an illusion. Likewise, perfection itself is no formless ideal but a positive, concrete reality, the rigorous imitation of Jesus in His love of the Father and all the children of the Father.[23] It is this twofold process that produces Christian perfection. Abnegation and imitation interact mutually, each actualizing the other. And a reading of St. Jerome's spiritual teaching in the light of this essential Christian principle will reveal the fundamental soundness of his spiritual doctrine.

Virginity

Virginity and continence form the second cardinal principle of St. Jerome's spiritual direction. So vigorous is his insistence on this point that his teaching has been frequently misunderstood, and he himself held up as the type of misanthrope that Catholicism is said to produce. To appreciate his insistence on chastity and to avoid misunderstanding him, two things must be kept in mind. First, St. Jerome's teaching is conformed to the traditional Christian teaching on virginity. Secondly, St. Jerome was forced to defend this traditional teaching against strong and persuasive opposition. Characteristically, his defense is equally strong. It is the first point that must be seen in some detail.

From the very beginning, for the Church, virginity is at once a protest against the insane fleshliness of pagan living, and an unmistakable sign of complete consecration to God. The purity of life entailed by Christian virginity was the glory of the Church and its proof of holiness in the world. Justin Martyr,[24] Athenagoras,[25] and Tertullian [26] contrast it with pagan moral standards and argue from it for the divine character of Christian holiness. At the same time, the stern requirements involved in virginity made of its practitioners a living and permanent call to all Christians to turn away from the laxity of pagan society and take up the cross of Christ. Nor did the Church ever lose sight of the positive character of this virtue, whereby in living a life of absolute continence a Christian followed Christ, His mother, and all the great saints in a most exact manner. Or that, by the virgin life, one "transmutes mortality into incorruptibility." [27]

But while esteeming this virtue highly, the Fathers of the Church were not blind to its possible and actual dangers. Cyprian, like Jerome himself, bears witness to abuses and scandals and lays down strict regulations concerning the virgins of the Church.[28] All of these writers insist on constant mortification and prayer as the only protection of such a form of life, for only through these will come the grace that is needed for it. "Perfect chastity is an extraordinary gift, and God only bestows it on those who sincerely desire it and beseech Him for it with unceasing prayer." [29] Gradually, too, it became manifest that only the strictest discipline would free the life of celibacy from the danger of abuses and, as a result, there developed communities of such persons living under superiors and according to a common rule.

The whole attitude of Catholic Christianity toward virginity and perfect chastity has its source in the twofold principle of Christian asceticism: *abnegat et sequatur*. The Christian consecration to a life of continence fulfils both requirements in the one choice. It is a supreme form of renunciation and a rigorous imitation of Christ, counselled by Christ Himself. Because it is an imitation of Christ, freely chosen for love of Him, it is preserved from renunciation for the mere sake of renunciation. Because it is the renunciation of what is of deep value in the sensible and temporal order, it is the perfect denial of self in order to follow Christ. Finally, it manifests here and now the life to come, when we shall love God completely and other things for love of Him, and there shall be neither marriage nor giving in marriage.

The preceding points form the general context for St. Jerome's doctrine on virginity and chastity. But his teaching has a definite contemporary background also. Much of what he writes is specifically directed against the evils of Roman social life and its dangers, which he describes realistically. Even more specifically what might be termed the synthesis of his teaching on the subject is brought out in his controversial works against Helvidius, Jovinian, and Vigilantius. These men represent an articulate expression of a whole wave of opposition to the ascetical movement that sprang up against Jerome and all that he stood for. Quite correctly, they realized that the heart of this ascetical life was the practice of virginity. Hence, to discredit this teaching and practice, and thereby undermine the whole ascetical movement, Helvidius undertook to prove that Mary had other children by Joseph. Such an attack was necessarily directed toward the destruction of the great exemplar of virginity held up by the ascetical writers. A few years later Jovinian, a monk who had left the monastic life, touched on the same point, but concentrated his efforts upon a conception of Christianity that would appeal to the seekers after pleasure, and to those desirous of a Christianity without the cross. Vigilantius, however, pointed his attack against clerical celibacy, holding that the whole idea of absolute chastity was a heresy—and, worse, a pharisaical cloak covering all manner of shamelessness. Monasticism itself he saw as a piece of cowardice, robbing the Church of necessary ministers and producing a body of useless men. It requires very little knowledge of St. Jerome to imagine the vehemence, scorn, and satire that would pour out in his answers to such as these. Typical is his remark to Jovinian: "Think of it! If you had never been born, the drunkards and riotous would never have been able to enter into paradise." [30] But the real importance of his anwers is that they offer a fairly complete formulation of his teaching on virginity. And it is this formulation, supplemented by his letters, that is presented here.

The primary point stressed by St. Jerome is derived from the very purpose of the ascetical life—the full service of God. It is based on the teaching of St. Paul: "He who is unmarried is concerned about the things of the Lord, how he may please God . . . the unmarried woman, and the virgin, thinks about the things of the Lord, that she may be holy in body and in spirit" (I Cor. 7:32–34). From this text St. Jerome draws his definition of a virgin: "one who thinks about the things of the Lord, that she may be holy in body and in spirit, since it avails nothing to have virginal flesh and be married in thought." [31] It is this distinction that divides the virgin serving the Lord from the married woman. The virgin is able to follow a regime of prayer and fasting. She is not called upon to devote her time to vanity and adornment in order to please her husband. Nor are her thoughts taken up with the cares of a household. Thus the virgin serves the Lord with singleness of mind and undivided love.[32]

Again and again, however, St. Jerome insists that the life of virginity is not a precept but a counsel. It is a call beyond the powers of human nature to live a life of angelic purity, and can only be done through the power of Christ:

What is demanded is commanded. What is commanded must necessarily be done, and if it is not done it is punished. But after all, that is an empty sort of command whose fulfilment rests on our free choice. Moreover, if the Lord had commanded virginity, by the same token He would have condemned marriage and removed the very seed plot out of which virginity springs. If He had cut off the root, how could He have expected the fruit? . . . Do not wonder, then, that set as we are amidst the delights of the flesh and the allurements of vices, an angelic life is not required but only recommended. When a counsel is given it is a matter of free acceptance. But if it is a command, then it is matter of required service.[33]

In support of this position, St. Jerome adduces the words of Christ: ". . . there are eunuchs who make themselves so for the kingdom of heaven's sake. Let him accept it who can" (Matt. 19:12). And, commenting on this passage, he states: "The master of the race in which all Christians run puts up a reward, and inviting contestants to run, He holds in His hand the prize of virginity. . . . He does not say you must run, willing or not, but whoever is willing and able may run and be victorious." [34]

St. Jerome also makes it clear that the real value of the virginal life in the eyes of God consists in the fact that it is freely chosen. The greater love that Christ gives to virgins is bestowed because they have willingly surrendered what was not demanded of them. For such a surrender is a great grace, since it offers up what is not commanded, and is not satisfied with rendering only what is required, and no more. Christ, therefore, lovingly takes to His heart those who have become eunuchs for the sake of the kingdom of heaven, for this offering makes them pure temples of God. Being unstained in mind and body, they are in truth a clean and whole burnt-offering made to God.[35]

The motive presented for this form of choice is the restatement of the traditional Christian teaching: the love of Christ. "Happy that conscience, blessed that virgin, in whose heart there is no other love than Jesus Christ. For He is wisdom and chastity, patience and justice, and all the virtues." [36] Through the practice of virginity one follows closely in the footsteps of Christ and gives herself to the highest of all loves.[37] "It is hard for the human soul not to love something, and of necessity our will must be drawn to some affection. And in this case spiritual love takes the place of carnal love. Desire is quenched by desire. Whatever diminishes the one increases the other. Therefore, as you lie on your couch at night, say, 'By night I have sought him whom my soul loveth.' " [38] To this motive is added the further consideration that this state is a great gift made possible for women by Mary. "In ancient days continence was found only in men, and Eve continued to bear her children in sorrow. But now a virgin has conceived in her womb, and the curse has been broken. Death came through Eve, life through Mary . . . and thus the gift of virginity flows forth more richly on women because it has its source in a woman." [39] In sum, the fundamental motif is the following of Christ and His mother, to whom are dedicated the first fruits of virginity in both sexes.[40] "For me virginity is consecrated in Christ and Mary." [41]

A careful reading of all these points makes it clear that St. Jerome is proposing only the traditional Christian teaching on virginity. While his statement of it is forceful and realistic, and permeated with scorn for his opponents, his doctrine itself does not differ from that of Ambrose or Cyprian. Yet it is only fair to recognize and deal with the strictures that have been laid against his teaching. Brushing aside the rather obvious charges of Manichaeanism that trail all ascetical preaching, it is apparent that the real point of attack is St. Jerome's view of marriage. Does he view it as a good, or simply as a necessary evil? Nor is the question without considerable foundation. First of all, it is true that his pictures of married life in contrast to virginity might well leave the impression that there is nothing of good in marriage. So much is this the case that even the ascetical Pammachius found it necessary to request an explanation on this very point.[42] What, then, are the facts of the case?

Whatever one may feel about St. Jerome's attitude toward marriage in general, he certainly may not be accused of heresy in his teaching on the subject. He explicitly disassociates himself from the heretical doctrine on it when he writes: "We do not follow the teaching of Marcion and the Manichaeans, and thus disparage marriage, nor are we deceived by the error of Tatian, the chief of the Encratites, who condemned all intercourse as unclean." [43] In defending himself against such charges, he makes his own mind equally clear. "Can one be said to condemn marriage who insists that it is a precept of the Lord that wives should not be put away, and that what God has joined together let no man put asunder?" [44] In the same letter he states that both virginity and marriage are gifts of God, and each has its own place in the life of the Church. Marriage must be allowed, otherwise nature is condemned; and how can he be said to condemn what he holds to be a divine gift? [45] Writing against Jovinian, he says: "It is only heretics who condemn marriage and despise the command of God; but we listen happily to every word the Lord says in praise of marriage. The Church does not condemn marriage but subordinates it. It does not reject wedlock but regulates it." [46] Enlarging on this last statement in his letter to Pammachius, he writes: "I protest with my last breath that I neither condemn nor have I condemned marriage." [47]

While it is clear that St. Jerome does not condemn marriage, it is equally clear that he does place it in a subordinate position. Yet this is neither strange nor un-Catholic. Virginity is a great Christian ideal. It is the perfect following of Christ; but its superior place does not mean that marriage is not a good. Indeed, if it were not a good, what greatness would there be in renouncing it freely for the sake of Christ? "No one compares a bad thing with a good." [48] Something of this idea may be seen in St. Jerome's explanation of the text from the epistle to the Corinthians: "Both he who gives his virgin in marriage does well, and he who does not give her does better." St. Jerome's comment is this: "It is one thing not to sin; it is another to do good. We forsake evil, and we do good. In this last lies perfection." [49] Thus St. Paul compares marriage to virginity as the good to the better. St. Jerome also uses a series of comparisons to bring out the same notion:

We are not ignorant of the fact that marriage is honorable and the bed undefiled. We have read the first ordinance of God, "Increase and multiply and replenish the earth." But while we receive marriage we prefer virginity, which is born of marriage. Is not silver still silver, even though gold is more precious? Or, is it a dishonor to the tree to prefer its apples to its leaves or roots? As apples are from the tree and grain from the stalk, so is virginity from marriage. [50]

And in confirmation of this he notes that the Church, while accepting marriage, subordinates it to virginity and widowhood. If married men are indignant with this approach, he writes, let them vent their anger not on him but on the Scriptures which teach it. [51]

So much, then, for the doctrine of the saint on marriage. But what is to be said about the actual picture of marriage that he draws in his epistles and controversial works? Here the case is not so easy, unless one takes into full account the man and his times. For, however sound be his doctrine, St. Jerome is too much the ardent defender and exponent of asceticism not to make full use of the low state of married life in Roman society in his defense of virginity. Able rhetorician that he was, the actual state of marriage in Rome would lose none of its dark side in his presentation of it. On the other hand, it cannot be claimed that the actual facts that he gives are only symbolic. The rank materialism produced by the corruption of Roman society had permeated the whole structure of social marriage. Jerome can support his case with actual reality. He is also aware that he is writing to highborn women and girls living in this atmosphere, and he recognizes that it would be all too easy for them to succumb to it. He therefore feels it incumbent upon him to stress this dark side, if they are to see clearly the dangers that confront them and realize the high state that they have sought for themselves.

Hence, admitting Jerome's rhetorical concentration on the seamy and sordid side of social marriage, it does not follow that such a contrast was without foundation. Whereas one might also wish that he had devoted some space to the noble side of marriage, the absence of such a treatment is not to be construed as a condemnation of marriage. What he does write must be read in the light of his character and his purposes. This may be illustrated by his much-criticized work against Jovinian.[52] In the introductory section of the First Book he tells us that his whole answer rests on the well-founded suspicion that Jovinian "upholds marriage so strongly in order to disparage virginity. Because when the lesser is equated with the greater, the lower profits by the comparison and the higher suffers." [53] In terms of such a suspicion, one can readily imagine the resulting reply and the emphasis that would be placed on virginity in contrast to marriage. This is intensified by Jerome's knowledge of the group that has gathered to support Jovinian in his teaching. "You have many lieutenants in your army . . . the gross, the fops, the exquisites, and the rabble-rousers who defend you with fist and foot . . . Amazons with bare breasts and naked knees and arms who challenge the men coming against them to a battle of lust." [54] To St. Jerome such a situation was not only Christianity without the cross but the struggle of gluttony and lust to overthrow the cross; and his reaction was characteristic, and should enter into our judgment of what he writes.

Prayer, Study, Mortification

Renunciation and virginity are the cardinal realities of St. Jerome's spiritual doctrine, but he does not neglect to set them in their proper and traditional framework of prayer, study and mortification.

Prayer. For the most part St. Jerome simply applies to the life of the ascetic the traditional life of prayer that had been developed by monasticism. According to St. Basil, and to some extent St. Pachomius, there were to be regular intervals of prayer at dawn, the third, sixth, and ninth hours, at nightfall and at retirement. These intervals were to be filled by the recitation of various prayers, the chanting of the psalms, and other responsories that were to be varied from time to time. [55] And it was this regularized order of prayer that was applied to the ascetical life in general by the Fathers of the Church, such as St. Athanasius. [56] Thus we find St. Jerome, in his letter to Eustochium, insisting:

We ought to have a regular order of prayer, so that even if we are occupied with work, the time itself will warn us. As everyone knows, there should be prayer at the third, sixth, and ninth hour, as well as at the break of day and in the evening. Do not take food unless it be preceded by prayer, nor leave the table until thanks has been given to the Creator. Arise two or three times in the night to meditate on passages of Scripture that you know by heart. In leaving the house, be armed by prayer. On returning from the street, pray before sitting down; and do not rest the body until the soul is fed. In every act, in every step, let your hand depict the cross of Christ. [57]

It is this same advice he gives for the training of the child Paula; and this is the rule of life he sets down for Demetrias. To this he adds constantly the Scriptural injunctions: "Pray always," "Pray without ceasing," "Let your conversation be in heaven."

Study. Hand in hand with prayer, St. Jerome prescribes constant study, particularly of the Scriptures. "Let reading follow prayer and prayer follow reading." [58] "Let sleep come upon you with the sacred page in your hand." [59] This is the example of the saintly Ambrose, who never retired until some portion of Scripture had been read, and whose days as a student were so ordered that they were divided into prayer and reading.[60] Jerome's own experience is used to affirm this practice, since, as a young ascetic unable to quell temptation and evil inclination, he betook himself to an arduous course of study, and now is able to gather sweet fruit from this seed of learning sown in bitterness.[61] This love of Scripture makes us partakers of wisdom.[62] Its constant perusal makes of our breasts the library of Christ.[63] St. Jerome also lays down a program of studies for the training of a young ascetic.[64] She is to learn, first of all, the Psalter, and then the rules of life set forth in the Book of Proverbs, as well as that of Job. After this she is to take up the Gospels, never to lay them aside again, as well as the Acts of the Apostles and the Epistles. Once she has enriched her mind with these treasures, she should memorize the Prophets, as well as the Heptateuch. So prepared, she is to take up the study of the Canticle of Canticles. In addition to the Scriptures, she should make her companions the writings of Cyprian, the letters of Athanasius, and the treatises of Hilary of Poitiers. All in all, a full program, but it represented an integral part of St. Jerome's spiritual direction from the very beginning. It was carried out in practice in the community established by Paula in Bethlehem.

Mortification. The last element of St. Jerome's spiritual doctrine to be considered here is mortification. On this point even the most casual reader of his epistles is aware of his detailed demands and, frequently enough, has heard them condemned for the ravings of a world-hating monk. What is not so well known is that St. Jerome himself answered this particular charge in his second book against Jovinian. This ex-monk had held that the ascetical doctrine and practice was a rejection of the goodness of God's creation. In reply St. Jerome presents the true picture of Christian mortification. It has its roots in the necessity for self-control which is required by man, to be truly man and not a beast. It is through the senses that vice enters into the soul, and the soul in turn is overwhelmed by the disorder so produced and is led captive by it. For gluttony is the mother of avarice, which fetters the heart to the earthly.[65]

Thus when these wedges of revolution have entered through the gates [of the senses] into the citadel of our mind, where then will be our liberty, our strength, our thought of God? Especially when the sense of touch pictures even past pleasures, and these recollections of vice force the soul to take part in, and after a fashion to practice, what it does not actually commit. A man deceives himself if he thinks that he can regale himself with an excess of food and drink and still be able to devote himself to the pursuit of wisdom—that is to say, that he can live in the midst of pleasures and not be netted by their vices.[66]

This whole point St. Jerome substantiates by an appeal to pagan philosophers, whose thought he gives in detail and from many sources.[67]

But the Doctor of the Church puts his real stress on the Christian reason par excellence—perfection. No Christian condemns what God has created. No Christian joins with Marcion and Tatian in hating and despising the works of the Creator.[68] "We praise every creature of God, and yet prefer leanness to fat, abstinence to luxury, fasting to fulness. . . . 'From the days of John the Baptist [who fasted and was a virgin] until now the kingdom of heaven has been enduring violent assault, and the violent have been seizing it by force'" (Matt. 11:12).[69] Or, as he wrote to Salvina, in the words of St. Paul: "'I chastise my body and bring it into subjection: lest perhaps, after preaching to others, I myself should be rejected'; and 'if Paul is fearful which of us shall dare to be confident?'"[70] Again, to Eustochium: "'Therefore mortify your members, which are on earth' (Col. 3:5). Because [the apostle] did so he could say with confidence 'It is now no longer I that live, but Christ lives in me.' He who mortifies his members and walks in this image is not afraid to say 'I am become like a winesack in the frost. Whatever there was in me of the moisture of lust has been dried up.' " [71] In like manner he writes to Demetrias that the devil uses our passions to tempt us, and to make an oven of our hearts which only divine grace and fasting can put out. "The celestial dew and strict fasting quench the heat of passion in a young girl and enable her to lead an angelic life." [72]

In his specific instructions on fasting, the saint is both understanding and balanced. Abnormal and extreme fasting is not required. One is not to fast until the heart pounds and we become so weak that we have to be supported by others.[73] The desires of the flesh must be curbed, but strength must be retained for study, psalmody, and vigils.[74] For "fasting is not the perfection of virtue but the foundation of the other virtues. So also with sanctification and chastity, without which one will not see God, they are steps on the way to the summit, but of themselves alone do not confer the crown on a virgin." [75] To Nepotian he writes: "Take upon yourself only such fasting as you can stand, and let it be pure, chaste, simple, and moderate." [76] His instruction to Furia is: "A little food that leaves the stomach unsatisfied is better than fasts of three days' duration. It is much better to take a little every day than to be satiated every so often. That is the best rain which falls upon the earth slowly. A sudden and exceedingly violent downpour heedlessly tears away the soil itself." [77]

In the course of his epistles on the ascetical life, St. Jerome applies this doctrine of mortification to many things: flesh meat, wine, clothing, appearances, social gatherings, servants. In some cases, such as in the use of wine, he calls for total abstinence; in others for moderation and sobriety, the avoidance of any self-indulgence. But throughout, he holds up as absolutely necessary the complete subjection of anything that attracts or stimulates the senses or detracts from modesty. This is the narrow road that leads to perfection, and there is no other. To Jerome, as to all teachers of Christian spirituality, mortification is the tool that every Christian must use if he would conform himself to the likeness of Christ. The more perfect the conformity sought, the more constant and extensive the mortification demanded. Only in this way does one take up his cross and follow Christ.

We have seen, in essence, the spiritual direction of St. Jerome: renunciation and virginity, with their handmaidens, prayer, study, and mortification. As he preaches it, it is a hard doctrine. He demands the greatest of effort, and is only content with the best. Neither compromise nor palliation is tolerated. And many who have read or heard of his spiritual doctrine have pictured him as a hard, unbending, and unattractive figure. They have seen him as devoid of human sympathies and lacking any consciousness of the beauties and joys of human life that God has given us. In the light of such a conception they wonder wherein does his sanctity lie.

Anyone who is satisfied with such an appraisal has not even begun to understand the many-faceted character of St. Jerome. His letters to his friends and spiritual children are bathed with a charm and radiance that alone explain how he could bind them so closely to the high ideal he taught. His eulogies on friends such as Nepotian, Paula, and Marcella show depths of tenderness and affection that he is neither ashamed of nor attempts to conceal. His letters of instruction, strong and unswerving in their spiritual direction, still bespeak an accurate understanding of the conditions in which his subjects live. Thus, his love and care for them is not a blind, unheeding thing, but one that foresees the dangers that will confront his spiritual children in the pursuit of their chosen vocation. His love for them is a love that wills only the highest good that man can achieve—Christian perfection. Greater love he did not know.

This last point is of essential importance to the appreciation of St. Jerome. He never lost sight of the fact that the vocation of a Christian is to be a saint. Each is called to that goal along a different path and by diverse gifts. The greatest of all gifts is to follow Christ perfectly—the aim of the ascetic life. And to the cultivation of that gift St. Jerome devoted all his energy and genius. All was demanded in order to gain all. Clearly it is a doctrine that will have no more appeal to our highly materialistic world than it had to his own, an age not too dissimilar from ours. But whatever be the age, the perfect following of Christ will always be the central theme of Christian spirituality, the pearl of great price, to buy which St. Jerome was happy to sell all that he had.

NOTES

[1] *Ep.* 46, 1.
[2] *De Civ. Dei,* II, 20 (condensed by Christopher Dawson in "St. Augustine and his Age," *A Monument to Saint Augustine*: New York, 1930).
[3] *Conf.* 8, 6 (trans. by C. Bigg, 1929).
[4] *Ep.* 22.
[5] Cf. *Epp.* 28, 29, 30.
[6] *Ep.* 22.
[7] *Ep.* 54, 2.
[8] Cf. *Epp.* 45 and 39, 2.
[9] *Ibid.*
[10] *Ibid.,* 7.
[11] *Ep.* 14, 3.
[12] *Ep.* 39, 6–7.
[13] Cf. *Ep.* 53, 10.
[14] Cf. *Ep.* 145.
[15] *Ibid.*
[16] *Ibid.*
[17] *Ep.* 66, 6.
[18] *Ibid.*
[19] *Ep.* 38, 5.
[20] *Ep.* 14, 3.
[21] *Ibid.,* 4.
[22] *Ep.* 22, 8.
[23] Cf. Pourrat, *Christian Spirituality* (transl. W. H. Mitchell and S. P. Jacques, London, 1922), I, 1–33.
[24] *Apol.,* I, 66.
[25] *Legat. pro Christ.,* 33.
[26] *Apologet.,* 9.
[27] Methodius, *De fest. Virg.* 4:2 (*PG,* 18).
[28] *De Hab. virg.*
[29] Origen, *Comm. in Matt.* 14:25 (*PG,* 13).
[30] *Adv. Jov.,* II, 37.
[31] *Ibid.,* I, 13.
[32] *Ibid.*
[33] *Ibid.,* I, 12.
[34] *Ibid.*
[35] *Ibid.*
[36] *Ep.* 130, 19.
[37] *Ep.* 22, 17.
[38] *Ibid.*

[39] *Ibid.*, 21.

[40] *Ep.* 48, 21.

[41] *Ep.* 22, 18.

[42] *Ep.* 48 and 49.

[43] *Adv. Jov.*, I, 3.

[44] *Ep.* 48, 4.

[45] *Ibid.*, 5.

[46] *Adv. Jov.*, II, 40.

[47] *Ep.* 48, 20.

[48] *Ep.* 22, 18; cf. *Ep.* 50, 5.

[49] *Adv. Jov.*, I, 13.

[50] *Ep.* 48, 2.

[51] *Ibid.*, 20.

[52] Typical of this criticism is the remark of its translator in the *Nicene and Post-Nicene Fathers* (VI, 346) : "The treatise gives a remarkable specimen of Jerome's system of interpreting Scripture, and also of the methods by which asceticism was introduced into the Church, and marriage brought into disesteem."

[53] *Adv. Jov.*, I, 3.

[54] *Ibid.*, II, 37.

[55] Cf. Pourrat, *op. cit.*, 94, 95.

[56] Cf. P. Resch, "St. Augustine on Praying the Psalms," *Amer. Eccles. Rev.*, 114 (1946), 424ff.

[57] *Ep.* 22, 37; cf. *Ep.* 107, 9 and 130, 15.

[58] *Ep.* 107, 9.

[59] *Ep.* 22, 17.

[60] *Ep.* 43, 1.

[61] *Ep.* 125, 12.

[62] *Ep.* 130, 20.

[63] *Ep.* 60, 10.

[64] *Ep.* 107, 12.

[65] *Adv. Jov.*, II, 7.

[66] *Ibid.*, 8–9.

[67] *Ibid.*

[68] *Ibid.*, 16.

[69] *Ibid.*

[70] *Ep.* 79, 7.

[71] *Ep.* 22, 17.

[72] *Ep.* 130, 10.

[73] *Ibid.*

[74] *Ibid.*

[75] *Ibid.*

[76] *Ep.* 52, 12.

[77] *Ep.* 54, 10.

St. Jerome and the Barbarians

JEAN-REMY PALANQUE

St. Jerome and the Barbarians

I T IS A MATTER of common agreement, in assessing the impact of Christianity upon the modern world, that the fourth and fifth centuries of the present era form an age apart. During this period, in both the East and the West, a theological and literary revival becomes so manifest that the whole epoch is generally referred to as the Golden Age of Patristic thought. At the same time, however, in the political sphere, the Mediterranean world had entered upon a crisis of such proportions as to mark the end of the ancient world and the beginning of the Middle Ages. Both Diocletian and Constantine, in the course of their relatively long reigns, used their political genius in an heroic but vain attempt to stem the tide of barbarian invasions. But, gradually, the wandering tribes from the north and east had won their way into the Empire, gaining trusted positions in the army and at the imperial court itself. The difficulties caused by such foreign penetration and the reaction of the Roman peoples against the atrocities and usurpations to which they were subjected so troubled the land that by A.D. 476 the Roman Empire can be considered as having come to an end in the West.

An important question thus arises as to the position taken by the Church in the face of this political catastrophe. Among the many prominent ecclesiastics whose sentiments in this regard have been preserved, none is of more interest than St. Jerome. The churchmen who preceded him, in the course of the fourth century, had not been faced with the breakdown of the Empire as such. The theologians of the East, Athanasius of Alexandria, Basil of Cappadocia, the two Gregories, and such articulate bishops of the West as Ambrose of Milan and Hilary of Poitiers, had passed on before the invaders seriously menaced the soil of Rome. The great writers of the fifth century came after the catastrophe, while the contemporaries of the invasions, living in the Eastern provinces and unmolested by the barbarians for the most part, gave little attention to the social and economic evils then visited upon the West.

Even among the Latins themselves, Pope Leo the Great, despite his immediate contact with the invaders, does not seem to have taken sufficient time to formulate his reaction to this crucial problem. The pamphleteer, Salvian, and the poet, Sidonius Apollinaris, are almost the only ones who registered open opposition to the infiltrations of the barbarians, vigorously deploring the trend of events, while holding out some hope for the future. But they appear to have been too fully preoccupied with the problems of the day. Thus their evaluations of events are hardly objective or unbiased.

It is necessary, then, to look to a previous generation for a proper estimate of the Christian reaction to this phase of history —to a generation which had experienced the *douceur de vivre* of the fourth century and the tragic aftermath of the invasions during the fifth. This is the generation of Jerome and of Augustine.

St. Augustine, of course, had vivid personal experience of the miseries of his day. He had seen the Vandals on African soil. He died in Hippo in A.D. 430 with the barbarians besieging his episcopal see. In his *City of God,* he had clearly analyzed the profound anguish troubling Christian hearts at the turmoil of the times. It was at once a *summa sociologica* for a new age, a tract on political philosophy, a discourse on world history, and a manual of Christian conduct. Animated with the grace of genius, this profound thinker furnished the Church with a pillar of fire that was to shine down through the centuries, with an intellectual tour de force that would inspire and hearten the whole of the Middle Ages.

At the same time, however, it would hardly be proper to overlook his immediate contemporary, St. Jerome.[1] For Jerome, too, was a man of keen intelligence and ardent sensibility, who was gravely affected by the troubles of the age. In considering the barbarians, Jerome gives evidence of having had personal contact and an early familiarity with the problem. And he was at once a thorough Christian and a humane and considerate patriot. An Italian, born on the northeastern frontier, he lived through the political developments that dominated the interval between the reigns of the sons of Constantine and those of Theodosius. He had first-hand knowledge of conditions in both the eastern and western halves of the Empire, and his life came to an end in the Holy Land of Palestine. Although the political difficulties of his century did not move him to the composition of a great or monumental work, his reflections on the demographic and political happenings of the times are well worth considering.

I

The initial catastrophe had taken place in A.D. 378. On the battlefield of Adrianople, Valens, the Roman Emperor, met his death, and the Roman world found itself faced with the first real barbarian breakthrough into its domains. The victorious Goths quickly spread themselves over the Danubian provinces, ravaging Moesia, Dacia, Pannonia, and Thrace, up to the very borders of Constantinople in the process.

Jerome of Stridon was then thirty years old. Born on the borderland between Dalmatia and Pannonia, he had lived a part of his life in the north of Italy. He had come down to Rome for his schooling, then travelled north again to Gaul, and wandered east as far as Antioch in Syria. There he had experimented with monasticism of the eremitical type. In 377 he had abandoned the desert, without, however, giving up his vocation to the ascetical life. He had been shocked and disheartened by the constant quarreling among the monks, whom he found more interested in arguing the theological meaning of the *hypostasis* and in anathematizing their fellows than in cultivating the harsher virtues associated with a retreat from the world. Jerome, become "despondent over this warfare, sick of body and soul, emaciated by fever and bad

temper," took leave of the hermitage because he found it "shat-
tered by the worst extremes of evil dispositions." [2]

Having at least partially recovered his health in Antioch,
Jerome took the road to Constantinople, where he first seriously
applied himself to the studies that would occupy the whole of his
mature career. He composed there the *Life of Paul the Hermit*
and embarked upon the translation of Origen's *Commentaries on
the Scriptures*. He spent some time on the composition of a
Chronicle of World Events, which he took bodily from the Greek
of Eusebius of Caesarea, carrying the record down to his own
times. And he managed to acquaint himself with the great ecclesiastical movements of the day, entering into friendly relations with
Bishop Paulinus of Antioch and Gregory of Nazianzus, at the
moment occupying the episcopal see of Constantinople.

But, even in the course of his travels in the East, Jerome did
not lose contact with the West, nor was he unaware of the evils
afflicting that half of the Empire. The text of his *Chronicle* for
the years A.D. 325 to 379—written on his own responsibility—
testifies to the fact that this intellectually inclined ascetic, intent
primarily upon theological pursuits and a monastic way of life,
had still not cut himself off completely from an interest in secular
history. Placing both spheres side by side in his account of the
ecclesiastical activities of the day, Jerome assured his readers:
"that while a citizen of heaven, he was still a patriot of the
Roman Empire." He still considered himself an heir of that civilization, "the principal events of which were here set down for
them." [3]

In the short, succinct paragraphs of which his *Chronicle* is
fashioned, Jerome was not in a position to pass judgment on the
parade of passing events. But a sentence, apparently just tacked
onto the preface, betrays the anguish produced in the hearts of all
at Rome by the victory of the Goths: "I content myself at this
date," Jerome wrote of the year A.D. 379, "reserving the remainder
of events from Gratian to Theodosius for a much larger historical
treatment. . . . For while the barbarians are spread throughout
our lands, all is uncertain." [4]

At the moment the Roman world in the West was having first-hand experience of the barbarian pressures. Neither Gratian nor Theodosius, for all their valor, could dislodge these new peoples, though they did manage to arrest their progress and, in part, to assimilate them. Encamped along the Danube as *federati,* these tribes remained as permanent guests of the Empire, docile most of the time but occasionally wild and unruly.

Meanwhile, the illusion of security was maintained by the indifference of the masses and the blindness of the Roman politicians. St. Ambrose, much closer to the threatened provinces than Jerome who was in Syria at the time, felt that this flood of invasions was the prelude to a new "deluge," in the midst of which he expected the Emperor Gratian to arise as a new "Noah." Ambrose, as a matter of fact, seemed to believe that the close of the fourth century might foreshadow the end of the world.[5]

At a greater distance from these troubles, Jerome could take a more sober view of the matter. Concluding his *Chronicle* with the year 380,[6] when the impending peril seemed momentarily checked by the victory of Theodosius, Jerome indicated his awareness of the significance of these barbarian infiltrations. He still had hopes that the intruders might one day be expelled; but he clearly understood that thenceforth the Empire would tread its way amid increasing uncertainties.

II

Fifteen years passed. The reign of Theodosius came to a glorious end, despite occasional insurrections and troubles. The Germans had not begun their terrifying incursions along the Rhone and Danube. The Franks and the Alemanni were still being deployed within the borders of Germany. The federated Goths remained loyal to their obligations and considered themselves the guardians of the frontiers. They continued to furnish recruits, even generals, for the imperial armies. But the death of Theodosius in January 395 was the signal for a fresh outbreak of disorders in the borderlands, as well as at the very center of the Empire.

During the months immediately preceding the death of that noteworthy ruler, most of the imperial troops from the East had been dispatched to Italy to deal with difficulties that had arisen on that peninsula. The Huns from the northeast took advantage of this situation to ransack the exposed Roman provinces in Europe and Asia. Some of them broke through to the Danube, overrunning Thrace. Others, scaling the lower reaches of the Caucasus, descended into Cappadocia and Syria. But, unlike their attack upon the Goths some twenty years earlier, which had sent the latter reeling in upon the Empire, this was not a well-organized adventure. It was more a raid of pillaging bands, intent entirely upon profiting from the momentary relaxation of vigilance on the part of the Empire. It did cause consternation in hitherto unmolested lands and magnified the sound of the word "Hun" into a threat sufficient to paralyze the countryside with fear. The Roman historian, Ammianus Marcellinus, depicting the Gothic invasion of 376, has well described the Huns at this later date when the terror of their very appearance struck the heart of the civilized world.[7]

There was in the making at this time another barbarian peril. It arose within the Empire itself and was the more disastrous on that account. The federated Goths, who had returned from Italy to eastern Illyricum, now took advantage of the death of Theodosius, and, in the spring of 395, they set out in marauding bands, overran Macedonia and Thrace and rode with impunity up to the very walls of Constantinople. Stilicho hastened from Italy to stop them. But the Oriental imperial court, jealous of its own power, commanded him to halt these operations and to evacuate the Balkan provinces. This lack of accord between the two halves of the Empire was indicative of a weakness that was soon to prove fatal for the whole Roman world. It is a key to Alaric's later successes: the rebellion he organized in Macedonia from 395 to 398; the depredations he carried out in Italy from 401 to 411. The immediate result was that the Visigothic soldiers, under this new chief, were able to ravage with impunity all of Greece, from Thermopylae to the Peloponnesus, right up to the moment when the Emperor Arcadius, without attempting to chastise him or curb his ambitions, was to hand him the command of the eastern Illyrian troops. Then, in 399, it was the turn of the Ostrogoths, encamped in Phrygia, who likewise rose in revolt.

In Constantinople, meanwhile, the situation was further complicated by a revolution within the palace itself and by subsequent uprisings in the city. In November 395, the troops that had returned from Italy assassinated the imperial minister, Rufinus. In July 399, the Eunuch, Eutropius, who had been all-powerful at court, was cast aside and sent into exile. Between July and December 400, General Gainas and his Gothic soldiers were made victims of an anti-barbarian campaign that spread through the capital. They were finally ambushed and annihilated. The five years that followed the death of Theodosius had thus proved to be a disastrously troubled period in Eastern politics.

III

Jerome had now been settled in the East for several years. He had returned to Rome in 382 to labor there for a short while as secretary to Pope Damasus. But upon the death of that pontiff in 385, he found himself compelled to leave the city. The attractions of the Holy Land, the convenience of the libraries which the Orient afforded, the closeness of St. Paula and her daughters, who contemplated emigration to Palestine, all conspired in his decision to settle permanently in Bethlehem. Here Jerome took over the guidance of a double monastery—a religious center that was to become a model of prayer, study, and hospitality. During thirty-five years of continual residence there, he produced his translations and his commentaries on the Scriptures, along with letters of spiritual direction and of controversy, that were to render his name illustrious throughout the Christian world. He devoted himself energetically to Scriptural exegesis and to theology, to combatting with unflinching energy the errors of the heretics, Helvidius and Jovinian, of his former friend, Rufinus, and the neo-Origenists, as well as of Pelagius and his newer heresy. But neither his interests in the Bible nor his theological controversies were able to occupy him so completely as to make him lose interest in the political events of the day. News of the Empire and the repercussions of its fateful happenings were continually breaking through the barriers of his remote retreat.

The monastery in Bethlehem was by no means a hermitage in the Thebaid. Numerous travellers and pilgrims stopped there on their way to Jerusalem. Couriers from Rome, from Gaul and Africa were constantly arriving with messages and information from across the sea. In his sympathies, by direct and epistolary contacts, the monk of Bethlehem was kept abreast of the world and its problems. His writings reflect his many worries and perplexities over the fate of his generation.

In a letter written during the summer of 400, Jerome gives a description of an invasion by the Huns that had taken place some five years previously:

Of a sudden, upon the swift appearance of the news carriers, the whole Orient trembled. For, from the far reaches of the Maeotide sea, between the frigid Tanais and the wild tribes of the Massagetes, there where the barriers of Alexander formed by the Caucasus Mountains had hemmed the barbarians in, suddenly broke forth a swarm of Huns. Coursing wildly about on fleet steeds, they quickly filled the countryside with carnage and terror, for the Roman army was out of reach at the moment, detained in Italy by the civil war.

Herodotus informs me that this people had held the East in captivity for twenty years under Darius, King of the Medes. They had exacted a yearly tax from both the Egyptians and the Ethiopians —may Jesus drive off such wild beasts from our Roman world! Unexpectedly, they swept down on all sides, their own swiftness outstripping the news of their coming. They spared neither religion, nor dignity, nor age, nor even the whimpering infant in its cradle. They put to the sword tender children who, unaware of the danger, cried out in glee upon being picked up or at seeing the shining weapons of their murderers.

Rumor has it that they were on their way to Jerusalem; that they were driving thither in search of treasure. At Antioch, long-neglected walls were hastily repaired after a too easy spate of peace. Tyre hurriedly destroyed its man-made connection with the mainland, willingly reassuming its true character as an island. Even we [in Bethlehem] were constrained to prepare ships and to hold ourselves in readiness on the shore, against the arrival of this enemy horde. We made ready to entrust ourselves to the danger of shipwreck from the incontinent winds rather than fall into the clutches of such barbarians, interested not so much in our own safety as in seeking the inviolability of our virgins. For, in our own land, we were having domestic difficulties that took precedence over an expedition against the barbarians.[8]

Jerome's account is in need of certain qualifications. These Mongolian Huns, roaming as nomads between the mouth of the River Don (the Tanais) and the Sea of Azov (Maeotide), and the country of the Massagetes to the east of the Caspian Sea, were certainly not the descendents of the Scythian tribes who had invaded western Asia in the seventh century B.C.[9] But they did follow the same route of invasion, seeking the passes through the Caucasus and tossing over all barriers until they reached the heart of Syria.

It is true that the marauding horsemen described by Jerome did prove a menace to Antioch, Tyre, and Jerusalem, plunging their populations into terror. His account here has the hallmark of direct, ocular testimony and is thus worthy of full confidence.[10] As he remarks, when the alert was sounded in Palestine, internal, political conflict had rendered impossible the sending of military reinforcements. His "*quaedem apud nos dissensio*" is clearly a reference to the conflict between the military courtier, Rufinus, and the barbarian general, Stilicho. The "*domestica bella*" is the revolt of Alaric. But the whole "invasion" really amounted to no more than a raid without particular consequence. Life at Bethlehem quickly returned to its original routine.

Jerome's narrative is actually part of a letter to Oceanus, which also served as a eulogy for Fabiola. The latter, a convert to Christianity after years of worldly living, had set out for Palestine, intent upon living a life of penance there together with Paula and Jerome. Desiring to find a solitude not far from the places sanc-

tified by the Mother of the Savior,[11] she had been received into
the women's monastery in Bethlehem. It was at this moment that
the terrifying incursions of the Huns intervened. The Romans in
Palestine prepared immediately to flee before these terrible enemies. Hastily gathering their baggage, they made for the sea.
Their ships were loaded and, despite a raging storm, each one
made ready to embark at the first approach of the danger—willing, as Jerome says, to face the risk of shipwreck rather than the
outrages of barbarians who thought of nothing but violence and
pillage.

Fortunately, the danger passed without incident, and, despite
the unrest it left behind, Jerome and his entourage installed themselves once more at Bethlehem—"kept in the Orient by long residence there and an inveterate love of the Holy Places." [12] But
Fabiola had not been fully acclimated. Having all her possessions
with her, she decided to abandon so dangerous a place and to
seek in Rome a new way of life devoted to penance and charity.

IV

Several months after Fabiola's departure, news reached Bethlehem that brought great sorrow to the already troubled heart of
Jerome. Young Nepotian, a nephew of Heliodorus, Bishop of
Altinum, died in the very flower of his youthful priesthood.
Sitting down immediately—it was in the middle of 396—Jerome
addressed a delicate and touching eulogy to the grief-stricken
uncle. The opportunity afforded him an occasion for a discourse
on the calamities of the times.[13]

His spirit weighed down by grief, the writer pauses to recall
"the recent miseries of our rulers and the catastrophes of our
days." He recounts the tragic deaths of the emperors of the
century: Constantine II, Julian, Jovian, Valentinian, Valens,
Gratian, Valentinian II; and that of the usurpers: Procopius,
Maximus, and Eugenius; then the fall of the ministers of Theodosius; Abundantius, Rufinus, and Timaxius.[14] But these were
merely recitals and generalities. They held no great importance.
Enlarging his canvas, Jerome hastened to describe "not the mere

disgrace of some unfortunate mortals, but the frailty of human circumstance," for it is only with horror, he says, "that the mind can contemplate the calamity of our age."

For twenty years and more now [since 376], between Constantinople and the Julian Alps, each day witnesses the shedding of Roman blood. Scythia, Thrace, Macedonia, Thessaly, Dardania, Dacia, Epirus, Dalmatia, and the two Pannonias are devastated and ravaged by the Goths, the Sarmatians, the Quadrati, Alanni, Huns, Vandals and the Marcomanni. How many matrons as well as virgins consecrated to God, persons of free birth and noble lineage, have become the playthings of these savages! Bishops captive, priests massacred along with clerics of every order, churches destroyed, the altars of Christ serving as mangers for horses! The relics of the martyrs disinterred—*on all sides sorrow, on all sides weeping, and the image of death everywhere multiplied. The Roman world falls round about us* and yet our proud necks are unbowed. What courage do you think the inhabitants of Corinth, of Athens, of Lacedemonia, of Arcadia and of the whole of Greece can now have, with the barbarians lording it over them? And yet I have but named a few cities in which there once reigned kingdoms of no little power. The East appears immune to these disasters, and yet the least rumor throws it into a frenzy. Why only last year, as you know, these wolves, coming from the far reaches of the Caucasus—not from Arabia alone, but from the far north—in short order overran numerous provinces.

How many monasteries have been molested, how many rivers have been reddened with human blood! Antioch was placed under siege along with numerous other towns bathed by the water of the Halys, the Cydnus, the Orontes, and the Euphrates. Whole troops of captives have been taken. Arabia, Phoenicia, Palestine, and Egypt know now the ravages of these destroyers. And I, *had I a hundred tongues or a hundred mouths, and a voice of metal* would not be able to sound forth the names of these multiple evils. I had not intended to write a history, but briefly to mourn over our calamities. Before the task of properly retelling these things, Thucydides and Sallust would have stood wordless.[15]

This recital is slightly exaggerated. The invasion had already commenced twenty years before this on the Danube and, by 378, had menaced the whole country between the confines of Constantinople and the Julian Alps.[16] But it was at this date that the provinces which Jerome enumerates so precisely had been overrun from "Scythia" (the Dobrogea of today) to both upper and lower Pannonia. Even if the disturbances had reached there anew with Alaric in 395, the land had had peace between 380 and 382. Hence, it had not been afflicted uninterruptedly during these twenty years.[17]

We are no longer obliged to consider as enemies of the Empire in the fourth century all those people whom Jerome accounts on the side of the Goths: the Sarmatians, Quads, Marcomanni, who were encamped on the border of Pannonia for so many centuries; the Vandals and the Alanni, who had come there to join them for a short while, together with the Huns, whom one fancies everywhere after the Battle of Adrianople.

The correspondent of Heliodorus is distracted by his own reveries, it appears, and by his habitual rhetoric. But at least he handed down an exact bit of information when he spoke of the invasions of the Huns during the preceding year, alluding to the description of the "Chaldean peoples [Assyrian, no doubt] in the prophet Habacuc." He describes these wolves as having come "not indeed from Arabia, but from the north, from the rocky borders of the Caucasus, invading the whole Orient even to Cappadocia [the land between the Cydnus and the Halys] and to Syria [between the Euphrates and the Orontes], after which Antioch was besieged." [18]

Here again, as in the letter to Oceanus, Jerome speaks from first-hand information, describing the monasteries captured by direct assault, the rivers splattered with blood, and the hordes of captives taken by the Huns. As he was writing to Italy, he wanted to show himself well informed when speaking of what had transpired in Europe; hence the *"Corinthios . . . Athenienses . . . Arcadus . . . quibus imperant barbari."* He is here certainly referring to the Goths under Alaric who had ravaged central Greece and the Peloponnesus, taken Athens, and destroyed Corinth.[19] Venice was already aware of the evils that had befallen

Hellas, and further of the disasters occasioned by the invasion of
379: the women violated, the clerics assassinated or taken into
captivity, and the churches either destroyed or profaned. Mixing
up in a single tableau the miseries of that day with those of
twenty years before, Jerome felt obliged to recall the *Aeneid*:

ubique luctus, ubique pavor, et plurimae mortis imago (II,
368). Finally, in the face of the lamentable spectacle which the
provinces of the East and West now offered him, he concluded
sorrowfully: "*Romanus orbis ruit*" the Roman world is rent
asunder.

V

Jerome's pessimism is exaggerated or, at least, premature. In
398 the Gothic peril seemed to have been averted: Stilicho had
driven Alaric from Arcadia and had surrounded him on Mt.
Pholoes; the revolt of the Moor Gildon—of which Jerome appears unaware—had likewise been suppressed; and Roman prestige appeared to have been restored on all its frontiers in both the
West and the East.

But this calm was not to endure. In 401, Alaric abandoned
eastern Illyricum, apparently at the suggestion of the Court at
Constantinople. He turned to the invasion of Italy. He was vanquished there in 402 by Stilicho who, in 406, wiped out in like
manner the hordes of Radagasius. But then, in 407, new Ger-
manic tribes spread out over the whole of Gaul, where a usurper
by the name of Constantine had arisen. Immediately Alaric
marched on the approaches of Italy once more. With the fall of
Stilicho the following year, he found himself its master. Favored
occasionally by the court at Ravenna, though more frequently the
victim of its rebuffs, he found himself alternately welcomed and
repelled by the Roman Senate. In turn, Alaric, supported or
abandoned at will the fanatic upstart, Attila, offering the Empire
peace at a price, then threatening to impose his designs by force.
Finally he hurled himself upon Rome, which he besieged, took,
and then pillaged for three whole days (August 410).

This was the first time in over seven centuries that the sacred

soil of the pomoerium had been violated by barbarians. Since the
fall of the Capitol to the Gauls under Brennus, the so-called walls
of Servius Tullius and the even more recent ones of Aurelius had
not had to submit to the assault of an enemy. What a humiliation
for the Eternal City! What shame for the vanquished Romans
and for all the inhabitants of the Empire! Jerome gives a realistic
account of the reaction. In six letters written between 407 and
414,[20] in several of the prefaces to his "Commentaries on Ezechiel" he makes allusion to these evils that had befallen the West
and of which he had been so quickly informed.

Writing in 407 to a certain Rusticus, who had been left behind
in Gaul while his wife Artemia was visiting the Holy Places in
Palestine, Jerome urged him to a life of penance. He encouraged
him in particular to the observance of continence with his wife,
something he had apparently promised. Among the arguments
Jerome offers him is a meditation on the straits into which he was
plunged by "the death of his friends and fellow citizens, the
destruction of towns and country estates," as well as by "the limit-
less disasters falling on his own province." [21] This is but a brief
consideration in comparison to the "fury of the barbarians and
the danger of captivity," which now lay between himself and his
wife.[22] The whole argument was epitomized in a very Roman
quotation addressed to this fugitive and victim of the invasions:

*"Tu vagaris in patria, immo non patria, quia patriam perdi-
disti."* (You wander about in your country—but indeed no
longer your country—for you have lost your home land.)

Two years later Jerome again gave a spirited account of the
Gallic invasions to the widowed Agerochia [23] in an attempt to
turn her from a second marriage. Besides reasons of a spiritual
nature militating against another marital venture, Jerome threw
into the scale the troubled conditions of the times which he believed more than sufficient for turning Christians away from setting up a household. "Is not this perhaps the beginning of the end
of the world?" Jerome asked, not hesitating to use the Gospel
admonition: "But woe to those who are with child, or have

infants at the breast in those days" (Matt. 24:19). Then he enumerated "a calendar of our present calamities":

Innumerable and most ferocious people now occupy the whole of Gaul. All the land between the Alps and the Pyrenees, all that is enclosed between the river Rhine and the ocean, is devastated by the Quadrati, the Vandals, Sarmatians, the Alanni, Gepides, Heruli, Saxons, Burgundians, Alemmani and—O pitiful republic!—the now hostile Pannonians. For the Assyrian has come upon them (Ps. 82:9). The city of Mainz, a noble town, has been taken and subjugated. Many hundreds of its inhabitants have been massacred in church. The people of Worms have been subdued after a long siege; and Rheims, that well-fortified city, together with Amiens, Artois, *extremique hominum Morini* [Aen. 8: 727], Tours, Nimes, Strasbourg, are all fallen before the onslaughts of the Germans. In the provinces of Aquitania and Novempopulaine, Lyons and Narbonne have each been devastated. All but a few cities have been ravaged either from without by the sword or from within by starvation. Not without tears can I mention Toulouse, which to the present has been spared destruction by the good graces of its saintly Bishop, Exuperus. Spain, itself on the verge of perishing, is in daily remembrance of the horrors brought by the invasions of the Cimbri, and suffers in fear and expectation the trials wreaked upon these other nations.[24]

We have here a precise and vivid picture of the great invasion of 407. The Rhine froze over that year and was crossed near Mainz on December 31, 406, by hordes of different tribes who threw themselves on the far-flung Roman provinces all the way from the Pyrenees to the ocean: Vandals, Quadrati, Gepides, and Heruli, Alemanni, Burgundians and Saxons making up the German element who took their stations between the Rhine and the Elbe, and even pushed further to the north of Pannonia. If the "Pannonians" are to be numbered among these hordes—they were already considered as citizens of the Empire, as Jerome attests with his *O lugenda res publica*—he has reference no doubt to the provincial people carried along some months before by the warriors of Radagasius, or at least to the ragged remnants of his warrior bands, originally thrown out of Italy and pushed back to the Danube. This invasion fanned out through the whole of Gaul, since Toulouse and even Spain were menaced. The low lands in all the provinces were picked clean, while the fortresses were besieged. The region around the Rhine, victim of the first assault, was particularly beset. Mainz, the city of Worms, and that of Nemetae (Spire), Strasbourg, Treves, and, in particular, Rheims and the sector right down to the coast towns on the English channel—Amiens, Artois, Morins in Flanders—were all, likewise, made victims of the plunder.[25]

VI

Italy too came in for its share of these terrors. Jerome goes on to detail the evils visited upon Illyria. "And now," he writes, "from the Black Sea to the Julian Alps, our own land is no longer our own. During the last thirty years, the frontier of the Danube has been destroyed. War has fallen upon soil in the very center of the Empire. The time for the tears of the ancients has passed. With the exception of a few old men, the people of today, born during the captivity or the siege, have no desire for a liberty they know naught of." [26]

The monk of Bethlehem is again speaking as if the barbarian domination had prevailed throughout the provinces of the Danube without interruption since the disaster at Adrianople. We know that this is an exaggeration, since the Ostrogoths as well as the Visigoths had long been encamped in Moesia and Pannonia as auxiliaries, actually "federated" in service to the Emperor. But he would have us understand (and on this account the testimony of Jerome is of great moment) that in the eyes of the Romans in these lands, the subjection of the Goths to the Empire was but a nominal thing. Actually these provinces were under their complete domination.[27]

Matters were to grow still worse in Italy, of course, where now the enemy was the master. "Who can believe, or what history honestly conceived must not maintain," Jerome exclaimed, "that Rome is battling on its own soil, not for glory but for its very survival. Indeed it is not even fighting, but trying to ransom its existence with its gold and household possessions." [28]

As a matter of fact, when Alaric marched on Rome for the first time in 408, the Senate had to buy him off by turning over to him 4,000 pounds of gold, 30,000 pounds of silver, 4,000 silk garments, 3,000 red tunics, and 3,000 pounds of spice, at the same time making appeal to the Court of Ravenna for the negotiation of a new treaty.[29] It was, of course, the vain and tortuous politics of Ravenna that had occasioned this revolt in the first place, and which was to cause Alaric's recourse to the offensive again in 409 and 410. In particular, it was Olympius, the *Magister Officiorum,* who had imprudently provoked the Gothic chieftain to his first two reprisals in 408 and 409. Besides the ministers who succeeded Olympius all too quickly in the course of palace intrigue, the blame falls very definitely upon the Emperor Honorius. But Jerome will not admit this. He says explicitly: "All this cannot be laid at the feet of our rulers, who are most conscientious men. It must be attributed to the wickedness of a semi-barbarian criminal who has armed our enemies against us with our own weapons and resources." [30]

This "semi-barbarian" is evidently Stilicho, the son of a Vandal, who was accused by his enemies of having turned the Empire over to the barbarians. But the accusation is most unjust. For it is precisely to Stilicho's total loyalty to the reigning dynasty, to his indefatigable energy, to his military ability, and to his talents as a statesman that the resistance of the Empire during the thirteen years following the death of Theodosius is to be attributed.[31] A whole faction had enviously hounded this *magister militum* of Honorius; at first in the court at Constantinople where Rufinus, then Eutropius and the two prefects, Aurelian and Anthemus, proved hostile to German and Italian interests; and then, in the West, where pagans and Christians combined in accusing him of betrayal and sacrilege.[32] Jerome reflects this state of affairs. He is, as a matter of fact, the earliest authority we have for this trend, which, eventually, brings about the downfall of a very competent minister. Succeeding events prove clearly that the disappearance of Stilicho in no way added to the strength of the Empire, nor did it in any way facilitate repression of the barbarians. On the contrary, it seems to have made Alaric all the bolder, once he had experienced a few striking successes.

But political passion pays little attention to either ethics or morality. And down the centuries, ancient and modern historians have striven to outdo each other in repeating the calumnies of the pamphleteers of the time, who were both badly informed and unfair. Instead, an effort should be made to sift out the evidence —exaggerated, it is true—offered by the man's self-appointed panegyrist, the poet Claudian.

In any event, by a curious coincidence, Jerome faced with the disasters of 409, engaged in the same type of historical reminiscence that had occupied Claudian after the victories of 402. He recalls the fact that Italy had been ravaged by the Gauls long ago, again by Pyrrhus and by Hannibal. But where Claudian, Stilicho's panegyrist, referred to his person as the new Camillus and the new Scipio,[33] Jerome suggested no such comparison. He is intent upon a return of Roman might, recalling from centuries past that the victory won by Brennus the Gaul was properly avenged by the Roman conquest of all Gaul and of Galatia; that the successes of the King of Epirus, and of Hannibal the Carthaginian, were promptly recompensed by the ignominious deaths that befell these conquerors and by the destruction of their ambitions.

The Roman Empire had already suffered an everlasting dishonor [he wrote] when Brennus the Gaul crossed down into Rome, having put our armies to route at Allia and devastated all before him. Nor was this ignominy avenged until Gaul itself, the fatherland of these Gallic warriors, and Galatia [Gallo-Graecia], wherein abode the despoilers of the East and West, were conquered. Hannibal, bringing his own tempest with him from the farthest corner of Spain, also devastated Italy. But upon viewing the city of Rome, he did not dare lay siege to it. Pyrrhus, likewise, was obsessed with respect for the name of Rome; and when he arrived to find the city in ruins, he stood in a section apart, not daring to consider himself as the conqueror of a place he had always been taught to look upon as the city of kings. And yet for this indignity—I will not call vainglory what has come to a proper end—the former, a fugitive in the face of the whole world, found death in Bithynia by poison; and the latter, upon returning home, died in his own kingdom. But thereafter, these lands paid tribute to the Roman people. Now, should events take a more favorable turn for us, there is nothing we could get from our present enemies other than what they have already stolen from us.[34]

Jerome felt he should almost despair of the world's future. Lucan had already asked: "What is it that can survive, if Rome is so weakened?" Quoting this poet, Jerome asked in turn: "What is there that will remain if Rome now perishes?" [35] And for the moment, it did seem that Rome might be marked for destruction. Apprised of Alaric's entry into Rome in 410, and of the death of many friends—victims either directly or indirectly of the barbarians—Jerome imagined it well-nigh time for the end of the world as predicted in the Sacred Scriptures. This is the mood in which he began his *Commentary on Ezechiel*. The same feeling is reflected in a note he wrote to Eustochium, the daughter of Paula:

Alas! with what grief have I heard of the death of Pammachius and of Marcella, during the siege of Rome, together with the passing of so many of my brethren and sisters. I sit here in consternation, moved to such a point that day or night I can think of naught but the fate of them all, dreaming of myself as a prisoner sharing the captivity of such holy souls. I dare hardly speak until I receive more definite news. For I am torn between hope and despair, tormented by the terrible things that have befallen our friends. But now that this glorious Light of the World has been tampered with; indeed, now that the very head and center of the Roman world has been defiled, and now that, with this City, the whole world is, in a way, faced with annihilation, *"I am dumb, and am humbled, and kept silent from good things"* (Ps. 38:3).[36]

Jerome used almost the identical terms in writing to Marcellinus, the tribune, and to his wife Anapsychia in 411: "On the

verge of starting my treatise on Ezechiel—to keep a promise I
have so often made my learned readers—at the very moment I
began to dictate, my soul was gravely troubled by the disasters
that had fallen upon the provinces in the West, and in particular,
upon the city of Rome itself; so that, to quote a well-known saying: "I could not find words, and I remained long silent, knowing that it was time for tears." [37]

Again in a passage written in 413, Jerome returned to a recital
of these tragic happenings:

Terrifying news comes to us from the West. Rome has been taken by
assault. Men are ransoming their lives with gold. Though despoiled,
they are still hounded, that after their goods they may pay with their
very lives. My voice is still, and sobs disturb my every utterance. The
city has been conquered which had once subjugated an entire world.
Indeed, it had died of hunger before being put to the sword, so that
there are few even to have been taken captive.[38]

Jerome then gave a description of the besieged dying of thirst,
and of mothers themselves destroying their newly born infants,
which he interspersed with Biblical and classical citations, quoting Isaias (15:1), the Psalms (78:1–3), and the *Aeneid* on the
fall of Troy:

> Quis cladem illius noctis, quis funera fando
> Explicet aut possit lacrimis aequare dolorem?
> Urbs antiqua ruit multos dominata per annos
> Plurima perque vias sparguntur inertia passim
> Corpora perque domos et plurima mortis imago
> (*Aen.* II, 361–365).

But Jerome's rhetoric is hardly as moving as the sober details of
the previous passage in which his passionate soul gave vent to
patriotic consternation. Rome was for him the land of his very
bones and marrow—the center of all civilization. It was, of
course, the city in which he had come to maturity; where many
of his closest friends, now in grave personal danger, were still to
be found. Pammachius had just died there. The widow Marcella
had been exposed to the recent horrors, and had undertaken the

most difficult precautions for the protection of the youthful Principia. She had died several months later.[39] Many had fled before
the advances of the Goths, finding refuge in Sicily, Africa, and in
the East itself. But, in Africa, as we have seen, they ran into
further difficulties. Proba, for example, widow of Olybrius, escaping with her granddaughter Demetriada before the actual taking
of Rome, boarded a frail ship and was taken captive by Heraclius,
who proceeded to sell the young woman in the markets of the
Syrian slaves.[40] The refugees likewise poured into Palestine.
Jerome describes their arrival in his *Preface to Ezechiel*:

Who would believe that Rome, which had spread over the whole
earth by means of its victories, could now fall so low as to be at once
the mother and the tomb for its own populace; that the shores of the
Eastern world, of Egypt and of Africa, once the proud possessions of
this governing metropolis, would now be laden with multitudes of her
children, reduced to the estate of servants and handmaids; that today,
this sanctified Bethlehem should welcome as beggars, nobles of both
sexes hitherto abounding in this world's goods! We ourselves, hardly
able to succor them, can but share their grief and mingle our tears
with theirs. . . .[41]

Particularly since the flight from the West, this overcrowding of
the Holy Land exposes the terrible savagery of the barbarians which
has given rise to the want and sufferings of these exiles. . . . We
cannot witness all this without tears and weeping, knowing that what
was once so great a power is now without learning or affluence and has
descended to such penury that it lacks shelter, food, clothing. . . .[42]

These refugees were actually a cause of embarrassment to the
monastery, for their coming coincided with the barbarian invasions threatening Palestine itself. Jerome spoke of it in his letter
to Marcellinus:

During the course of this year, after I had written three volumes,
we are exposed to a sudden invasion not unlike that which your Virgil
so aptly describes in his *lateque vagantes Barcaei*; and of which the
Holy Scriptures also speak in reference to Ismael—*contra faciem
omnium fratrum suorum habitabit*. For the barbarian, swiftly overrunning the borders of Egypt, Palestine, Phoenicia, and Syria, de-

scended on us like a flood, sweeping all things before him. By the mercy of Christ we are just about able to escape his ravages. . . .[43]

As no other historical source makes mention of this invasion, which certainly took place in 411,[44] it is most probable that it amounted simply to a raid of pillaging Arabs come up from the south, particularly since Jerome makes reference to Ismael and speaks of the borders of Egypt and Palestine before those of Phoenicia and Syria.

These alarms, the influx of refugees, the sorrow occasioned by the news from Italy and from Africa—where the uprising of Heraclius took place in 412—all combined to disturb the labors of the Hermit of Bethlehem. Yet he continued with his studies, regularly completing the treatises that he had planned. In another of his prefaces, he explains his frequent procrastinations:

I remember reading once as a child that "there is nothing so easy that it will not become difficult if one approaches it unwillingly." I confess that it is a long time now since I have promised you these *Commentaries on Ezechiel,* and I have not been able to keep my promise, distracted as I am by the multitude of people arriving here daily from all over. For there is not a single minute even when we are not occupied with groups of brethren or do not have to share the solitude of our monastery with a vast crowd of strangers, so that we either have to shut our gates or relinquish our pursuit of the Sacred Scriptures, for which purpose they were originally opened. As a consequence, it is in the busy, indeed furtive, hours of the night, now lengthening with the approach of winter, that I try to dictate what I can by lamp light. It is thus that I try to overcome the weariness of a distracted mind with the work of exegesis. I am not boasting of our hospitality towards the brethren, as some will no doubt observe, but simply giving you in detail the reasons for my delays.[45]

Thus this continually active sexagenarian, despite his many troubles, furnished his friends with a good example of his state of mind. Though frequently interrupted, his *Commentary on Ezechiel* was pushed to completion and served as a proper complement to the work he had done on Isaias and the other Prophets.

It was immediately followed by the *Commentary on Jeremias*.[46] Jerome, for all his despairing protest and his references to impending doom for this miserable world, did not allow himself to fall victim to his own alarms. It is a primary lesson to be taken from any consideration of Jerome's life and doings. Amid the worst tribulations, one must look to the good things of the past and labor for those who are to live in a much better future. This ancient exegete thus places before the scholars of all time a model of fidelity to his tasks and of detachment that is not lacking in grandeur.

VII

The prefaces and letters of St. Jerome suggest several considerations on the course of human events which it will be proper to mention in bringing this essay to a close. The first is an admonition regarding penance. Each catastrophe that afflicts the earth should warn men against running after the pleasures of the world. It is not at all astonishing, of course, to see Jerome, the great champion of virginity and asceticism, using the troubles of his times as a pretext for counseling virgins against marriage and widows against a second espousal. It makes good sense. Why should one encumber herself with a family when one faces the prospect of having to leave all behind and live in exile?[47] What good will it be to take a husband who tomorrow will be obliged to leave for battle, or to flee in disgrace before the enemy?[48] There is here, of course, a touch of bourgeois prudence or of self-concern a little too foreign to our taste. But as a propagandist, Jerome is only too happy to find here an argument from circumstance that so conveniently strengthens his contentions in favor of continence.

Jerome likewise presents us with a great lesson in humility. These evils demonstrate the fragile estate of worldly possessions. Life itself is a small thing in the hands of God, and we are so liable to forget the supremacy of divine Providence. There are too many who remain deaf to the lessons of reality. In 396, Jerome had cried out: "The Roman world is crashing down, and still our proud necks are unbowed." [49] In 413, he repeated the same charge: "Alas! the whole world is falling, and still our sins are not decreasing." [50] Modern man, likewise, should not linger among the blind but should profit by the warnings of Providence. He ought to see in the destruction of worldly possessions a reminder of the only real and lasting grandeur, that of Almighty God. The poet had long ago subtly advised the school of Stoics:

> Sic fractus illabitur orbis
> Impavidum ferient ruinae.[51]

But the Christian, properly judging this superficial austerity, should be able to face these disasters with a serene heart and with an awe not unmixed with hope.[52]

Finally, Jerome sets before us a challenge of perfection. In line with the moralists of all ages, he saw a divine chastisement in the evils visited upon the Roman Empire. He found the cause of the disastrous defeats that fell upon Rome in the unworthiness of its citizens. Taking refuge once more in the language of the Old Testament, he spoke of the divine anger directed against the folly of human behavior:

We know that God has been long displeased. Nor have we tried to placate him. It is because of our sins that the barbarians have grown strong, because of our vices that the Roman armies have been overpowered. And, as if this were not a sufficient catastrophe, civil wars are now taking the lives of almost more men than fell before the enemy's sword. O miserable Israelites! In comparison, Nabuchodonosor might be considered a servant of the Lord. Unhappy are we who have offended God to such an extent that His wrath has descended upon us in the savagery of the barbarians.

Ezechias did penance for his sins, and in one night a hundred and eighty-five thousand Assyrians were destroyed by the avenging angel. Josephat sang the praise of the Lord, and the Lord granted a victory to his glorifier. Moses overcame Amalec, not with a sword, but with his prayers. If we wish to be lifted up, let us prostrate ourselves.[53]

A spirit of detachment, a spirit of prayer, a spirit of faith— these are the remedies that Jerome prescribed. In a word, it is an integrated spiritual economy that he opposed to the breakdown brought by temporal disasters. It cannot be said that Jerome resigned himself to the downfall of the Empire; or that he "had gone over to the barbarians," as did Salvian some fifty years later. But, having shed bitter tears over the fate of his country and of his fellow citizens, Jerome continued to pursue his scholarly labors. He placed himself beyond the horizon of human events in the hope of thus leading his contemporaries to virtue, even to an heroic way of life.

It may be said that Jerome treated the political problems of his day in rather cavalier fashion. It is true that he took too little cognizance of them. For he never criticizes the rulers of the Roman Empire. A respectful subject of the Theodosian dynasty, he rendered due homage to the godliness of its princes and did not rise in judgment against their methods of government. Only once do we see him belabor the unpopular general Stilicho, holding him responsible for the victories of Alaric. And this was an unjust accusation.[54] But in general, Jerome did not bother with the problems involved in the survival of the Empire.

Having suggested that the calamities of the present might portend the end of the world, Jerome thereafter avoided all dabbling with that possibility. He busied himself as if the world were to perdure, giving up all thought as to how the generations of tomorrow might conduct themselves. It was only essential for him that the Christian man should live his faith, reaching down into the depths of its spiritual resources. In the midst of impending catastrophe—a condition that not infrequently afflicts the course of human events—without dogmatism or dialectic, Jerome offered a sure remedy for human uncertainty. But his message has meaning only for the soul that wants to disengage itself from passing things and turn to the eternal.

NOTES

[1] Cf. F. Cavallera, *Saint Jérôme, sa vie et son oeuvre* (Louvain, 1922).

[2] P. Monceaux, *Saint Jérôme, sa jeunesse* (Paris, 1932), 229: Engl. transl. by F. J. Sheed (Sheed and Ward, New York, 1937).

[3] F. Cavallera, *op. cit.*, I, 68.

[4] *Chronicon* (ed. Helm), 7.

[5] Cf. *Expositio evangelii sec. Lucam*, 10, 11 (*in occasu saeculi sumus*) and 14 (*finem mundi videmus*). For the position of St. Ambrose, see J. R. Palanque, *Saint Ambrose et l'Empire romain* (Paris, 1933), 57–59.

[6] For the date, see Cavallera, II, 20.

[7] Ammianus Marcellinus, 31, 2.

[8] *Ep.* 77, 8 *ad Oceanum* (ed. Hilberg, *CSEL*, 55, 45–46). For the date, see Cavallera, II, 46.

[9] And not under Darius at the end of the sixth century, B.C. Besides, Herodotus (*Hist.*, I, 104, 106) places them in the time of the Pharao Psammetichus I (664–610), the contemporary of Assurbanipal (669–626).

[10] This is confirmed by Claudian, *In Rufinum*, II, 28–35.

[11] Cf. *Ep.* 77, 8 (the sentence preceding the passage quoted above).

[12] *Loc. cit.* "Nos in Oriente tenuerunt jam fixae sedes et inueteratum locorum sanctorum desiderium."

[13] This is *Ep.* 60 to Heliodorus. Its date is fixed by the historical allusions which it contains; see Cavallera, II, 44.

[14] *Ep.* 60, 15–16 (*CSEL*, 55, 568ff.).

[15] *Ep.* 60, 16–17.

[16] If one can believe the testimony of Claudian, it had already begun on the Danubian frontier in 395; for it is he who speaks of the barbarian *gentes* crossing the river where it had frozen over: *In Rufinum*, II, 26–28.

[17] Habacuc 1:6–8: ". . . a bitter and swift nation, marching upon the breadth of the earth, to possess the dwelling places that are not their own. They are dreadful and terrible. . . . Their horses are lighter than leopards and swifter than evening wolves. . . ." The last verse naturally suggested the passage to Jerome as an apt description of the horsemen of the Huns.

[18] In 409, Jerome will use the same quotation again for his description of the invasions in Gaul (*Ep.* 123, 16).

[19] Cf. Claudian, *In Rufinum*, II, 36–46.

[20] These are *Epp.* 122 (A.D. 407), 123 (409), 126 (411), 127 (413), 128 (413), 130 (414). For the dates see Cavallera, II, 52–54.

[21] *Ep.* 122, 4 (*CSEL*, 56, 70).

[22] *Ibid.*

[23] Geruchia, according to Hilberg (56, 72); but Cavallera restores the name Agerucia-Agerochia given by several MSS. (Cav., I, 315, n. 1).

[24] *Ep.* 123, 15 (*CSEL*, 56, 91).

[25] This date is confirmed by other sources: Orosius, VII, 38, 40; Prosper, 1230; *Chron. Gallica* (MGH, AA, IX, 652); *Consularia Ital.*, ann. 406; Zosimus, VI, 3, I.

[26] *Ep.* 123 (*CSEL*, 56, 93).

[27] *De bello getico*, 166–176.

[28] *Ep.* 123, *loc. cit.*

[29] Zosimus, V, 41.

[30] *Ep.* 123, 17.

[31] This is the opinion of E. Stein, *Geschichte des spätr. Reiches*, I (Vienna, 1928), 348.

[32] Cf. Rutilius Namatianus, II, 42–52: "Proditor arcani . . . imperii . . . nec tantum geticis grassatus proditor armis; ante sibyllinae fata cremuit opis"; "et (comparing him to Nero) hic mundi matrem pertulit, ille suam" (II, 59–60). Cfr. Orosius, VII, 38–40; Philostorus, XII, 2.

[33] Claudian, *de bello getico,* 430–432 ("Brenni rabies"); 386–389 ("ferus Hannibal"); *In laud. Stilichonis,* III, 31–32 ("cedente . . . Pyrrho"); Praef. (particularly 21–22: "noster Scipiades Stilicho quo concidit alter Hannibal"). Cfr. also 640–642, where recalling the invasions of the Cimbri, he salutes Stilicho as a new Marius.

[34] *Ep.* 123, 17.

[35] *Ibid.,* 16.

[36] *In Ezech.,* I, praef., *(PL,* 25, 15).

[37] *Ep.* 126, 2 *(CSEL,* 56, 144).

[38] *Ep.* 127, 12 *(ibid.,* 154).

[39] *Ibid.,* 13–14.

[40] Cf. *Ep.* 130, 7 *(ad Demetriadem).*

[41] *In Ezechielem,* III, praef. *(PL,* 25, 75).

[42] *In Ezech.,* VII, praef. *(PL,* 25, 199). This was written in 412–414, according to Cavallera (II, 53–54).

[43] *Ep.* 126, 2 *(CSEL,* 56, 144).

[44] After his *diu tacui* (referring to the taking of Rome in 410), Jerome wrote *hoc autem anno,* which must be 411.

[45] *In Ezech.,* VII.

[46] These works were completed in 416 (Cavallera, II, 55–56). Jerome was approaching his 66th year; he was to die in 419 at 72.

[47] This idea is expressed in his letter to Demetriada *(Ep.* 130, 5).

[48] *Ep.* 123, 17 (to Agerochia).

[49] *Ep.* 60, 16 (see note 16 above).

[50] *Ep.* 128, 5 (to Pacatula: in *CSEL,* 56, 161).

[51] Horace, *Odes,* III, 3, 7–8 (quoted in *Ep.* 130, 7).

[52] Cf. Rom. 12:12, "gaudentes in tribulatione"; 5:3–5, "tribulatio patientiam operatur, patientia probationem, probationem spem."

[53] *Ep.* 60, 17 *(CSEL,* 54, 572).

[54] See note 33 above.

St. Jerome as a Humanist

EDWIN A. QUAIN, S.J.

St. Jerome as a Humanist

IN THE middle of the ninth century, in the valley of the Loire, the monks of the scriptorium of Tours were presented with a difficult problem. It would appear that they had succeeded in borrowing from their brethren of Corbie a fine old manuscript of the works of the Roman historian, Livy. The book was a treasure indeed, being then almost four centuries old, and the canny owners gave strict orders that it should be used and returned in the shortest possible time. They were taking no chances on anyone forgetting where it really belonged. The Director of the scriptorium at Tours sat at his high desk in the sun-swept hall where so many famous books were saved for future ages, and pondered his problem. The usual method of setting a scribe to the task and allowing him in leisurely fashion (with time out by day and night for the singing of the Office, the *Opus Dei* of all the sons of Benedict) to finish the work, was out of the question. Corbie would not wait, and unless the work were done with speed and dispatch, Tours would not be able to list among its treasures the story of the Glory that was Rome.

He made his plans and chose eight of his cleverest scribes. He divided the copy, gave to each his share of snow-white parchment, and exhorted all to adhere strictly to the beautiful script of Tours that was becoming the vogue in France and the envy of all their brethren across the land. The scribes chosen were young and vigorous, and they had been carefully trained from their earliest days in the monastery of the great St. Martin to form each letter according to the style so carefully cultivated at Tours. To make assurance doubly sure, the director lightly wrote their names on the new parchment, and they set to work. All had been foreseen, one would think, to check any spurts of individuality that would betray the eightfold parentage of the book.

At the end of the task, the Director must have shaken his hoary head and muttered in his beard at the sparks of individuality that fairly leapt from the page. In his annoyance, he seems (fortunately for us) to have forgotten to erase the names of each that he had written on the parchment. In spite of the rules and conventions of the scriptorium, the famous book, now in the Vatican Library, clearly betrays the fact that one day in the Middle Ages the unquenchable individuality that God imparted to the force that is the human soul broke through the bonds of rules and regulations and left its personal signature upon the page.

One scribe leaned his pen slightly to the right, another to the left. A third obviously misjudged the space he would need in Turonian minuscule to copy the last page of his uncial model. He begins to spread his words and letters, in his generosity, until about ten lines from the end he realizes he is going to be pressed to make it fit. From then on he crowds his letters and uses all the abbreviations he can find. To his undoubted chagrin, he ended up with two words left over. Still another scribe finished his own portion in a burst of speed, and then the end of that of one of his confreres.[1]

The laws of the script, originated to curb individual vagaries, fell before the impact of sheer personality. Try as he may, the educator is always dealing with something that heredity, environment and sheer personal bent have set upon the path that a man will inevitably follow. No matter how similar the training, personality, God's initial gift to Man, will lead each man his own way. The most rigid regime of education cannot refashion the minds and hearts of any two men so that the light of inherent personality will not shine through. God did not pour us all into the same mold, and the lathe of education can but shape and smooth as best it can, making the most it may of the fragile, friable clay that we are. Two men, no matter how similar their backgrounds and education, will always develop in their own individual fashions.

St. Augustine and St. Jerome are two of the greatest figures in the history of the Church, and both were formed in the traditional Roman system of education, the Seven Liberal Arts. If Cicero could have come back and stepped into the schoolroom of the one in North Africa or the other in Rome, he would have felt perfectly at home, although, perhaps, somewhat distressed at the flighty manners of these later sons of Romulus. Grammar and Rhetoric—that is, the poets and orators—were read and explained, conned and memorized. Dialectics followed, and an introduction to philosophy was fed the thirsting minds of eager young men. The quadrivium of Arithmetic, Geometry, Astronomy and Music followed, and as an "elective" the student might go on to Law. From there Augustine turned to the teaching of Rhetoric, while Jerome travelled to Gaul and laid the foundations of the studies that were to make him famous throughout the Mediterranean world even in his own lifetime.

It has been well said that the history of thought in the Middle Ages is the history of what happened to the ideas of St. Augustine. The philosophy of history, the theology of man, music and morals, education and the human soul—all these problems were examined, pored over, thought through and expressed in the glowing prose that flowed so readily from the pen of the greatest figure the Church produced in North Africa. For Augustine, in spite of the busy, almost turbulent life that he led, was above all a profound and adventuresome thinker. Jerome was in his monastery at Bethlehem separated from the Bishop of Hippo by far more than the seas and mountains, deserts and plains of the Mediterranean world. Jerome was a scholar, imbued with the learning of classical antiquity.

He thought till the end of his days in the literary mold of the pagans. He was the most learned man of his time in Hebrew and Biblical lore, the Father of the study of the Sacred Scriptures. No original thinker, neither philosopher nor theologian, he was a man of letters, a controversialist, a learned and painstaking commentator, a scholar of gigantic proportions. No man among the early figures of Christianity put greater store on learning, and there were few who so keenly realized the crying need for Christianity to appear before the pagan world, not merely as a *cult* but also as a *culture*.

Jerome brought to his life's work the mind of a litterateur, and while Augustine was turned to God by the reading of Cicero's *Hortensius* (an introduction, *Protrepticon*, to philosophy) Jerome, as a result of what he had gotten out of his education, naturally turned to literature, to the literature of Christianity, to the Bible, the revealed word that God had spoken to mankind. The mental preoccupation of his whole life as an ardent student of Classical literature, and later as a commentator of Sacred Scripture directed his mind to the multifarious details; his voluminous learned commentaries sought to explain the minutest point of God's message to man. Jerome saw the Many where Augustine's penetrating mind saw the One; Jerome manipulated his facts, while Augustine leaped to general conclusions. Jerome's translation of the Bible, becoming *textus vulgatus*, the commonly accepted version of the Scriptures, helped to teach the Middle Ages the language in which to express the thought of Augustine.

Jerome's earliest education was begun in his home town of Stridon, where he was taught, as a mere infant, the letters of the alphabet, short syllables and then words; soon came reading and writing and elementary counting. At the age of twelve years, however, a larger world opened before the eyes of the country boy when his parents, who were comparatively wealthy, sent him to Rome, the capital of his world, where his teachers were to be the most famous of the times. It was here that Jerome began the humanistic education that was to win him, for all time, a high place among Christian Humanists.

Fifty years later, when Rome was sacked by Alaric and the Goths, tears of anguish were to stream down the cheeks of the old hermit of Bethlehem when he thought of the temples and basilicas of Rome crashing down before the destructive horde from the North. He groaned as he thought of the noble center

of the Empire one mass of flames with the people of Rome wandering over the face of the earth as exiles and the Capitoline covered with soot and smoke.[2] Jerome had learned to love the Eternal City, and that love must have begun on the day when, as a
child, he first came upon Rome from the north, after the long
journey from Stridon. In the school of Aelius Donatus, foremost
grammaticus of the fourth century, he was to learn to love Virgil,
and Rome for him was the city of Aeneas, who found this haven
of destiny after wanderings and woes unnumbered over land and
sea. In his youthful enthusiasm he could stand before the rostrum
in the Forum whereon Cicero had awed the multitude with his
almost divine eloquence. At the most impressionable time of his
life he lived in the midst of the pageant of Roman history, before
the mighty Colosseum, the triumphal arches of the Caesars and
the hallowed temples of a growing Christian Rome. The literature
he learned at the feet of the *Magister* lived and breathed in the
streets of the metropolis of the world.

Here were sown the seeds of the humanism that was to be a
part of his character till the day he closed his eyes in death at
the scene of the Birth of Him who was born the Son of God. His
youthful mind was impregnated with the beauties of classical literature; he learned a scholar's love of books, and here began the
collecting of the library that was his pride, gathered *summo studio
ac labore*.[3] He learned to seek for the earliest and most accurate
text, a habit that was to flower in later life when he had the hardi-
hood, in the face of long and respected tradition, to go back to
the original Hebrew text of the Bible, stating that the version of
the Septuagint was merely the work of man and not, as was
believed, almost verbally inspired by God. Jerome the Humanist
was born on the banks of the Tiber.

Jerome was proud of his Roman education. In his *Chronicon*,
an annalistic history of the world which he wrote in later years,
among mention of kings and rulers he records the fact that in
354 "Donatus the grammarian, *my teacher in Rome*, and Victorinus the rhetorician were famous at this time. And Victorinus
even had a statue erected in his honor in the Forum." [4] When

over fifty he blandly assumed that his enemy Rufinus had some smattering of classical learning, and he asks: "I suppose as a boy you read Asper's commentary on Virgil and Sallust, Volcatius on Cicero's speeches, Victorinus on his dialogues, and the works of *my teacher Donatus*, on Virgil and Terence." [5] When commenting on the remark of *Ecclesiastes* that there is nothing new under the sun, he remembers that Terence had said something similar, and then takes the opportunity to retail a *bon mot* of Donatus: "When *my teacher Donatus* was explaining this verse, he said: 'Down with those who have expressed my ideas before me!' " [6]

A brilliant pupil is an all too rare joy in the life of a teacher, and Donatus must have delighted in the chance that brought him the spirited lad from Stridon. Jerome fairly devoured all that his teacher had to offer. The zeal with which he applied himself to his studies is attested by the marvellous ease with which, long years after, he can quote, adapt and apply the literature he learned as a boy. Donatus was an authority on Terence and Virgil, and we have already seen that Jerome read Cicero's speeches and dialogues and studied detailed commentaries on them; Sallust he knew, and Plautus, Lucretius and Horace, Persius and Lucan. His works till the end of his days are dotted with passages from these and other ancient authors.

Of Greek he learned only the elements at Rome, but he perfected his knowledge of that tongue at Antioch and in the desert. The day had passed when Greek was a second mother tongue for educated Romans. Most of his knowledge of the Greek philosophers came from Latin sources, but this does not prevent him from parading his erudition in the midst of his controversy with Rufinus, whom he accuses, quite unfairly, of being comparatively ignorant. Thus when some remark of Rufinus suggests cosmological lore, Jerome says: "Did you want me to talk *de natura rerum*, if this were really the place for such a disquisition, I could give you the Epicurean view according to Lucretius, or that of Aristotle for the Peripatetics, Plato for the Academics, or Zeno for the Stoics." [7] He insists that he was so thoroughly imbued with this learning when he was young that he could no more forget it than wool that has been steeped in dye could lose its color, or the wine-jar lose the flavor of the wine, thus, incidentally, echoing Horace. Again turning to the imagery of the ancient poets, he avers that he would have to drink the waters of Lethe in order to forget what he had learned so well. It is clear that Jerome thoroughly enjoyed the years of his early studies.

The most famous rhetorician of the fourth century was Victorinus, who as a Christian lost his chair at Rome by a decree of Julian the apostate in 362. Jerome, who left the school of Donatus the following year, was thus too late to sit under this great master. Whoever his teacher was, Jerome was an excellent pupil, for, of all his early studies, his course in rhetoric seems to have made the deepest impression on the formation of his mind. The budding orator in the schools of Rome was trained in the multitudinous precepts of Cicero's *De inventione*, and went on to their application in the writing and delivery of original speeches. This was the time-honored practice of *controversiae*, examples of which have come down to us in the works of Seneca the Elder. They were exercises in Declamation, which generally took as their subject an imaginary case at law. Either side might be assigned to a student in the interest of improving his power of expression. Some of the subjects that have come down to us reveal the unreality of the exercise. There would seem to have been no limit to the use of the imagination, even to the invention of laws and documents with which to prove one's case. As a scholastic exercise, it can readily be seen that the *controversia* would be an extremely valuable means of translating rhetorical theory into practical use and for promoting nimbleness of wit and adroitness in argument. The delivery of a *controversia* in the presence of a critical teacher and a heckling group of fellow students was an ordeal. Jerome in his old age recalls that even then he sometimes dreamt that he was a boy again, dressed in his best toga, with his hair neatly curled (he mentions this when what hair he has left is white!), standing before his audience to deliver a *controversiola*. With a sigh of relief he awakens, grateful that he is freed from such torture.[8]

In a letter written [9] in 396 to Nepotian, a nephew of his school-mate Heliodorus, Jerome looks back indulgently twenty years to a letter he had written to the uncle, and admits that it was done in the rhetorical mode of the *controversia*. "When I was a mere boy and had first come out to the desert, I wrote a letter to your uncle Heliodorus, to persuade him to join me. It was full of tears and complaints to show him the love his hermit friend bore him. Being very young and fresh from the schools of rhetoric, I told my tale in the manner of a scholastic exercise. But now I'm an old man, my hair is white and my forehead is wrinkled. . . ." The letter rings the changes on the sorrow of young Jerome, separated from an old friend. He used all the *loci communes*, contrasts, comparisons, *homoioteleuta* and antitheses. He imagines the sorrow of the parents, servants, nephews and friends who will be stricken at the thought of Heliodorus' departure, but he bids him manfully scorn them all. Even though his aged father should lie prostrate on the doorstep, the true Christian must step over him and be gone to the call of the desert solitudes! Jerome cites all the objections that could be offered, and with great flourish of argument, example and citation, wipes them all away—and achieves a production that would have won acclaim in the schools.

In 406 he wrote a letter,[10] presumably to a woman and her daughter in Gaul, to heal the estrangement between them. Some of his enemies later suggested that he had made the whole thing up, just for practice. Vigorously he asserts that he was constructing no straw man but was dealing with an actual case, but perhaps he doth protest too much.

The importance of these years of rhetorical training on the mind and character of St. Jerome can hardly be exaggerated. In the perennial Roman tradition, the *ars bene dicendi* overshadowed the entire educational curriculum. It was a relic from the days of the Republic, when a career as an orator laid open the path to the highest positions in the State. But the days of the Empire had come, and what had been a means became an end in itself. Rhetorical tricks that were meant to be a delectation to the ear of the audience became commonplaces of all composition.

According to the standards of the fourth century, all written and spoken words were best expressed in accord with the rules and precepts of the schools. Even though Jerome in his maturity saw the artificiality of the stylized and often stilted procedure, yet the training of his youth caused him, even on the most spiritual of topics, to mold his thought and marshal his arguments after the fashion of the schools. The resounding periodic sentences, the clever turn of phrase and the pithy epigram sprung to his lips as he hastily dictated his letters. The accents of the schools of rhetoric haunted him till the day he died.

This, however, is no proof of insincerity in St. Jerome. In view of the intense training he had undergone in the school of rhetoric, it would not be unlikely that Jerome wrote according to rhetorical form no matter what he was writing, since that was the way in which he had been taught to write and speak and he knew no other way of effectively expressing his thoughts. The elaborate *exordia*, the artificial arrangement of his arguments, the *exempla*, *figurae verborum et sententiarum* were to a man of Jerome's education the normal and natural way of conveying his ideas.[11]

The third part of the trivium, Dialectics, made far less impression on Jerome. He can on occasion exhibit his knowledge of the minutiae of dialectics, as when he gives the seven classical forms of arguments and swears that he had not read such matter since he was a boy at school.[12] He is here merely trying to prove the tenacity of his memory when Rufinus had reproached him with filling his pages with Horace and Cicero and Virgil. But we may take his word for it that he was not sufficiently interested in philosophy to go back to it once he had finished his course in dialectics.

Philosophy to Jerome was just so much more literature; he knew the thoughts and theories of the ancient sages, but he never found it necessary to model his life on their ideas. The motivating and controlling forces in the life of Jerome came from Scripture. He had little bent for speculation. He was interested in the ideas of the past only as a window into the culture of the past. It is striking that when Pelagianism forced itself on his attention he argues against it altogether from texts of Scripture to prove that man could not, of his own powers, remain free from sin. In Jerome we will find none of the speculative genius of Augustine, who forms the heart of the Church's doctrine on Grace when dealing with this same Pelagius.

This was the education of St. Jerome in the schools of secular learning. His brilliantly imaginative mind turned naturally to poetry, and he shows none of Augustine's preoccupation with mathematics and geometry and the relation of both to philosophy. The dour and pessimistic theories of Manichaeism for a time attracted the youthful Augustine, but in his impatience with slipshod thinking, he turned with eagerness to the architectonic grandeur of Platonism. Still unsatisfied, he only found rest for his mind and heart in the Beauty ever ancient, ever new. No such weighty problems ever troubled the mind of Jerome, whose youth was given over to the delights of his literary studies. His literary humanism grew out of his education just as the mind of Augustine, immersed in the same atmosphere, flowered into the greatest speculative intellect of the Patristic age. The problem of humanism for Jerome lay in reconciling his love for beautiful literature with the somewhat rude and pedestrian style of the Scriptures. For Augustine it presented itself as a matter of principle, the dichotomy between Truth and falsehood, between the Real and the fanciful, between the Eternal and the transitory.

Jerome was baptized at the age of nineteen years at the hand of Pope Liberius. Such a delay was customary at the time, being predicated on the somewhat cynical attitude that since baptism removes both Original Sin and actual sin, the young man should be allowed to pass through the turbulent years of adolescence, and in his maturity take the step that would wash away the faults of the past. In Jerome's case, however, the faith that he had imbibed from his infancy was always a strong force in his life. Nowhere better than at Rome, where the brilliant pageantry of the Church was all around him, could such feelings have been nourished and fostered. At school he learned of the Rome of Aeneas and Romulus, of Tullius and the Scipios, of Cicero and

Caesar, but all the time he was living in Christian Rome, where the souvenirs of the Apostles and Martyrs were daily impressed upon his mind. The depth and solidity of his faith is mirrored in a passage that is precious in its implications of tender devotion in the youthful Jerome to the relics of the recent Christian past.

When I was a boy in my studies at Rome, a group of us of the same age and like intentions used on Sundays to visit the tombs of the apostles and martyrs. We used to go down into the tombs that were dug in the depths of the earth, and as we walked along the dark passages, the bodies of the martyrs lay on shelves along the walls. It was so dark down there that we seemed to be fulfilling the word of the prophet: "Let the living go down to hell." A faint light occasionally tempered the horror of the blackness, coming it would seem, not through a window, but it was as if the light itself pierced a hole through the earth to reach the spot. Then, as we returned to the surface, stepping carefully in the midst of the darkness that all but swallowed us up, we were reminded of the line of Virgil: "Fear and the very silence itself struck terror into our souls." [13]

These repeated, awesome visits to the Catacombs by a boy of sharp, imaginative perceptions who was filled with the haunting, prophetic and pathetic lines of Virgil, give us a picture of the character of Jerome that was in its large lines now formed for life. As Jerome was then, so he was to remain for the rest of his life. Endowed with insatiable curiosity, passionately anxious to know and to learn, never capable of totally divorcing his classical literature from his ardent Christian faith and love of Christ, he remained the Christian Humanist in whom both piety and poetry were equally handmaids before the throne of God. [14]

In the days of his study of rhetoric, Jerome had run about ("*percurrebam*") Rome to the Law Courts, and sat fascinated before the real-life spectacle of what he, as a boy, was merely playing with. [15] He may indeed at that time have dreamed of a career at Law, but at the end of his studies in Rome his course appears to have been set. With his faithful friend Bonosus, he departed for Treves in Gaul, where he stayed for the better part of a year.[16] Now Treves at the time was the residence of the Emperor Valentinian, but the glamor of the Court must have made less impression on him than the numerous monasteries there, relics of the exile of St. Athanasius. It was surely during this voyage to Gaul that Jerome's mind was made up and he decided to become a monk. His irrepressible curiosity was at work in the course of his travels, and the few details he gives us record the mores of a savage tribe ("*gentem britannicam*") who were given to cannibalism, and another passing note refers to the linguistic and ethnic origin of one of the Rhenish peoples. There he began the study of the Christian writers, and we know that with his own hand he copied a commentary on the psalter and a voluminous work on Synods, both by Hilary of Poitiers. These works are mentioned in passing in a later letter, and it is not unlikely that he read and copied other works among the Christian authors. There would have begun the Christian portion of his treasured library.

The young man who turned south once again to visit Stridon, which he had left some ten years before, was an educated and serious figure. He had acquired in the intervening years the culture of both pagan and Christian Rome; he had enjoyed the broadening effects of travel with a congenial companion of like tastes and ambitions, and now he knows the path that he is to follow. In Aquileia, near to Stridon, he rejoins some of his old companions from Rome, and for some six years devotes himself to further reading in the Christian writers, the fruit of which was to appear in the *De viris illustribus* he wrote in later years. His spiritual growth in these years was immense, but his popularity in certain quarters seems to have left something to be desired. The decision was apparently made suddenly, for soon we find him on the road again. This time, he travelled east to Antioch. Here his studies continued, and he added to his fragmentary knowledge of Greek; an interval of the hermit's life in the desert intervened until his passionate desire for learning led him once again to become a pupil, this time of the great St. Gregory Nazianzen in Constantinople.

In these two saints, so much alike in sensitivity of character, love for learning and a passionate desire to discover, develop and spread the truth of Christ's teaching, we have two of the great figures in a century that can boast of a veritable galaxy of gigantic Christian leaders. Besides them, in the West were Augustine and Ambrose, Damasus and Gregory of Tours; in the Eastern sky there shone that brilliant triad, Gregory of Nazianzus, and the brothers, Basil and Gregory of Nyssa. All were born and labored in this fourth century when heresy, both in the East and the West, made brothers of them all in the mighty struggle that meant so much for the growth and stability of the Church of Christ. It is but another indication of Jerome's scholarly instinct that he turned to the East, to Gregory and his colleagues, with a view to bringing to the West the learning of that great theologian.

Some three years had been spent in Constantinople when Jerome returned to Rome, where he immediately attracted the attention of Pope St. Damasus. Damasus came to rely heavily on the learning of his assistant and saw him as the man who could check the flood of Latin versions of the Scriptures which were arising everywhere. At this point the clear and definite orientation of Jerome's life was determined, and he devoted the rest of his days to the translation and elucidation of the Word of God. By this time, he was completely at home in Greek, and so he set about the task of adding Hebrew to the languages he controlled. The labor and toil the cultured Roman (for so he ever after considered himself) had to expend in the study of the harsh, guttural He- brew tongue all but discouraged him, but he tells us that, at the end, he could thank God from his heart that from such bitter seeds of study he could reap such sweet fruits of learning.[17]

Jerome's linguistic and theological preparation was now com- plete, and with pardonable pride he could boast that he was *homo trilinguis, Latinus, Graecus et Hebraeus*.[18] He held in his hands the keys to all the literature that was then important for his chosen field of labor, and the humanist that had been formed in Rome and Treves, Antioch, the desert of Chalcis and Constantinople, rose to the task that was to make his name famous throughout all the Christian world.

II

The career of St. Jerome seems quite naturally to have progressed from Roman schools to Scriptural studies in Gaul, Antioch, the desert, Constantinople, Rome again—and, finally, to the birthplace of Christ in Bethlehem. But it would be an error to imagine that all this was achieved without much heart-searching and pain. The hierarchical structure with which we are today familiar, of a preparatory education in secular literature followed by studies of theology and Scripture, was not so clearly organized nor so readily accepted in the early centuries of Christianity.

From the very first moment of its contact with pagan Rome, Christianity felt the anomaly of having its members immersed in a mythology that was essentially alien to the teachings of Christ. The mind of Christendom clearly saw the chasm that lay between the materialistic deism of Lucretius and the idea of a personal and benevolent Providence, between the deification of dissolute emperors and the Incarnation of the Divine Word.

The obvious need for Christianity was a distinctively Christian system of education, but the times were such that men were daily concerned about their very lives, and the leaders of Christianity had to be satisfied with teaching the doctrine of Christ and preserving the earliest Christians in the purity of His message. The warning voices of Tertullian and Cyprian, of Arnobius and Minucius Felix were continually raised against the dangers that lay hidden in the literature of paganism, but Christianity found itself impaled on the horns of a dilemma.[19]

In the eyes of sophisticated Rome, Christianity was negligible as an obscure Eastern cult without a literature or a culture of its own. Rome's first reaction was one of scornful ridicule; the teachings of Christ were indeed foolishness to the gentiles. Christianity made its first conquests among the common people, but when intelligent Romans came under the yoke of Christ, the need for an intellectually respectable justification of their faith became of paramount importance. But to produce Christian literature, men had to be educated, and the only medium of education lay in attendance at the pagan schools, which taught doctrines that endangered the purity of the teachings of Christ.

The solution was not simple, because there was much to be said for the advantage of an educated body of Christians who could stand the peer of any man. There always lay the alternative for Christians to live completely detached from the world around them. But this would frustrate the essentially missionary nature of the faith. Still it was far from certain that pagan literature inevitably concealed a snare for Christian souls. We must remember that in the early days of the Faith in Rome and throughout the Empire, all men came from paganism of one form or another to the feet of Christ. *"Fiunt, non nascuntur Christiani,"* as Tertullian insisted. The culture of Rome was far from being an insurmountable barrier to humble faith. Perhaps there were many, like Virgil, *anima naturaliter Christiana,* but that may be but another way of saying that *Romanitas* was an ideal soil for the flowering of *Christianitas.* The goodness, the nobility, the "divinity" of the natural man as expressed in much of Roman literature was at the same time a source of hope to Christian thinkers and an omen of danger, lest Beauty beckon too strongly to herself and draw man, all unknowing, to the abyss.

All the great figures of the early Church were trained in these pagan schools, and while they themselves had come through unscathed, as is the wont of human nature, they feared lest others be not as strong as they. They wavered from time to time in their views, but the burden of their cry is one of ominous warning. Meantime Christian children sat side by side with pagans in the traditional schools, and their leaders hoped that the resulting influence would not do too much harm to their souls.

Christians in the fourth century had risen to positions of eminence in these very schools. In 362 the Emperor Julian sought to curb this—to his mind—untoward influence, and issued a decree that no one who did not believe in the ancient pagan gods was to be permitted to teach anywhere throughout the Empire. The measure was ostensibly aimed at purifying the schools from a baneful influence, but in one of his letters he exposed his true

motives and averred that while Christian teachers were pro-
scribed, he was willing that Christian children should continue to
have the opportunity of learning the truth while they were still
at an impressionable age! [20]

So, in a state of doubt and hesitancy, Christian leaders failed
to provide any other education, and boys like Jerome absorbed
the ethos of paganism from their earliest years. The Mind of the
Western Church did not yet have, in the fourth century, a man of
sufficient speculative power to achieve a solution *in theory* of this
problem. In the East, St. Basil had realistically averred that the
pagan gods were dead, and Homer a handbook of morality. The
all-important quest for the Christian was the salvation of his soul,
and whatever could be adapted to the promotion of that end was
to be loved and pursued with might and main. The poets and
orators of paganism could be used to cultivate and refine the
minds of Christians, just as Moses and Daniel had learned the
wisdom of the Egyptians and Persians before they rose to the contemplation of divine truth. "Let us then in our study of literature
follow the example of the bees; for they do not visit all the flowers
indiscriminately, nor do they take their fill from a single blossom.
Thus if we are wise we will gather [from pagan literature] whatever is allied to truth, and shun the rest." [21]

The problem was essentially that of rising to an adequate conception of Christian Humanism. The true humanist cherishes a
lofty conception of human nature, in that the specifically human
qualities are believed capable of the highest possible development
in a human way. The Christian humanist is always conscious of
(and glories in) the supernatural destiny of Man; well he knows
that what we have of the *naturalia* is, in a sense, the foundation
upon which is built the edifice of the supernatural life, but he
does not see this natural foundation as smothered or obliterated
by our divine destiny. Rather is the lesser thus exalted and made
more glorious. Each human faculty has a pleasure and a joy connected with its normal, natural functioning. This is a truly *human*
joy, and the humanist aims at intellectual joy, as man knows all
that his mind is capable of grasping; at moral peace and content-

ment, when his conscience finds rest and satisfaction, reconciled to the truth that his mind has understood; and artistic pleasure, as his taste is satisfied in the joy of the beautiful.[22]

Humanism in the traditional, historical sense is surely to be found in St. Jerome. If ever there was a mind formed on the literary ideals of antiquity, impregnated with its mythology, history, poetry and oratory, the budding hermit of Bethlehem can lay claim to that title. But Christian Humanism of the type which the logic of events required in the fourth century must mean a clear and unmistakable stand on the conflict between Christian supernaturalism and pagan materialism. On this topic St. Jerome has much to say.

We would perhaps be going beyond the facts if we were to claim that he evolved the complete, theoretical justification of the matter for the West. His was not the speculative mind that could achieve that; but he made his contribution, which Augustine after him applied and adapted.

Jerome's handbook of Christian Humanism is to be found in his letter to Magnus, official Orator of the City of Rome.[23] The latter had written to Jerome, objecting to Jerome's right to use *exempla* from pagan writers in his own works, and thus "pollute the purity of the Church with the mire of paganism." It is in this letter that we see Jerome as the conscious Humanist. He cites the example of Moses and the Psalmist, who manifest great knowledge of the books of the gentiles. There is Solomon, who in the beginning of Proverbs sets out to explain matters that are in the province of philosophers and dialecticians. St. Paul himself quoted the ancient poets and drew an argument for the Faith from an inscription on the Areopagus of Athens. Whereupon Jerome entitles him *"ductor Christiani exercitus et orator invictus."*

From the Bible he turns to the early Christian writers and shows that they too used the weapons of paganism against itself, as did Origen and Methodius against Celsus and Porphyry. The attacks on Christ made by Julian the Apostate would naturally (if Jerome were to undertake their refutation) be refuted with the words of the philosophers and historians. Among the Jews, both Josephus and Philo showed an amazing knowledge of ancient philosophy. Then there passes in review before us that mighty company, both Greek and Roman, closing with Tertullian, whose *Apologeticus* contains all the wisdom of the world; Lactantius, whose works are an epitome of the eloquence of Cicero, and Hilary, "bishop and confessor of my own times," whose name is in honor among men of learning. Thus Jerome finds in great and noble leaders a precedent for his own use of pagan antiquity in the battle for the truth of God.

Finally Jerome approaches a general principle which, because of the enormous popularity of his letters in the Middle Ages, became a *locus classicus* in the justification of the use of literature by Christians.[24] The principle is based upon the precept of Deuteronomy that a Jew might marry a captive gentile woman if first he had shaved her head and eyebrows and clipped her nails. On the basis of this symbolical practice, Jerome asks: "Why then should it be a cause of surprise if I should desire to make an Israelite of this captive maiden, that is, to adapt to God's truth this wisdom of the world which I admire because of the beauty of its content and the charm of its expression?"

About fourteen years previously, in a letter to Pope Damasus, he had made use of the same allegorical interpretation even more pointedly:[25]

This worldly wisdom is described in Deuteronomy under the symbol of the captive maiden, about whom the voice of God prescribed that she might become the bride of an Israelite if her head and body were shaved and her nails clipped; when she had thus been purified she might marry the warrior who had won her as a prize of war. Now if we take these prescriptions literally, surely they make no sense. But this is precisely what we usually do metaphorically when we read the books of the philosophers, or when some of the books of the wisdom of this world come into our hands. If we can find in them anything that is useful, we apply that to God's revelation; anything we discover that is useless, such as remarks about idols, or love or on merely worldly pleasure, we shave away and clip and cut, as we do with our nails.

Here we have the main point of Jerome's justification of Christian Humanism, whereby a Christian might use pagan learning as a weapon in the defense of Christianity. It must be stressed that this is merely an indirect solution of the problem; he is not urging anyone to turn to the classics; he is merely permitting such a study. In the course of this, he has let slip a remark that is precious for us in our knowledge of his character. While he is presumably allowing the use of pagan learning as an instrument for the defense of truth, perhaps inadvertently he betrays his old-time love of the literature he had learned so well in his youth. Note that he wants to make use of the "wisdom of the world which I admire because of the beauty of its content and the charm of its expression." Now its beauty and charm was immaterial when it was being, in a sense, made to bear witness against itself. But, Jerome here shows the weak spot in his armor, and like many a Christian Humanist since his day, he has betrayed his love for what, in his calmer moments, he knows he ought to deprecate.

A further development of his thought is to be found in his commentary on the Prophet Daniel,[26] which opens with the words: "The Lord delivered Joakim the King of Juda into the hands of Nabuchodonosor, and part of the vessels of the house of God. And he carried them away into the land of Sennaar to the house of his god and the vessels he brought into the treasure house of his god." Jerome's explanation of this tells us that Nabuchodonosor could only take away a part of the vessels of the temple and not all of them, since the "part of the vessels of God" are to be interpreted as *dogmata veritatis*. And thus it happens that you will find some truth in the teachings of the pagans. For "if we look into the books of the philosophers, we are bound to find in them some part of the vessels of God. In Plato you will find mention of God as the creator of the world; in Zeno, the leader of the Stoics, you will find mention of hell and the immortality of the soul. . . . But because the pagans mingle truth and falsehood . . . they have only a part of the vessels of God, and only fragments of the whole and perfect truth." Thence he concludes that the portion of truth possessed by the pagans and mirrored in their literature can be reclaimed by Christians as belonging to the universal truth of God. What is God's belongs to the children of God.

On this point, it is clear that Jerome has taken a further step. Not merely is a Christian permitted to read the classics, but insofar as they contain truth, he is almost obliged to rescue from pagan captivity what belonged to God in the first place. We can well imagine that Jerome must have gotten a good deal of satisfaction from this added reflection. Now with a good conscience he could read his philosophers and poets, his orators and historians, and feel that he was thus only fortifying the breastworks of the Lord with the ruins of the arms of the enemy. Beyond this he could and would not go.

The personality of Augustine, however, more forthright intellectually, achieved two further refinements of the argument. Where Jerome would perhaps have scrupled, his contemporary tells the story of the Hebrews who, on escaping from the bondage of Egypt, took with them some of the gold and silver idols of the Egyptians and used them for the vessels of the temple of God. He says that they did this not only on their own authority but at the behest of God:

And so the teachings of the gentiles possess not only many superstitious vanities which we, on emerging from the company of the heathen, ought to hate and detest, but also they have the liberal arts, which can readily be adapted to truth, and certain very useful principles of morality, since they have some notion of the worship of the true God; these things are like gold and silver which the pagans have not mined, but have refined from certain ores of divine providence and dedicated them to the use of the demons. So, when a Christian departs from their unhappy company, he ought to take with him the truth which they have and use it for the preaching of the Gospel.[27]

This theme of *Spoliatio Aegyptiorum* became the watchword of the Middle Ages when Augustine's *De Doctrina Christiana* was the *vade mecum* of all Christian humanists. With care and accuracy, Augustine surveyed the whole sky of worldly learning and saw it all as the proper possession of the Christian. And not only did he permit the use of pagan literature, but he claimed that wordly learning was necessary for the Christian if he were to understand the word of God. Thus the Christian must know the literature, oratory, history, astronomy, mathematics and philosophy of the ancients if he is to grasp the poetry of the psalms, the rhetoric of St. Paul, the historical books of the Old Testament and the astronomical data of the Pentateuch. "All these human inventions and traditions which are necessary for human life, should not only not be avoided by Christians, but carefully studied and committed to memory. . . . Although the things which pertain to the worship of demons should be repudiated, the truly human values (*ea quae homines cum hominibus habent*) should be adopted." [28]

With Augustine, Christianity has a program of education. The whole classical tradition has been absorbed into Christian Culture. *Scientia* has been allied to *Sapientia*. Save for fitful regressions in the course of the Middle Ages, Christian Humanism becomes the normal attitude of men and institutions who seek the eternal salvation of souls through the means of secular learning. The Gentile Maiden has become an *ancilla* in the household of the Lord, and the gold and silver of the Egyptians adorn the human temples of God.

III

St. Jerome was a very impulsive man. When we think we have him neatly catalogued and typed, his temperament (and he *was* somewhat temperamental!) bursts forth and rudely destroys our nicely constructed edifice. He never wrote an autobiography, but from his letters we have a picture of a man who was imaginative, impressionable, given to exaggeration, quick to judge and, often, too quick to condemn. Out of such a volume of material we are bound to evoke evidences of inconsistency. It is possible that he deliberately changed his mind; on the other hand, he may have forgotten what he had once written, but very likely his vivid imaginative power from time to time saw various aspects and difficulties in a position he had taken. The result is that, particularly on the matter of the use of pagan learning, he suffered uncomfortably from scruples.

Later in the same letter to Pope Damasus, he remembers the temptations that lie amid the allurements of paganism, and he fears lest the Christian may become the slave of the gentile maid. For the most part he feels quite capable of reading literature without harm to his own soul, but he is afraid of giving bad example. Hence he warns his reader that St. Paul spoke of this danger: "Shall the weaker brother for whom Christ died perish because of your worldly learning?" Having, just a few pages previously, justified the use of the classics, he now thunders: "Is not St. Paul here telling you that you must not read the philosophers, orators and poets? is he not forbidding you to take pleasure in their works? God forbid that a Christian should utter the words 'Omnipotent Jupiter' or swear by Hercules or Castor. These are not the names of gods but of monsters."

Jerome had not read his Horace and Juvenal in vain but had absorbed their spirit of Satire, adding it to his own keen eye for the shortcomings of human nature. Thereupon he launches into an attack on some of the less fervent clergy of his times:

In these our own days, we see priests who never read the Gospels or the Prophets but spend all their time in singing the love songs of the pastoral poets, and they cling to Virgil, *a thing that is permissible for boys at school,* but these priests commit a deliberate sin in thus neglecting their duty. We must be careful lest in our affection for the captive maiden, we ourselves be led into idolatry. If we are enamored of her beauty, we must purify and cleanse her of every stain, lest one of the little ones of Christ should be scandalized when he hears the voice of a Christian singing the verses in honor of idols.

Perhaps here there comes to his mind his own backsliding, and he realizes the impropriety of one given to the pursuit of perfection in the monastic life, spending time on the frivolities of secular literature. To be sure, "that is quite unobjectionable for boys at school," but now he has put aside the things of a child. When an urgent letter arrives from across the sea, begging for his advice on the education of Eustochium, a child destined for the religious life, he calls for his *amanuensis* and hurriedly dictates his reply. The letter is really a treatise on the state of Virginity, in which he warns her against the pitfalls of vanity and pride, of which, he implies, many religious were the victims. For her, the Word of God should be meat and drink, and he is none the less a humanist for not urging her to read Plautus. Here of course, he is concerned with the immediate problem before him, and he does not conceive of himself as setting a general norm for all Christians.

The closest that Jerome comes to outlining a system of Christian education is in the letter to Laeta [29] in which he gives detailed instructions for the rearing of her daughter Paula. It is clear from the beginning that Paula is to be dedicated to God from her childhood and every precaution is to be taken to protect her from the slightest taint of worldliness. Details are given as to her food and dress, companions and amusements that portend a Spartan existence for the little girl. Even as a baby she is to play with lettered blocks that will help her to learn the alphabet, and (shades of modern "progressive" educationists!) thus her play will be part of her education. Next should come simple spelling, and soon she will form the letters, and later syllables, with someone guiding her hand, on wax tablets. The first words that she learns should be useful, not merely baby words, but the names of the Prophets, Apostles and Patriarchs, and in these her memory is to be trained. The character and learning of her teacher is stressed and the example cited of Philip of Macedon, who commissioned Aristotle to be the teacher of his son, the future Alexander the Great.

At this early age, her attention may tend to wander, and little presents should be given her as a reward. Further, it would be good that she have companions in her school work to stir rivalry, and she should be allowed to know the triumph of leading the class or the chagrin of being at its foot! A healthy *aemulatio* never did any harm to the growing minds of students.

When she comes to the age for studying literature, however, Jerome's curriculum is wholly Scriptural, and there is not a word of mention of the beloved authors of his own youth! She is to begin with the psalter, and her songs are to be those of David; the maxims of Solomon and the wisdom of Ecclesiates are to fill her youthful mind; patience and fortitude she will learn from Job, whence she will turn to the Gospels that are to be the companions of her life. The Acts and Epistles of St. Paul will form her will and heart, and the Prophets and historical books are to be committed to memory. Finally, when she is old enough, the allegory of the Canticle of Canticles is to be explained to her. When she is thus fully imbued with the wisdom of God's revelation, then she may turn to the works of Cyprian, the letters of Athanasius and the books of Hilary, so that both her mind and soul, her taste and her piety may be nourished from the same sources.

Never is she to know the pleasure of wearing jewels or silks, but she is to delight in the books of the Bible, and these even are not to be written in gold on purple parchment, but in a simple and careful script. It is clear that the young lady is to be trained on hardy fare. This was written in the year 400. Some thirteen years later he writes to Gaudentius [30] on the education of his daughter Pacatula, and it has been said that Jerome learned in the interval the art of being a grandfather. The curriculum is much the same, but greater concessions are to be made to human nature; rewards are to be promised her for doing well in her studies—a honey cake, some flowers, some simple jewels and the dolls that she would delight in; as a final reward, the kisses and affection of her parents and relatives are to be so connected with progress in her studies that she will come to love what she is forced to do. The saintly hermit has learned something about little girls.

The Bible as the source of a completely human education, then, is Jerome's plan for a liberal education. Well he knew that sharp-nosed critics would ferret out the inconsistency between this, his theory, and the practice of his own life. In fact, at this very time, he was teaching Virgil, Plautus and Terence, the lyric poets and the historians to boys who had been entrusted to his care "that they might learn the fear of God." [31] Thus hoist by his own petard, he boldly claims that the Bible contains its own equivalent of a course in the Seven Liberal Arts, and he can find all the wisdom of the philosophers in the Old Testament. "Isaias tells us not only of the birth of Christ from a virgin, of His life and miracles, but also of His death and burial, His Resurrection, and of His whole doctrine. Why should I talk of Physics, Ethics and Logic? All that the human mind can speak or understand is to be found in the pages of Holy Scripture." [32] In the psalms are contained "all that the philosophers are wont to say in their disputations on Physics, Ethics or Logic; for Physics we only have to turn to Genesis and Ecclesiastes, for Ethics to any part of the Bible, and Dialectics are to be found all through the Gospels and in the epistles of St. Paul." [33]

So it would appear that a perusal of the voluminous works of St. Jerome will show him to be at times an ardent humanist, completely enamored of the literature of Greece and Rome, and the allusions, ideas and images of the ancients will dot his pages. On the other hand, we will also find him eschewing the wisdom of the pagans and finding the sum of all learning, human and divine, in the pages of Scripture. There is no doubt of the permanence all through his life of a fierce desire for learning in all forms (*eruditionis voluntas* and the *contentio discendi* are ever for him, strong impelling forces in every undertaking), and he remains a man so impressed with the importance of the *naturalia* that every power and faculty of his soul and mind is dedicated to the enlargement of his knowledge of whatever God has made it possible for man to know, either through the exercise of his own mind or through the gift of Revelation. The result is that we can say that Jerome is sometimes a humanist and sometimes very unlike a humanist, but at all times he is a learned man and the greatest scholar the early Church produced.

The inconsistency stems from the fact that he dealt with this problem at different periods of his life, in very different emotional states and under disparate provocations. He was ever a strongly emotional character, as his deep and abiding friendships and his equally virulent antipathies will testify. When we add to this the tendency to exaggeration fostered by the rhetorical cast of his mind, we see as altogether in character, his divergent discussions of the same subject. Jerome never sat down and wrote an *ex professo* treatise *de doctrina christiana* as did Augustine; he never formulated his views on this matter definitively, and the only sources we have from which to reconstruct his views are the letters which spread over forty years of his epistolary life.

IV

Jerome's famous Dream, which took place in the desert of Syria when he had first embarked on the eremitical life, has won more emphasis than it really deserves from the critics of his inconsistency in both ancient and modern times. Haled before the throne of Judgment he was apparently condemned as a Ciceronian and denied the accolade of Christian; on being condemned, he was flogged, and only won a reprieve having given the promise that he would never again read the books of the gentiles.[34]

It is most important to consider the context in which this experience is related to us; Jerome was writing his famous treatise to Eustochium on the religious life and outlining the dangers of the path that lay before her—temptations of the flesh, to avarice, pride and affection—incidentally, in his best satiric manner, retailing some of the vanities of too-worldly nuns. To clinch finally the case against worldliness, he recounts this experience of a fever-racked dream which bears signs of a diabolical temptation to despair. The intensive course of mortification on which he was at the time engaged could very well have induced an attack of scruples over the apparent uselessness of his former life, concerned as it was almost exclusively with secular learning. Whatever the precise nature of the seizure, it is clear that Jerome believed in its reality, but to deduce from this the settled view of his life as to pagan learning is surely unfair.

In later years he himself made very light of the dream,[35] and in view of that, there is no reason why we should hold this temporary aberration, related to us in a moment of undoubted emotional stress, as an epitome of his views on pagan literature. A learned and painstaking scholar has compared Jerome's works,

for echoes of the classics, before and after the dream, and he concluded: [36]

. . . making all due allowance for the dream, Jerome's attitude . . .
appears if not wholly consistent, at least easily intelligible. It was that
of a man classically trained, seeing the strong points but also the
weaknesses of the secular literature; in his youthful enthusiasm led
first to an admiration and then to a strong, though temporary, aver-
sion to the classics; and, finally, with the sanity of maturer life and
the influence of the culture of the Greek East, able to walk with a
surer step, realizing that the complete acceptance of the new faith
did not necessarily involve the total rejection of what was of value
in the old literature.

One of the most penetrating students of the Middle Ages in
modern times, a scholar to whom is due, more than to any other,
the present enthusiasm for the language and literature of the centuries of Faith, Ludwig Traube, thus characterizes Jerome: [37]

In spite of his dream and his oath, Jerome remains what he always
was: Grammarian, Philologist, Classicist, hunter of citations, the
Christian Aristarchus, who never gave up reading and citing the
classics. He became one of the most powerful influences on the language and literature of the Middle Ages, since Jerome translated the
Bible not merely *fideli sermone* but also *puro sermone*.

In the final analysis, then, we find St. Jerome wavering at
different periods of his life with regard to the theoretical basis of
Christian Humanism. There is no doubt that humanism naturally
appealed to his temperament, but emotional preoccupations and
a deep consciousness of the weakness of human nature prevented
him from taking a calm and detached view of the matter. He saw
all human knowledge as a means of furthering the understanding
of God's Revelation; he realized that the spread of that Revelation infinitely outweighed in importance the pursuit of human
learning, but sometimes he wavered, captivated by the beauty
and charm of the gentile maiden. In spite of his deep humility
and distrust of himself, he often revelled in the humanistic joy in
beautiful literature, and, in his own eyes, thus fell from his ideal.

The growth of the tradition of Christian Humanism is one of the most striking manifestations of the continued vitality of the pursuit of learning in the Middle Ages. In this supremely important phase of the history of culture, Jerome occupies a position of paramount importance. For it is to Jerome and his works and the tradition that he engendered that the great scholars of succeeding centuries look back with admiration and respect. Cassiodorus, in his *beata solitudo* at Vivarium, instructs his followers in the masterly commentaries of the hermit of Bethlehem. Alcuin, who came from the quiet of his monastery of York to the thriving school at Aachen, learned to love and admire the first Scripture scholar of Christendom. Lupus Servatus continued Jerome's labors in his passion for manuscripts and accurate texts. Great was the admiration of John of Salisbury for Jerome in the long life in which the boy from Britain crossed the sea to become the glory of Chartres and Paris, and perhaps the best educated man of the Middle Ages. Thus the humanists of the Middle Ages pay honor to Jerome.

But even the Renaissance, in spite of its haughty disdain for the "barbarism" of the Middle Ages, took Jerome to its heart. The iconography of Jerome would read like a history of mediaeval illumination and Renaissance painting and woodcutting. Perugino and Verrochio, Raphael and Guido Reni, the Caracci and Lorenzo Costa, El Greco and Tintoretto, Domenichino, Rubens, Van Dyck all with loving care portrayed Jerome, the monk, the scholar and the teacher.[38] The earliest printed books of the Renaissance contained masterly woodcuts by Cranach and Dürer. As a result, moderns are familiar with the calm and emaciated figure, always, it seems, accompanied by the recumbent figure of the lion, which enshrines the beautiful fable that Jerome once found the animal with a thorn in its paw. The kindly hermit extracted the thorn and eased the pain, thereby winning for himself a lifelong companion and protector. Fables have a way of crystallizing in brilliant fashion the reputation of centuries. It was an uncanny instinct that associated the fiery temperament of the lion with the monk of the Eastern deserts whose long life was punctuated with some mighty struggles and some correspondingly mighty roars of indignation.

With justice, then, may modern times look to St. Jerome as the exemplar of the Christian Scholar and Humanist. For in God's design, His creatures are destined to reach the highest perfection of all the faculties they have from the hand of God. He desires the perfection of all the powers that He has given to man, the sanctification of the whole human being, soul and mind, and, since any additional perfection of the mind is an adornment of the soul, of the whole human being. True Christian Humanism will be an integration of all the forces of nature and Grace, all the powers of mind and soul, since men are destined by means of their whole nature to enjoy eternally Him in whom are contained all the treasures of wisdom and knowledge.

NOTES

[1] E. K. Rand & G. Howe, "The Vatican Livy and the Script of Tours," *Memoirs of the American Academy in Rome,* I (1915).

[2] Jerome, *Epistolae,* 107, 1; 126, 2; 127, 12; 128, 5; *Comm. in Ezechielem,* Praef. (*PL,* 25, 15).

[3] *Ep.* 30, 22.

[4] *Chronicon,* Year 354.

[5] *Adversus Rufinum,* I, 16 (*PL,* 23, 428C).

[6] *Comm. in Eccles.,* 390 (*PL,* 23, 1071A).

[7] *Adversus Rufinum,* III, 29.

[8] *Adversus Rufinum,* I, 30.

[9] *Ep.* 52, 1. The letter to Heliodorus is *Ep.* 14.

[10] *Adversus Jovinianum,* 389 (*PL,* 23, 356).

[11] The consolatory letters of Jerome are written in the traditional style of the *consolatio.* He enumerates famous cities that have fallen, kings who have died, and looks for consolatory ideas in the writings of Hesiod, Naevius, Ennius and Virgil. He refers explicitly to the *rhetorum praecepta* as to the topics that should be treated in such a *laudatio funebris.* In these letters he is certainly sincere, at times all but heartbroken, but he consistently uses all the apparatus of rhetorical form. He never got over his love for the nicely turned phrase and the neat epigram. The pagans of his time were extraordinarily interested in the niceties of style, clinging to this, perhaps, when they saw the structure of official paganism collapsing around them. They accused the Christians of *rusticitas,* and it was to combat this charge that Jerome wrote his *De viris illustribus,* a catalogue of the famous philosophers, orators and learned men of Christianity. In his zeal, Jerome included a few heretics, at which St. Augustine remonstrated. Jerome was not pleased.

[12] *Adversus Rufinum,* I, 30.

[13] *Comm. in Ezechielem,* XII (*PL,* 25, 377).

[14] F. Cavallera, *Saint Jérôme, sa vie et son oeuvre* (2 vols., Louvain, 1922), I, 15.

[15] *Comm. in Ep. ad Galatas*, 405 (*PL*, 26, 365).

[16] *Ep.* 3, 5; 5, 2.

[17] *Ep.* 125, 12.

[18] *Adversus Rufinum*, III, 6.

[19] G. Bardy, "L'Eglise et l'enseignement pendant les trois premiers siècles," *Rev. des Sciences Religieuses* (Strasbourg), XII (1932), 1–28; "L'Eglise et l'enseignement au quatrième siècle," *ibid.*, XIV (1934), 525–550 and XV (1935), 1–27.

[20] *Codex Justinianus*, X, LIII, 7. Cf. *Epistolae Juliani*, #42. Julian, in his violent hatred of Christianity, did not realize that the day of paganism was past and that the future belonged to the Church. This edict was repealed after his death by his successor. Cf. *Cod. Theodos.*, XIII, 3, 6.

[21] St. Basil, *On Literature to Young Men* (*PG* 31, 569).

[22] G. G. Walsh, S.J., *Medieval Humanism* (New York: Macmillan, 1942), 2. The always perceptive Henri Bremond says: "Christian Humanism, the only one which occupies itself with the theology of salvation, does not believe in the sufficiency but in the efficacy of human merit; it does not preach the pride, but the joy of life, it desires the blossoming, but not the freeing of the individual consciousness." *A Literary History of Religious Thought in France* (transl. by K. L. Montgomery), I, 10.

[23] *Ep.* 70.

[24] Deut. 21:10–13; cf. *Traditio*, III (1945), 224.

[25] Ep. 21, 13. Cf. Hrabanus Maurus, *De Clericorum Institutione* (*PL*, 107, 396).

[26] *Comm. in Dan.* (*PL*, 25, 495C).

[27] St. Augustine, *De Doctrina Christiana*, II, 60. Cf. Exodus 3:22; 11:2; 12:35.

[28] St. Augustine, *ibid.*, II, 40–56.

[29] *Ep.* 107.

[30] *Ep.* 128.

[31] *Apologia Rufini*, II, 8–10 (*PL*, 21, 591).

[32] *Comm. in Isaiam*, Prologus (*PL*, 24, 18B).

[33] *Ep.* 30, 1; *Comm. in Eccles.*, 1 (*PL*, 23, 1064A).

[34] *Ep.* 22, 30.

[35] *Adversus Rufinum*, I, 30–32.

[36] A. S. Pease, "The attitude of St. Jerome towards pagan literature" (*TAPA*, 50 (1919) 167).

[37] L. Traube, *Vorlesungen und Abhandlungen* (München, 1909), II, 66.

[38] Cf. Ansgar Pöllmann, "Von der Entwicklung des Hieronymus-Typus in der älteren Kunst," *Dem heiligen Hieronymus. Festschrift zur fünfzehnhunderten Wiederkehr seines Todestages* (Beuron, 1920), 86–170.

The Study of St. Jerome in the Early Middle Ages

M. L. W. LAISTNER

The Study of St. Jerome in the Early Middle Ages

To assess in the space of a brief essay the influence through a thousand years of so versatile a scholar as St. Jerome is manifestly impossible. No informed person at the present day would regard that long epoch which we call the Middle Ages as static. And even in the field of study which Jerome made peculiarly his own and in which his authority endured longest without serious challenge new ideas and new methods developed, which widened and deepened the stream of Biblical exegesis, even though its authors were not unmindful of the source from which that stream had taken its rise. If the present chapter confines itself almost wholly to the eighth and ninth centuries, the setting of such chronological limits is not without justification, for that epoch marks a fundamentally important stage in the growth of Jerome's influence. It would indeed be difficult to exaggerate the significance of the age of Charlemagne and his successors to the end of the ninth century for the rediscovery and subsequent transmission of both pagan and Patristic literature. Had it not been for the students in that age and, in particular, for the ceaseless activity of monastic and cathedral scriptoria, much that we still possess would have been irretrievably lost. True, the number of surviving uncial and half-uncial manuscripts of individual works by Jerome is not negligible. Two extant codices of his translation of Eusebius' *Chronicle* were copied in Italy a generation or little more after his death. His essay in literary history, *De viris illustribus*, which with the continuation of Gennadius enjoyed an enormous

235

vogue throughout the Middle Ages, and some of his letters survive in a few manuscripts copied before A.D. 600. The oldest manuscripts or fragments of manuscripts containing one or other of his Biblical commentaries belong to the seventh century. These and others which have long since disappeared were the exemplars that were rediscovered and sedulously copied in the age of Bede and with greater intensity in the Carolingian era. Still, the total of surviving Jerome manuscripts dating from the fifth, sixth, and seventh centuries is very modest, less indeed than that of early manuscripts containing works by Augustine or even by Hilary of Poitiers. No doubt the intensified interest in Jerome during the Carolingian age was partly cause and partly effect of activity in the scriptoria; but one must reckon also with a certain degree of reorientation among students of theology. That admirable scholar, the late Cuthbert Turner, in a posthumously published volume, indeed went so far as to remark: "Even of the greater writers, it was the Carolingian movement which substituted the study and circulation of the works of Augustine and Jerome and dethroned in their interest the favourite writer of the seventh and early eighth centuries, Pope Gregory the Great." [1] This judgment, though an overstatement, contains a measure of truth. But even Bede's profound devotion to Gregory's teaching did not prevent his becoming familiar with much of Augustine and even more with the works of Jerome. Nor did the increased study of these two Fathers in the ninth century lead to wholesale neglect of the Gregorian writings. On the other hand, in the various doctrinal disputes that engaged the attention of churchmen in the age of Charlemagne and for some time after, the works of Augustine, and to a somewhat less degree of Jerome, afforded more copious material for the disputants to use in support of their arguments than did the treatises and homilies of Gregory. The treatment of even the relatively brief period with which this chapter mainly deals does not pretend to be exhaustive; but at least the main lines of St. Jerome's influence in various directions can be established and then illustrated by reference to Bede and to the Carolingian divines.

For his library in the episcopal palace at Seville St. Isidore composed a series of short poems. These were placed above the cases in which his books were housed, so that the user could see at a glance what author or authors were to be found in each section of the library. He penned three dactylic hexameters for the bookcase in which reposed the works of St. Jerome, echoing a sentiment that had already been expressed by Cassian: [2]

> Jerome, adept translator skilled in divers tongues,
> Honored in Bethlehem, the world rings with thy name;
> So with thy books our library shall bruit thy fame.

Nearly two centuries later the Venerable Bede refers to Jerome as the "translator of sacred history" and "the admirable translator and teacher of the Sacred Scriptures." In the ninth century testimonies to Jerome's eminence meet one at every turn. One writer calls him the "translator of the Divine Law," another, "the most blessed Jerome, incomparably learned in so many languages and books." For Alcuin he is "the interpreter of Sacred History and the greatest teacher (*maximus doctor*) and defender of the Catholic Faith." The Spanish Paulus Albarus who calls Jerome "that saint and abyss of learning" composed a poem of some length in his honor. The poetry is mediocre, but the sentiments are unimpeachable. The redoubtable Hincmar of Rheims more specifically says of Jerome that he was "most expert in Hebrew, Greek, and Latin," while Hrabanus Maurus, some time abbot of Fulda and later bishop of Mayence and himself a most industrious compiler, expresses his admiration for the genius and learning of this Latin Father, which he displayed in translating and expounding Holy Writ. Jonas, bishop of Orléans, with terse daring dubs him "the library of Mother Church." These various utterances, which could be multiplied greatly, are doubly significant: they show the veneration with which the scholars of the eighth and ninth centuries regarded Jerome, but they also indicate their reasons for it. He is the translator of the Bible; he is versed in the original languages in which the Old and the New Testament were composed; and he is a man of outstanding erudition. These are the more obvious grounds for the reverent admiration with which he came to be considered for centuries after his time, but they are by no means all.

Although his fame as a translator rests primarily on the Vulgate, which was in part a new translation of the Scriptures from Greek or Hebrew, in part a revision of older Latin versions of the Bible, he was also, together with his friend and later enemy, Rufinus, largely responsible for giving to the West Latin renderings of Greek theological works that otherwise would have remained unknown there for centuries. Thus, his version of Eusebius' *Chronicle*, to which he himself made certain additions at the end, became a standard work which directly or indirectly underlies later chronicles of world history. Continued by chroniclers of the fifth century, Jerome's Latin version, as befitted a standard book of reference, was in constant demand by those chroniclers and historians who did not confine themselves to contemporary or near-contemporary history, but included some treatment of pre-Christian and early Christian antiquity. The list of such writers is long and extends over many centuries from Isidore and Bede to Marianus Scottus, Hermann of Reichenau and Sigebert of Gembloux. Indeed, the last-named says expressly of himself, *"imitatus Eusebium Pamphili,"* though he used the Latin version, not the Greek original. Jerome's translation of the *Rule of Pachomius* was highly influential in the formation of Latin monastic rules. It was to a great extent through him that Western Europe became familiar with some at least of Origen's thought and teaching, partly because Jerome translated a number of Origen's homilies into Latin, partly because, as is now very generally recognized, much of his own expository writing in his Biblical commentaries is not original but adapted from the Greek Father.[3] And there were other Greek authors whose works were made accessible to the West by Jerome; indeed, in some cases, as with the treatise on the Holy Spirit by Didymus the Blind, the Greek original is lost and we depend for our knowledge of the book on Jerome's version. Amongst his contemporaries he had met with much criticism for his methods as a translator and their strictures were not confined to his Vulgate. He had stated some of the difficulties and briefly indicated his guiding principles in the letter to Pope Damasus prefacing his version of the Gospels and in the foreword to his translation of Eusebius' *Chronicle*. A dozen years later he wrote a long and reasoned defence of his position to his friend Pammachius. It is a classic exposition of the true art of translation. It rejects outright the type of literal rendering from one language into another which does violence to both meaning and style, but which is unhappily still too common even in our own day. "For I myself not only admit," he writes (*Ep.* 57), "but freely proclaim that in translating from the Greek (except in the case of the Holy Scriptures where even the order of words is a mystery) I render sense for sense and not word for word." In the Middle Ages the voice of criticism became stilled. *Epistle* 57 was read but aroused no controversy; and in the thirteenth century, when Roger Bacon discussed the value of studying many languages and the proper art of translation, he recalled the wise opinion of Jerome on that subject.[4]

When writers of a later age speak of Jerome as "interpres," they are no doubt thinking in the first instance of him as the author of the Vulgate. But they also had in mind, we may be sure, the other sense of the word which it still bears in English; for of all of Jerome's own works it was his Biblical commentaries that were most widely read, quoted, and excerpted by the scholars of the earlier Middle Ages. "Carrying on his inquiry with the Lord's inspiration, he was rewarded by penetrating to the marrow and very vitals of Sacred Scripture." [5] The evidence is unequivocal. A survey of writers who flourished in the eighth and ninth centuries shows more frequent use of the commentaries than of any other books by him. The number of extant manuscripts and the contents of medieval libraries so far as they are known lead to the same conclusion. St. Jerome had expounded all the prophetic books, Ecclesiastes, the first Gospel, and four of the Pauline Epistles, Galatians, Ephesians, Titus, and Philemon. His *Hebrew Questions* were in effect a commentary on Genesis; and, as is now certain thanks to the researches of Dom Germain

Morin, he had written a brief commentary on the Psalter as a whole, and also a series of homilies, intended primarily for his fellow monks, on a number of individual Psalms. The earliest manuscripts, seven in number, of these homilies, were copied in the late eighth and ninth centuries, an excellent example of the way in which Carolingian industry preserved writings which might otherwise have perished.[6]

In the eighth and ninth centuries theological writing was in the main of two kinds, expository and controversial. The elucidation of books in the Old and New Testament canon attracted many students, and, as might have been expected, the quality of what was produced varied greatly. All the commentators, however, had one thing in common: they were essentially traditionalists rather than innovators. The earliest of them was also the greatest; but the Venerable Bede himself advises his readers that he is following in the footsteps of the Fathers, and his Biblical commentaries are full both of direct quotations from Patristic literature and of adaptations from the same source. Still, Bede had not only read widely; he had digested and thought through what he had studied. The result was that his works, though their thought is so largely derivative, nevertheless bear the imprint of his own mind and personality. The same was true of Paschasius Radbertus, for many years abbot of Corbie. He too was a scholar of unusual erudition who reproduced what he had gleaned from many earlier commentators; and the library of the monastery over which he presided was, and continued to be for centuries, unusually rich in works both sacred and profane.[7] Still, Paschasius, like Bede, to some extent transmuted what he borrowed and also enriched his writings by his own reflections. He had many predecessors, headed by Jerome, to consult when he set himself to expound the Gospel according to St. Matthew; but when he elucidated the Book of Lamentations he was breaking new ground, even though his commentary was firmly based on the teaching of the Fathers. The allegorical, moral, and anagogical interpretation of Holy Scripture is no longer in fashion.

But at least one must recognize that these two representatives of early medieval scholarship were the most distinguished exponents of the method in the early Middle Ages. The Biblical commentaries of other writers in that epoch are as a rule little more than collections of quotations from the Four Doctors and occasionally one or two other Patristic sources. Thus the expositions by Claudius of Turin and by Hrabanus Maurus are essentially *collectanea,* even though both add some comment of their own. Hrabanus is quite frank on the subject. He remarks of his *Commentary on St. Matthew* that he had composed it, not because a fresh treatment was urgently needed, but because a work like his, which tried to bring together in a single treatise the teaching of many earlier authorities, might be a boon to poor readers who were cut off from the resources of an adequate library and therefore were not in a position to study the early commentators for themselves.[8] Hrabanus' justification seems sound enough. While every monastic house, and cathedrals also, would have some books, larger collections which had accumulated a substantial number of treatises by such prolific authors as Augustine or Jerome were relatively few in number; and, moreover, the hazards of borrowing were serious in an age of much political unrest. Another factor which must not be overlooked is the standard of education which commonly was low even amongst the religious. Thus, Christian of Stavelot, who composed his commentary on St. Matthew towards the end of the ninth century, states expressly in his preface that he is following the guidance of St. Jerome; but he adds that much that was to be found in his works, and by implication in the writings of other Fathers, was too advanced for the pupils whom it was Christian's duty to instruct. We may note also that Paschasius, in his more elaborate exposition of the same Gospel, from time to time inserts grammatical notes and comments on the meaning of particular words and linguistic usages. The pronunciation of foreign words might give the student serious trouble; and so we find a monastery teacher in the eleventh century writing down specific instructions for the reader. In a manuscript of St. Jerome's letters copied by Otloh of St. Emmeram at Regensburg he has appended the following note on the first folio: [9]

It should be noted that the Greeks pronounce certain syllables differently from the way in which they are written, especially diphthongs. Thus the diphthong ai is spoken like short e—for instance, kai is pronounced ke—and oi like i, ou like u, and long e like i.[10]

Yet another author, Angelomus of Luxeuil, in the foreword to his commentary on Genesis explains that he has drawn on the Fathers and on the traditions that he has learned, since some works were inaccessible to him. He added some comments and illustrations of his own and expressed the hope that readers who have not the leisure to study the Fathers for themselves will find his shorter compendium an aid to understanding. Angelomus is a little disingenuous. The truth is that much of what purports to come from authors of the fourth century is actually quoted by him at second hand; for he relies extensively, though usually without acknowledgment, on Bede. This exemplifies the real problem that confronts any student of medieval literature when investigating the sources supposedly used by a given author. Not infrequently the original source is reproduced at second or even third hand, being derived from an intermediate author or, alternatively, from one of those *collectanea* garnered from various writers which were so popular in the Middle Ages. Authors who frequently referred to their authorities by name or indicated borrowed material by noting its author's name in the margin, as Bede and Hrabanus sometimes did, were the exception rather than the rule.

It is clear that both the greater and the humbler theologians who tried their hand at Biblical exegesis were familiar with some at least of Jerome's commentaries; it is equally clear that the width of their reading and the depth of their understanding varied greatly. Bede was probably acquainted with the entire corpus of Jerome's Biblical expositions; indeed there are only two, on Jeremiah and on Ephesians, from which I have been unable to trace direct citations. Alcuin also had read widely in the same author, although Schönbach's assertion, that he quoted Jerome more often than any other Father, goes too far.[11] His *Commentary on Ecclesiastes,* it is true, is little more than an adaptation of his predecessor's treatise. But in his other works his indebtedness to St. Augustine is noticeably greater. Among the many early authorities pondered over with reverent care by Paschasius was Jerome, the Biblical commentator. Minor exegetes turned to the same source of guidance and information, as far as the resources of their libraries and perhaps book-collections in neighboring monasteries permitted.

Of all of Jerome's commentaries those that enjoyed the widest circulation were unquestionably his expositions of Isaiah and of St. Matthew. This is proved not only by the frequency with which these particular works are cited by authors of the eighth and ninth centuries, but also by the survival of numerous manuscripts of early date. The commentary on Isaiah, of which nearly thirty manuscripts copied before A.D. 900 are extant, was the longest and most carefully elaborated of all of Jerome's books in this category; furthermore, it treated an exceptionally difficult author. The constant comparisons instituted in it between the Hebrew text and the Greek versions of LXX, Aquila, Symmachus, and Theodotion interested only one or two exceptional scholars of the earlier Middle Ages, notably Bede and also to some extent Paschasius. But the Biblical commentaries, to which may be added the treatises on Hebrew names and on Palestinian geography, were a mine of information about Old Testament names and places and about their allegorical meaning. Besides, the judicious mixture of literal or historic, allegorical, and anagogical interpretation had a special appeal for the medieval student. The commentary on Matthew, though much briefer and, as we know from Jerome himself, rather hastily composed, owed its popularity—I know of eighteen early codices and there may be more—not only to the authority of the writer but to the fact that it explained the weightiest of the three Synoptic Gospels. The commentary on Jeremiah, again, expounded a difficult author and text, but Jerome never lived to complete it. Yet scholars, like Hrabanus and Servatus Lupus, misled by an error of Cassiodorus, sought for the later books of this work. It is a curious fact that, while manuscripts of early date are plentiful, actual citations or borrowings from this commentary are seemingly few. Yet we can be sure that it was read and studied by the more advanced students of theology, otherwise copies would not have been multiplied.[12] If it was more rarely quoted, one reason may well be that in it St. Jerome concerns himself primarily with textual problems, while his interpretation is mainly literal; for it is only here and there that he also offers an allegorical or anagogical interpretation. Three authors of the ninth century who were demonstrably familiar with this exposition were Alcuin, Smaragdus of St. Mihiel, and Hrabanus.[13] It was also one of the works by Jerome from which extracts were taken by the compilers of the *Liber Glossarum* at the turn from the eighth to the ninth century. The monastery in which this huge and remarkable combination of dictionary and encyclopedia was put together was in all likelihood Corbie in Picardy. Among extant manuscripts copied in its scriptorium in the ninth century is one of the commentary on Jeremiah.[14] By far the greatest number of Jerome glosses in the *Liber Glossarum* were taken from the treatise on Hebrew names, but not a few were culled from the commentaries on the four Major Prophets, Hosea, Jonah, Ecclesiastes, St. Matthew, and the Pauline Epistles. A few come from the *Hebrew Questions* and from individual letters, and there are besides a good many left unidentified by the editors.

Though the three commentaries that we have named seem to have enjoyed the greatest popularity, the remainder were also in considerable demand. Of more than a hundred manuscripts or parts of manuscripts containing one or more of the commentaries on the four Pauline epistles seventeen were copied before A.D. 900, although only two of these contain the exposition of all four epistles together.[15] The treatise on Galatians especially was often copied alone. In addition, many manuscripts of varying date which ostensibly preserve Jerome's work actually contain the commentary by Pelagius in one recension or another. Jerome's treatises on the minor Prophets, at least in early manuscripts, were often copied singly or in small groups, since they varied considerably in length.[16] Similarly the commentaries on the major Prophets, if the script was large and the size of the codex moderate, filled more than one volume. Thus, a manuscript of the early ninth century copied in Rheims (now Rheims, MS 75) contains only books 1–9 of the commentary on Isaiah, another written at Cologne (now Cologne, Dombibliothek 51) at about the same date preserves books 7–14 of the commentary on Ezekiel, the companion volume (books 1–6) being apparently lost. The last-named work in its complete form fills two manuscripts of the ninth century from the St. Gall scriptorium (now MSS 117 and 118).

St. Jerome had been the most redoubtable controversialist of his day; indeed, the intemperance of his onslaughts on opponents had at times shocked even his friends. The truth is that he had the defects of his qualities. He was the unfaltering upholder of orthodox doctrine in the Church of the fourth and early fifth centuries, and to him the spreading of false or even questionable doctrine was the mark not merely of a misguided mind but of moral baseness. As an old man, whilst referring specifically to his attacks on Pelagius and his followers, he defended his attitude by saying: "I am the enemy not of men, but of error." [17] The earliest of his seven controversial treatises were a dialogue intended to controvert the heretical teaching of Lucifer, bishop of Calaris in Sardinia, and the better known tract on the perpetual virginity of the Blessed Virgin Mary directed against the errors of Helvidius. A decade later (393) he published his famous rebuttal of Jovinian's views on the life of virginity, marriage, and asceticism. The tract against John of Jerusalem and the treatise in three books attacking Rufinus were in essence products of the controversy over the writings and teaching of Origen, and the longer work led to a final break in the once friendly relations between Rufinus and Jerome.[18] The unfinished tract against Vigilantius combats his views on the worship of saints and relics. Finally, near the end of his life. Jerome was aroused to compose his dialogue in three books against the Pelagians. The intellectual vigor and stylistic elegance of this book are truly remarkable from a man nearing his seventieth year and in very indifferent health. This book and the incomplete commentary on Jeremiah, in short, demonstrate clearly that Jerome's mental powers remained unimpaired to the end.

To the theologians of the early Middle Ages these controversial works would not all be of equal interest. The Origenist controversy, especially insofar as it involved personal differences between Jerome and Rufinus, was no longer a living issue. Still less so was a dialogue written to refute the opinions of a group of schismatics long since forgotten; for Luciferianism had become extinct within fifty years of its author's death. It is not surprising, therefore, that these works by Jerome have left comparatively little trace in the medieval period. There were copies of the dialogue in the libraries of Reichenau, St. Gall and Rheims (MS 385) in the ninth century, at Chartres in the eleventh, and at Bec in the twelfth. The treatise against Rufinus seems to have reached England rather early and was known to Bede. More than a century later Sedulius Scottus included extracts from it in his *Collectaneum,* a miscellany of anecdotes and excerpts from pagan and Christian writers on literary and ethical themes. It is mentioned about the same time by Remigius of Lyons, but without actual citation, and his contemporary, Prudentius of Troyes, quotes a passage from the second book.[19] Copies of it are listed in the twelfth-century catalogues of Corbie, Bec, and Prüfening.

St. Jerome's other controversial works appear to have been more widely read, mainly because they discussed or provided material arguments and illustrations for doctrinal disputes. It will be recalled that a series of controversies arose in the later eighth and the ninth centuries which, though they left the mass of the population untouched, caused serious concern to ecclesiastical authority because of their actually or potentially dangerous character. Thus, the Adoptionist heresy originated in Spain and met

with vigorous opposition from orthodox prelates, like Beatus of
Liébana and Etherius. But the dispute did not remain localized;
for when the chief heresiarch, Elipandus, was joined by Felix of
Urgel, whose see was located in territory then under Frankish
control, both the emperor and the theologians within his realm
were drawn into the controversy. No less a person than Alcuin
composed treatises to rebut the false doctrines of both Elipandus
and Felix; he also corresponded with Beatus on the questions at
issue.[20] More important, because it brought into the open the
growing differences on fundamental issues between the Eastern
and the Western Churches, was the Trinitarian dispute which
arose out of the proper definition of the Procession of the Holy
Spirit. The teaching of Western churchmen, that the Holy Spirit
proceeded from the Father and the Son, was soundly based on
their reading and interpretation of the Latin Fathers and became
the accepted belief of Western orthodoxy. But it was rejected by
the Greek Church. Nor was this the only serious altercation
between East and West. The question of image-worship had
aroused acute dissension in the Byzantine world. There Iconoclasm was succeeded by tenets which went to the very opposite
extreme, and these were sanctioned by an Oecumenical Council
held in 787 at Nicaea of historic memory. To Charlemagne and
his advisers, though political motives may also have played some
part in forming their decisions, both Iconoclasm and the extreme
form of image-worship which succeeded it in the East with
ecclesiastical approval seemed worthy of condemnation. The so-
called *libri Carolini,* whether Alcuin or some other was their
author or compiler, took a middle line: the saints deserve and
should receive veneration, but their images and pictorial like-
nesses were set up in churches only to remind the worshipper of
their good lives and deeds. The reply of Frankish theologians,
supported by ample reference to Patristic literature, to the Acts of
the Nicene Council in due course received Papal approval. But
even so the question was not finally settled in the West. Claudius
of Turin, not satisfied with the *via media* sanctioned by Pope and
Emperor, in certain writings emerged as an outspoken Iconoclast;

his views were attacked and refuted notably by the Irishman Dungal and by Jonas, bishop of Orléans.

The addition of the words, "and from the Son" (*filioque*), to the definition of the Holy Spirit in the creed, which had already received the sanction of Gregory I, was formally approved at the Synod of Aachen (A.D. 808) and somewhat later was also incorporated in the confession of faith used in the Roman service. The orthodox teaching of the Western Church concerning the Trinity had been stated fully some years before by Alcuin in his treatise, *De fide sanctae et individuae Trinitatis,* which derives its authority from the Latin Fathers and, above all, from St. Augustine. The dogma concerning the Procession of the Holy Spirit, however, continued to call forth writings from Alcuin's successors in the Frankish empire, their arguments being taken from the same fourth-century sources as his. What was still a controversial topic owing to the attitude of the Byzantine Church reached its peak in 866, when the Patriarch of Constantinople, Photius, in an encyclical charged the Western Church with unorthodoxy on various counts. The chief was once again the Western definition of the Procession of the Holy Spirit. A year later Pope Nicholas I invited leading divines in the Frankish Church to compose a reasoned refutation of Photius' criticisms. Not all the writings called forth by the Papal request have survived; but the *collectaneum* of Patristic excerpts assembled by Aeneas of Paris and the profounder and more closely reasoned treatise against the Greeks by the learned monk of Corbie, Ratramnus, are still extant.

But the most extensive body of controversial literature in the ninth century drew its primary inspiration from the teachings of the monk Gottschalk. He challenged the then accepted teaching of the Church on the subject of predestination, basing his views on his reading and his own particular interpretation of St. Augustine's anti-Pelagian tracts. Various shades of opinion found expression in the literary battle that ensued. Some scholars shared Gottschalk's opinions or supported his arguments; others, notably Hincmar of Rheims, Hrabanus Maurus, and Amalarius of Metz, rejected them vigorously and challenged his understanding of

Augustinian works. Some, again, attempted to take a middle position between the two extremes of full approval and outright rejection. In the end the controversy centred less on the mistaken teaching of Gottschalk than on the work of one of his opponents, John Scotus. John's *Liber de praedestinatione* was indeed a philosophical refutation of the monk of Orbais. But his approach to the doctrinal questions involved and his proposed solution were alike in sharp opposition to the accepted teaching of the Church in the ninth century. John's book provoked keen disapproval and was formally condemned by the synods of Valence (A.D. 855) and Langres (A.D. 857). As might have been expected, the chief Patristic source to which the participants in the predestination controversy turned to a greater or less degree, according to their learning and scholarly opportunities, was St. Augustine. The writings of St. Jerome were little in evidence, save in the *collectaneum* by Prudentius of Troyes. The excerpts that he gathered, however, were from the Biblical commentaries on Isaiah and Ezekiel, on some eight of the minor Prophets, and on the Pauline epistles. He refers, as we have already seen, to the treatise against Rufinus and quotes twice from that against Jovinian, but he does not seem to have been familiar with Jerome's anti-Pelagian dialogue. Indeed, clear evidence for the use of this work in the controversial literature of the ninth century is hard to trace. It is quoted in Lupus' *Collectaneum* (III, 19), but early manuscripts are few, and the book does not often appear in library catalogues. It was to be found in the ninth century at Reichenau, Lorsch, Lyons, Wuerzburg and St. Gall; [21] at Bobbio in the tenth, and in Bec and Prüfening in the twelfth.

In the controversial literature evoked by the disputes with the Byzantine Church three of Jerome's treatises are occasionally quoted. Dungal and Jonas reproduce a number of extracts from the treatise against Vigilantius. We almost seem to detect a certain national pride, when the latter quotes Jerome's *obiter dictum* on Gaul: "Gaul alone has had no monsters, but has always been famed for men of wisdom and eloquence." [22] The same sentence is introduced by Richer in the tenth century into the discussion of the peoples of Gaul with which his *History of France* opens. Passages from the treatise against Helvidius make up the ninth chapter of Ratramnus' essay on Christ's nativity. But of all these treatises that against Jovinian was easily the most popular. Quotations from it in writers from Aldhelm and Bede to the end of the ninth century are plentiful, several manuscripts of early date survive,[23] and it is listed in some twenty or more library catalogues between the early ninth and the twelfth century. Occasionally this treatise was followed in the same codex by a work which the catalogues describe as *Apologeticus ad Pammachium,* for example, at Reichenau (Carlsruhe, Aug. 94), St. Riquier, and Lorsch in the ninth century, and at Bec and Zwiefalten (now Stuttgart, *Cod. theol.* 221) in the twelfth. The tract in question was St. Jerome's letter to Pammachius (*Ep.* 48). In it he defended his attack on Jovinian, to which some of Jerome's friends appear to have taken exception, partly on account of the violent tone of some passages, partly because of his extreme views on marriage; and in the course of his defense he quotes at some length from the treatise.

We turn finally to Jerome's correspondence which from the very first seems to have been greatly admired and prized. Some of his letters, as we know from his own statement, were actually published by himself; for he alludes to a group of them which he had addressed to Marcella and to another written to various correspondents. The care, moreover, with which they were composed and the elaboration of the subject matter in the longer epistles especially prove clearly that their author intended them for publication. Stylistically his letters are the most perfect of Jerome's original works. Complete collections of them were probably for a long time a rarity. It is deeply to be regretted that their most recent editor, Hilberg, did not live to publish a full discussion and elucidation of their text transmission.[24] But certainly single letters or groups, like the correspondence between Jerome and Augustine, were often copied and circulated separately, as is shown by several surviving manuscripts of early date.[25] The reason for copying certain of these epistles singly is readily understandable. Many of them, though in form letters, in content were short treatises in which Jerome expounded some Scriptural passage, laid down rules for the religious life, or discussed, often with a wealth of illustratory matter, questions of discipline or ritual practice. By the beginning of the ninth century, if not before, large libraries, like those in the abbeys of St. Gall or Lorsch, appear to have owned complete or nearly complete sets of the letters. References to particular epistles or quotations from them occur with some frequency in the literature of the early Middle Ages. While Aldhelm, as far as we can tell, knew only a very few, Bede quotes from a dozen or more, and Alcuin too had considerable acquaintance with this body of Jerome's writings. References or quotations become more frequent in the ninth century, but a single example, to illustrate a general trend, must suffice. Unquestionably one of the best Jerome scholars in that age was Amalarius of Metz. His important treatise, *De ecclesiasticis officiis,* dealing primarily with Christian ritual and the offices of the Church, is no mere *collectaneum* of excerpts but a well constructed dissertation. But it is based on an extensive study of Patristic literature and its author shows an unusual familiarity with the works of St. Jerome. He cites from the commentaries on Isaiah, Ezekiel, Daniel, Joel, Hosea, St. Matthew, Galatians, Ephesians and Titus, and these quotations deal with a wide variety of topics: explanation of passages in Scripture, public penance, various ritual observances, warnings against unorthodox or even heretical practices or beliefs, the offices of priest and deacon and their institution, and the ritual dress of the Jewish High Priest. But Amalarius also derived material for his monograph from ten of Jerome's letters, using them in most cases for some specific topic. Thus, we find extracts from *Ep.* 41 concerning the heresy of Montanus; from *Epp.* 52 and 146, addressed to Nepotian and to Evangelus respectively, in which Jerome discoursed on the duties of the clergy and on the status of deacons and presbyters; from *Ep.* 64 regarding the vestments of the High Priest; from *Ep.* 65 which is a commentary on the forty-fourth Psalm; from *Ep.* 71, an exhortation to Lucinius in Spain to visit Bethlehem and to lead an ascetic life; from *Ep.* 78 which discusses the forty-two resting places (*mansiones*) of the children of Israel during their wanderings in the desert; and from *Ep.* 130 laying down rules of conduct for those about to enter on a life of virginity. The remaining two letters quoted by Amalarius are less specialized in their content, *Ep.* 77, a eulogy of Fabiola, and *Ep.* 108, a letter of consolation to Eustochium on the death of the Elder Paula. Both these epistles were greatly and rightly admired in the Carolingian age as model letters of their kind. Much read also were Letters 22 and 107. The former was perhaps the most famous of all the epistles, if only because it contains an account of St. Jerome's famous dream. But this letter to Eustochium became the classic expression of the reasons which should influence those who vow themselves to a life of virginity, and of the rules that should govern their life and conduct. Letter 107, advising Laeta on the best method of bringing up her little daughter, together with Letter 128 to Gaudentius on the same general subject, contain St. Jerome's views on female education. Though the opening sections of the *Epistle to Laeta,* which concern themselves with the early stages of formal education, echo the enlightened views already expressed by Quintilian three centuries before, the remainder are pure Jerome, and the two letters are therefore in some sense a supplement to Epistle 22.

Although we need not doubt that the elegant latinity of the *Correspondence,* to which reference has already been made, attracted the more discriminating literary figures of the Carolingian age, they seem to have concentrated only on its content; for their own style does not seem to have been affected to any noticeable degree. But in the twelfth century the literary excellence of the letters made a great appeal to one of the greatest of medieval scholars. John of Salisbury, both in the *Policraticus* and the *Metalogicon,* from time to time refers to Jerome by name, when invoking his authority in support of some fact or piece of information. But, as can readily be seen by consulting the indexes of Clement Webb's admirable editions of these works, direct verbal reminiscences and quotations from Jerome, but without mention of his name, are far commoner. John had made a profound study of Jerome's writings and evidently was familiar with many of the commentaries and controversial treatises. But it is the *Correspondence* that he echoes most often. He was, in short, thoroughly steeped in the latinity of the letters and constantly introduces into his own prose elegant expressions or pithy turns of phrase that he has taken directly from St. Jerome.

As the Middle Ages progressed, new approaches to Biblical exegesis were opened up. Younger schools of commentators adhered less rigidly to Patristic teaching and tradition than their predecessors.[26] Yet this implied neither disrespect nor neglect of the Fathers. *Florilegia* compiled in the earlier period of scholasticism in the twelfth century contain extracts from writers like Ambrose, Augustine, Jerome, Gregory I, and even Bede together with sentences from Anselm of Laon, William of Champeaux, or Ivo of Chartres.[27] By the thirteenth century, too, greatly renewed interest had got under way in the original languages of the Old and New Testaments and in comparing the Hebrew with the Vulgate version. This, amongst other things, brought with it fresh study of Jerome, the one Latin Father who had put such linguistic problems in the forefront of his Biblical exegesis. Indeed, it may be said that now more than ever before St. Jerome came to be regarded par excellence as the authority on the literal or historic sense of Scripture, just as St. Gregory the Great counted as the classic exponent of the *sensus moralis*. A fourteenth-century tractate on the art of preaching, attributed to Henry of Hesse, begins by defining the four senses of Scriptural interpretation. Jerome is the representative of the literal sense, Gregory of the moral, Ambrose of the allegorical, and Augustine of the anagogical.[28] What the writer of the tractate lays down at the beginning of his work is not, of course, peculiar to him; it represents the accepted teaching of the age.

Thus, there was every reason why libraries should possess at least some of Jerome's many writings. The larger collections, as, for example, in Christ Church and in St. Augustine's, Canterbury, would be likely to own a complete or near-complete set of his works, and some of these besides in multiple copies.[29] The number of surviving manuscripts of different treatises by Jerome, copied between A.D. 1100 and 1500 is enormous; it runs into many hundreds. And, if the majority were plain copies for workaday use, some were fine examples of calligraphic and illuminated codices. An example of such is the superb manuscript of Jerome's commentary on Isaiah in the Chapter library of Durham Cathedral (B.II.8). A product of the Durham scriptorium during the second quarter of the twelfth century, it is written in a beautiful round hand of the period and adorned with illuminated capitals and occasional figure subjects, including several of the prophet Isaiah and one of Jerome himself holding an inscribed scroll.[30] Such a portrayal of him is characteristic of earlier medieval miniatures and resembles the representations of the four evangelists at the same period. The more elaborate pictures of the saint belong to the end of the medieval period and the sixteenth century. In them he appears in one of three characters: He is depicted as a Doctor of the Church, in company with Ambrose, Augustine, and Gregory I; or as the translator of the Bible and its expounder; or he is shown in the desert, usually in an attitude of prayer and penance.[31] All three types had their roots in the distant past; yet in historical development the first and second were reversed. The third, though based on Jerome's practice of asceticism as reflected in his *Letters* and his controversial treatises, and indirectly even in his short biographies of the three monks, Paulus, Hilarion, and Malchus, and thus never forgotten, was nevertheless subordinate to the other two in the literature of the early Middle Ages. It is surely not without significance that of the more than five hundred manuscripts of these *Vitae patrum* that still survive, the majority were copied in the twelfth century or later. And of the one hundred and twenty-four listed by the most recent investigators as worthy of study in connection with a new text-critical edition that is projected only seventeen or eighteen were copied before circa A.D. 900.[32] The testimonies of scholars in the eighth and ninth centuries, which were quoted at the beginning of this essay, their quotations from the works of Jerome, and the

evidence of the extant manuscripts, combine to show that to
Bede and his contemporaries and to the Carolingian divines St.
Jerome was first and foremost the translator of the Bible and an
expositor of unexampled learning and unswerving orthodoxy.

NOTES

[1] C. H. Turner, *The Oldest Manuscript of the Vulgate Gospels* (Oxford,
1931), p. xix.

[2] Hieronyme, interpres variis doctissime linguis,
    Te Bethlem celebrat, te totus personat orbis,
    Te quoque nostra tuis promet bibliotheca libris.
For Isidore's library in general cf. C. H. Beeson, *Isidorstudien* (Munich,
1913), pp. 135–166.

[3] Jerome's debt to Origen is considered at length by Pierre Courcelle, but
he probably goes too far in minimising Jerome's knowledge of Greek literature, profane and theological, before Origen's time. See his *Les Lettres
grecques en Occident* (Paris, 1943), pp. 37ff.

[4] Roger Bacon, *Opus maius* (translated by R. B. Burke), I, pp. 75–76.

[5] "Medullas et ipsa viscera scripturae sacrae investigando, domino inspir-
ante, penetrare promeruit." Hincmar in J. P. Migne, *Patrologia latina* (here-
after quoted as *PL*), 125, 246C.

[6] For the *Commentarioli in Psalmos* and the *Tractates* on various Psalms
see *Anecdota Maredsolana*, III (Maredsous, 1895); also G. Morin, *Études,
Textes, Découvertes* (Maredsous, 1913), pp. 220–293.

[7] Cf. note 14 below.

[8] Cf. *Monumenta Germaniae Historica: Epistulae Aevi Carolini*, 3, p. 388,
27ff.: ". . . quasi magis commodum, cum plurimorum sensus ac sententias
in unum contraxerim, ut lector pauperculus, qui librorum copiam non habet,
aut cui in pluribus scrutari profundos sensus patrum non licet, saltem in isto
sufficientiam suae indigentiae inveniat."

[9] See Bernhard Bischoff in *Studien und Mitteilungen zur Geschichte des
Benediktinerordens*, 51 (1933), p. 124.

[10] "Sciendum est, quoniam Graeci quasdam syllabas pronuntiant aliter
quam scribunt, precipue diptongos: ut ai dyptongon quasi per e brevem
ut kai quod sonat ke, et oi pro i, et oy pro u et H vocalem sono i producta
exprimunt."

[11] A. E. Schönbach, *Sitzungsberichte der K. Akademie der Wissenschaften
zu Wien*: Phil.-Hist. Klasse, 146 (1902–3), Abhandlung 4, p. 49.

[12] This is the only one of the commentaries available so far in a good
critical edition. See *C(orpus) S(criptorum) E(cclesiasticorum) L(atinorum)*,
59. The editor, S. Reiter, lists more than twenty early manuscripts headed
by a half-uncial codex of the late sixth or early seventh century (Lyons
468 + Paris, Bibl. Nat., N.A. 1602) and by seven folios of a seventh-century
codex that was once at Fleury and now reposes in the Municipal Library at
Orléans (MS. 192, foll. 21–27). He also lists more than fifty manuscripts
varying in date from the eleventh to the fifteenth century. For Cassiodorus'
mistake and its perpetuation see the discussion by Reiter, *op. cit.*, pp. vi–x.

[13] Alcuin: *PL*, 100, 180D; Smaragdus: *PL*, 102, 41A, 378A, 378C–D;

Hrabanus used Jerome's book for his own commentary on Jeremiah and refers specifically to it in the preface to book 13.

[14] Cf. *Glossaria Latina* (edd. W. M. Lindsay et al.: Paris, 1926), I, SI 507 and ST 42. The number of extant manuscripts of Jerome's works copied at Corbie in the late eighth or in the ninth century is remarkable, viz.: Paris, Bibl. Nat. 11627 (Isaiah), 11631 (Letters), 12153 (Jeremiah), 12155 (Ezekiel), 12161 (*De viris illustribus*), 13347 and 13348 (*Hebrew Questions*), 13349 (Ecclesiastes), 13354 (*Against Jovinian*). Also Leningrad F.1.3 (Isaiah) and Vatican City, Vat. lat. 340 (Pauline epistles).

[15] See Alexander Souter, *The Earliest Latin Commentaries on the Epistles of St. Paul* (Oxford, 1927), pp. 101–104; for the pseudo-Jerome commentary see *ibid.*, pp. 207ff.

[16] For example, of the ninth-century manuscripts from Reichenau now in Carlsruhe, MS. 74 contains Jerome on Jonah, Nahum, Sophonias, and Haggai; MS. 113 contains Hosea and MS. 257 Amos; MSS. 148 and 212 contain Obadiah, Zechariah, Malachi, and Hosea; MS. 226 preserves the same Prophets as MS. 74 with the addition of Joel and Micah. In Munich, Clm 14082 (9th c.), the commentaries on four minor Prophets are associated with the exposition of Daniel.

[17] *CSEL*, 59, p. 221, 12–13: "neque enim hominum sed erroris inimicus sum."

[18] See the clear and judicious discussion of this quarrel by Francis X. Murphy, *Rufinus of Aquileia* (Catholic University of America, 1945), chapters III and VI.

[19] *PL*, 115, 1338C.

[20] For Alcuin's letter to Beatus see Wilhelm Levison, *England and the Continent in the eight century* (Oxford, 1946), pp. 314–323.

[21] Cf. the extant manuscripts of the ninth century, Lyons 602, foll. 1–94, and St. Gall 132; Vatican City, Pal. lat. 178 (Lorsch).

[22] *Against Vigilantius*, 1. Cf. Jonas' quotations from this work in *PL*, 106, 310B and C; 327B; 352C; 371D; 378D; 382C; Richer I, 3.

[23] Carlsruhe Aug. 94; Laon 266; Lyons 602, foll. 95–142; Paris, Bibl. Nat. 13354 (from Corbie).

[24] The text of the letters, edited by Hilberg, will be found in vols. 54–56 of *CSEL*.

[25] E.g., Milan, Ambros. Libr. O 210 sup.; Leningrad Q.V. 9 and 10; Verona XVII (15); Naples VI.D.59, all of the sixth century. Also Ghent 246 (7th c.) and the Orléans fragment of the same date (MS. 192, foll. 29–30).

[26] Cf., for instance, chapters III–VI of Miss Beryl Smalley's book, *The Study of the Bible in the Middle Ages* (Oxford, 1941).

[27] Cf. Martin Grabmann, *Geschichte der scholastischen Methode*, II, pp. 141ff., and particularly, Heinrich Weissweiler, S.J., *Das Schrifttum der Schule Anselms von Laon und Wilhelms von Champeaux in deutschen Bibliotheken* (Münster i.W., 1936), p. 102.

[28] See Harry Caplan in *Publications of the Modern Language Association of America* 48 (1933), pp. 345ff.

[29] Cf. M. R. James, *The Ancient Libraries of Canterbury and Dover* (Cambridge, Eng., 1903), pp. 38–40 and 219–221.

[30] See R. A. B. Mynors, *Durham Cathedral Manuscripts* (Oxford, 1939), No. 68 with Plate 42 in colored reproduction.

[31] Karl Künstle, *Ikonographie der christlichen Kunst*, II, pp. 299ff.

[32] Cf. W. A. Oldfather et al., *Studies in the Text Tradition of St. Jerome's Vitae Patrum* (University of Illinois, 1943), pp. 4–5; 11–17.

St. Jerome and the Canon of the Holy Scriptures

PATRICK W. SKEHAN

St. Jerome and the Canon of the Holy Scriptures

TWO DEVELOPMENTS of recent years in the Latin Church for which St. Jerome wrote mark both a final victory for his approach to Biblical studies, and by the same token the recession, for the first time in a millennium, of the direct influence of his Vulgate version. The new Latin psalter approved for the public prayer of the Church [1] can be said with confidence to be the most accurate reflection of the complete sense of the original *Psalms* that has been available for public prayer since the second century B.C. It is based on the Hebrew text, critically appraised, and it therefore reduces the influence of the Septuagint rendering at a point where the weight of tradition was too strong for St. Jerome himself. The explicit endorsement of vernacular versions based directly on the original languages of the Old and New Testaments [2] for private reading represents a renewal in our day of the endeavor of St. Jerome to secure that the current Biblical texts derive as directly as possible from the main source.

At a time when the Vulgate, particularly for the Old Testament, seems likely to become more and more a scholar's tool, and less the received Scriptures of everyday use, it may seem ungrateful to devote a special article, not to some phase of the fifteen-hundred-year reign of that remarkable version, but to the one point on which the Church has not followed the formal teaching of her greatest Scriptural Doctor, namely, his presentation of the canon of the Holy Scriptures. Yet the writings of St. Jerome contain so much that is informative for the historical setting in which the canon of the Scriptures received its final formulation by the Church that the subject can hardly be passed over. And in the familiar distinction between his theory and his practice with regard to the canon, there are remarkable instances of his docility toward the voice and practice of the Church, the more exemplary when we find them in one who could be, when the occasion demanded, an intransigent controversialist.

We can begin with what may be termed the precritical period of St. Jerome's writings, which extends beyond his final settlement in the East (hence approximately A.D. 374–390). During these years the source of St. Jerome's Scriptural citations is substantially the Old Latin version as it was current in Italy at that time. Certain favorite texts are selected which are to be found recurring again and again as often as the occasion seems to call for them, throughout the remainder of Jerome's life. Among these, some are drawn from books of the Bible which he later questioned or rejected, at least in theory. These are a testimony to the practice of the Latin churches known to St. Jerome in his youth, and they are in favor of a wider canon than he would later admit. The impress of his early training never wore off completely. There is something of a parallel with his attitude toward the classics; so that when he is citing sources, whether religious or profane, he constantly falls back on values gained in his youth, even though these run counter to the more rigid and narrower theory which he sets up for the guidance of others in his mature age. In addition to the formal citation of texts, through the constant Biblical allusions of this earliest period there run a number that rest on Old Testament narratives which he later excludes, sometimes very emphatically, from the canonical writings.

In the class of favored quotations we may remark a text used by St. Jerome for the first time in his letter (*Ep.* 22) to Eustochium in the spring of A.D. 384. To characterize the married state as one which meets with divine approval he cites *Hebrews* 13:4, "Let marriage be held in honor with all, and let the marriage bed be undefiled." Since this assumes the sanctity of marriage, and since in its Greek and Latin forms [3] it can be taken as a categorical statement as well as a precept, it is used in the former sense by St. Jerome. It was evidently a standard quotation before his time for use against the Montanists and Manicheans. Despite the later reflection by St. Jerome of contemporary doubts about the *Epistle to the Hebrews,* he never forgoes the use of this text. In the controversy with Jovinian (A.D. 393) he not only acknowledges its use by his opponent (*adv. Jovin.* I, 5), but accepts it himself (*ibid.,* 3; *Ep.* 48, 2). He cites it as Scripture (*Ep.* 69, 4) in A.D. 398; accepts it again (*Ep.* 79, 10) and quotes "the Apostle" for it (*Ep.* 66, 3) in other writings of about the same period. It recurs (*Ep.* 130, 12) in A.D. 414.

Similar treatment is accorded the section of the *Book of Wisdom* (4:8–14) which opposes the attributes of age and wisdom, and makes the latter quality a compensation for brevity of earthly life in those who die young. We first meet with this in a letter (39, 3) of consolation addressed to Paula late in A.D. 384. Its language is appropriate to soften the poignancy of her grief at the death of her daughter Blesilla. A later letter (54, 2: A.D. 394–5) uses *Wisdom* 4:13 in referring to this same death. The death of the young Nepotian calls forth (A.D. 396) a letter of sympathy in which parts of the same text are twice employed (*Ep.* 60, 2, 10).[4] In A.D. 399 a letter (75, 2) to Theodora consoles her for the loss of her husband, with "For, as it is written in a book of Wisdom" to introduce our text. In this letter, no quotation of any secular writer is in evidence. From about the same time comes the very similar letter to Salvina, in which (79, 2, 6) the same passage is again twice drawn upon for its consoling value. Another favorite text from the *Book of Wisdom* is *Wis.* 6:6 (7), *quia potentes potenter tormenta patientur.* We first meet with it in letter 14, from A.D. 376–7. It turns up in the commentaries on *Ecclesiastes* (I., *PL,* 23, 1023: c. A.D. 387), *Ephesians* (III., *PL,* 26, 515 A.D. 387–89?), and *Sophonias* (*ad Soph.* 3:8–9, *PL,* 25, 1379: A.D. 389–92?). It recurs in a context where it is selected for its controversial value, in the treatise against Jovinian (II, 25; A.D. 393). It is used again (*Ep.* 78, 25) in the summer of A.D. 400; and an adaptation of it in conjunction with

Luke 12:48 is to be found in the commentary on *Jeremias* (III. 11, A.D. 414–?).

The fact of St. Jerome's use of "deuterocanonical" texts during the early period is familiar enough. We have no statement from him at this time on the question of the canon. Had he been pressed to give one, it is hard to see how it could have differed much from the lists adopted at Hippo (A.D. 393)[5] and Carthage (A.D. 396, 419), or that of Pope Innocent I (A.D. 405). If he does not cite *Baruch*, for example, this can as easily be viewed as accidental as its omission in the lists, where it is apparently true that the book was looked upon as a sort of appendix to Jeremias. What is characteristic of this period is Jerome's unhesitating acceptance of books and parts of books which he later quite definitely rejects. A first such instance is his letter 1, 9 (A.D. 374) in which *Susanna* and the *Hymn of the Three Children* are alluded to along with *Daniel*. Letter 3, 1 (A.D. 375) speaks of Habacuc on the basis of the Bel narrative; this is repeated in letter 22, 9 (A.D. 384). Such texts are not used for their precise wording, but St. Jerome appeals to circumstances of the narrative for which he found accommodative applications. He includes like references to II *Macc.* 7 (*Ep.* 7, 6; A.D. 375–6), Susanna again (*Ep.* 14, 9, A.D. 376–7; also *contra Helvidium* 4, in A.D. 383) and Judith (*Ep.* 22, 21; A.D. 384). A curious parallel comes in his acceptance of Thecla (*Ep.* 22, 41), whose story he later repudiates in *de viris illustribus* 7 (see the citation below). Before A.D. 385 *Tobias* is not used, nor, rather surprisingly, is *Ecclesiasticus*, which we encounter fairly often later on. Both these latter books are employed in the commentary on *Ecclesiastes* (c. A.D. 387): *Tobias* 12:7 (*PL*, 23, 1074), *Ecclus.* 1:33 (*ibid.*, 1084), and *Ecclus.* 27:29 (*ibid.*, 1094), the latter as by *ipse Salomon*.

The "precritical" period we have thus far been considering can be said to end abruptly only in the sense that our evidence becomes obscure some time after St. Jerome's final journey to the East. The gap of seven years between the 45th and the 46th of his collected letters, combined with the nature of his literary work between A.D. 386 and A.D. 392—much of it is compilatory in character, or is translation work—makes it difficult to follow directly and in clear temporal sequence the transformation which led up to the statements in the *"Prologus galeatus"* and in *de viris illustribus.*

Howorth dates the change in St. Jerome's attitude on the canon to 390 or 391; and he sees in this change an effect of Jewish influence (which in part it surely is), possibly connected with St. Jerome's conflict with the partisans of Origen's heretical views.[6] For this second explanation there is a chronological difficulty, in that the outbreak of the Origenistic controversy for St. Jerome dates to A.D. 393. Also there is no likely link between the question of the canon and the opposition to Origen; the more so as Origen's direct formulation of the canon of the Old Testament is actually the narrow, Jewish one which St. Jerome now comes to accept. A date about A.D. 390 for St. Jerome's change of view on the canon can be inferred from the fact that neither the commentary on *Ecclesiastes*, already referred to, nor those on *Ephesians, Galatians, Titus* and *Philomen* (c. A.D. 387–89) show any hesitations regarding the "deuterocanonical" testimonies they allege.[7] In the series of commentaries on *Micheas, Nahum, Habacuc, Sophonias, Aggeus* (c. 389–392), the practice in citations remains much the same as in the earlier works;[8] but for the first time the prologue to the commentary on *Habacuc* leaves the canonicity of the "Bel and the Dragon" narratives (*Daniel* 14, Vulg.) an open question.[9] This seems to be the only documentation for the idea of a more limited canon in the period leading up to *de viris illustribus* (A.D. 392–3), apart from the prefaces themselves to *Jeremias, Daniel* and *Samuel*.

We shall now examine the standard references to St. Jerome's formal teaching on the canon; then we shall try to account for that teaching as a consequence of the trend of his own personal studies, while taking note of how the teaching, once given, affected St. Jerome's own practice and the attitude of his friends. For comprehensive statements regarding the canon, we have three to draw upon. They are not, as will be seen, entirely consistent; and the first applies only to the Old Testament. It is contained in the "*Prologus galeatus*," or *Praefatio in libros Samuel et Mala-chim*, and it lists the Biblical books as follows:

Genesis, Exodus, Leviticus, Numbers, Deuteronomy; Josue, Judges, Ruth, Samuel (1, 2), *Kings* (3, 4), *Isaias, Jeremias, Ezechiel,* 12 *Minor Prophets; Job, Psalms, Proverbs, Ecclesiastes, Canticle of Canticles, Daniel, Paralipomenon* (1, 2), *Esdras* (1, 2), *Esther.*

Then comes a general statement that anything else is apocryphal, that is, non-canonical (*ut scire valeamus, quidquid extra hos est, inter apocrypha esse ponendum*). This is followed by an explicit rejection (*Igitur . . . non sunt in canone*) of *Wisdom, Sirach* (*Ecclus.*), *Judith, Tobias* and the *Shepherd*(!), and it is said that the first, but not the second, book of *Maccabees* is to be found in Hebrew. The dating of this testimony is subject to some doubt, both for an absolute date (surely before A.D. 393), and relatively to the translation of other Old Testament books. Cavallera,[10] arguing from the language of the preface to *Isaias*, places the work on the Prophets first, and supposes that the rendering of *Samuel* (and its prologue) follows these. Stummer [11] opposes to this the language of the preface to *Samuel-Kings*, and concludes for the priority of that section and therefore of our list. As will be seen in what follows, Cavallera's order appears more plausible to the present writer.

The second general testimony is that in letter 53, to Paulinus, from July of A.D. 395 (Cavallera). The books here named are:

Genesis, Exodus, Leviticus, Numbers, Deuteronomy, Job, Josue, Judges, Ruth, Samuel (1, 2), *Kings* (3, 4), 12 *Minor Prophets* (in the Hebrew and Vulgate order), *Isaias, Jeremias, Ezechiel, Daniel, Psalms, Proverbs, Ecclesiastes, Canticle of Canticles, Esther, Paralipomenon, Esdras-Nehemias.* New Testament: *Matthew, Mark, Luke, John; Epistles of Paul* (to seven churches, to *Titus,* to *Timothy,* to *Philemon; Hebrews* is left doubtful [12]); *Acts;* 7 *Epistles of James, Peter, John, Jude; Apocalypse of John.*

The list is concluded with an exhortation to Paulinus to make these books the sole preoccupation of his life (*inter haec vivere, ista meditari, nihil aliud nosse, nihil quaerere*).

The third list is in the letter (107) to Laeta, from the period A.D. 400–402. One section (12) gives the books of the Holy Scriptures in the order in which St. Jerome recommends that they be read and studied by a growing child who has been dedicated by her parents to a life of virginity. Hence no inference is to be drawn from the order of the books; and indeed, the only point regarding the canon which can safely be derived from this text is that St. Jerome was consistent in maintaining at this time the general position outlined for the Old Testament in the two earlier statements. He says:

Let her first learn the Psalter, devoting herself to these songs only, and let her be trained for life from the *Proverbs* of Solomon. From *Ecclesiastes* let her grow accustomed to spurn worldly things; let her follow the examples of patience and virtue in *Job*. Let her go on to the Gospels, and then never let them out of her hands; let her drink in the *Acts of the Apostles* and the Epistles with wholehearted eagerness. And when she has enriched the storehouse of her breast with this wealth, let her commit to memory the *Prophets*, the *Heptateuch*, the *Books of Kings* and *Paralipomenon*, and the scrolls of *Esdras* and *Esther*; then at last she may without danger learn the *Canticle of Canticles*—lest if she read it at the first she should be injured by not discerning the bridal-song of the marriage of the spirit under its fleshly words. But let her avoid all the apocrypha; and if she will read them occasionally not for the truth of their teaching, but to show respect for the miracles they describe, let her know they were not composed by those whose names are given in the titles, there is much mixed in with them that is faulty, and it is a task for great prudence to seek gold in the mud.

Apart from the absence of the "deuterocanonical" Old Testament books, we may notice certain other features of this list. *Ruth* is presumably to be included with *Judges* and hence in the "*Heptateuch*." *Samuel* is included under *Kings*. *Daniel* (but not *Baruch*) is undoubtedly to be classed under the Prophets. In the New Testament, the position of *Hebrews* is not made plain; and we miss any mention of the *Apocalypse*, though this is probably not deliberate.[13]

As between the *prologus galeatus* and the letter to Paulinus, it will be noted that the former gives the Hebrew canon of the Old Testament uncompromisingly and in an arrangement solidly supported by Jewish tradition. The latter makes no change as regards the number of Old Testament books to be included; and the presence of *Job* after the Mosaic books finds warrant from Jewish and Syrian sources. But the grouping of the Prophets is a concession to the influence of the Septuagint tradition in two respects: the presence of the *Minor Prophets* at the beginning, and the inclusion of *Daniel* in this category at the end. Among Greek writers, these same features are found combined in St. Jerome's friend Epiphanius; [14] and several features of the same arrangement are suggested again by the letter to Laeta (note also the position of *Esdras* and *Esther*). There is, then, on the part of St. Jerome, a willingness to let the Septuagint tradition influence his theoretical position, within limits. The letter to Paulinus shows that even when he is laying down a theory based on the Hebrew, he will accord to material drawn from the Greek a substantially equal recognition in practice. He says for example:

Daniel, at the end of his most holy vision, says that the just will shine like the stars and those with understanding, that is the learned, like the firmament. You see what a difference there is between the justice of the unlettered and that of the learned. The one group are compared to the stars, the others to heaven—though according to the *hebraica veritas* both can be understood of the scholarly, for as they have it we read . . .

The final quotation is from the Vulgate and the Hebrew; but the argument is based on the text of Theodotion, as that used for *Daniel* by the Church. The same citation had been used without qualification to convey the same distinction in his *Commentary on the Epistle to the Ephesians* (A.D. 387–89?), in the words introducing book III (*PL*, 26, 515).

With regard to the position of St. Jerome on the canon of the New Testament, the letter to Paulinus leaves little room for questioning. Its testimony is later than the *de viris illustribus* (A.D. 392–93). The latter has a whole series of indications, in its first nine articles, which might lead us to expect a denial by St. Jerome of canonical status to a number of New Testament books. Some of these articles worked their way into Vulgate manuscripts as prefaces to the books to which they refer. This furnished a basis for later writers to question the canonicity of *James* or *Hebrews*, for example, down to the sixteenth century. The articles (9:18) bearing on the Epistles of John were not used in the Biblical codices. In the order in which they appear in the *de viris illustribus*, the pertinent passages are as follows:

1. Simon Peter . . . wrote two epistles known as catholic epistles; the second of these is said by many (*plerisque*) not to have him for its author, in view of its divergence from the style of the first. (There follows an indication of Peter's connection with the Gospel of Mark, and then a formal rejection of the Gospel of Peter and a group of similar books—*inter apocryphas scripturas repudiantur.*)

2. James, called the brother of the Lord . . . wrote a single epistle, which is among the seven catholic epistles. Of this it is affirmed that it was published by someone else under his name, though gradually, in the course of time, it has secured recognition.

4. Jude, the brother of James, left a short epistle which is among the seven catholic epistles. And because in it he takes a quotation from the book of Enoch, which is apocryphal, it is rejected by many (*plerisque*). However, its antiquity and the use made of it have earned it recognition and it is counted among the Holy Scriptures.

5. Paul . . . wrote nine letters to seven churches . . . and to his disciples, two to Timothy, one to Titus, one to Philemon. But the epistle known as "to the Hebrews" is believed not to be his, because of its divergent style and diction. (Here Jerome enumerates Barnabas, Luke, Clement, and Paul himself writing anonymously, as possible authors. Pursuing this last possibility, he adds—) Himself a Hebrew, he had written fluently in Hebrew, his own language; in consequence, what had been eloquently written in the Hebrew was rendered more eloquently into Greek. This they allege to be the reason why the Epistle is seemingly different from the other epistles of Paul. There is also on record an Epistle to the Laodiceans, but it is rejected by everybody.

6. Barnabas . . . wrote one Epistle, for the edification of the Church, which is current among the apocryphal writings.

7. Luke . . . wrote a Gospel . . . also . . . The Acts of the Apostles . . . Therefore the Journeys of Paul and Thecla . . . we reckon among the apocryphal writings.

9. John . . . wrote a Gospel . . . also one Epistle . . . which is accepted by all informed churchmen. The other two . . . are said to be the work of John the Presbyter, for whom a separate burial-place is pointed out in Ephesus at the present time, though some think that there are two memorials of this same John the Evangelist. In the four-teenth year then after Nero . . . he wrote the Apocalypse. (The 'John the Presbyter' story is given on the authority of Papias, who is then quoted for it in the article (18) devoted to Papias' own writ-ings.)

The *de viris illustribus* is of course a compilatory writing.[15] In outlining in controversy with Rufinus his view of the function of a commentator, St. Jerome maintains (*adv. Rufin.*, I, 16) the right of the commentator to set forth divergent and opposing views, with the reasons alleged for them, so that the "prudent reader" may make his own choice. It is evidently a similar policy he follows in the present instance, when he draws on Eusebius and others for his account of the first generation of Christian writers. In addition, his discussion of the *Epistle to the Hebrews* in letter 129 (see below) makes it altogether clear that the ques-tions of authenticity and canonicity were understood by St. Jerome to be susceptible of independent treatment. Moreover, during this same period, St. Jerome included in his *Liber de nominibus hebraicis* the proper names which occur in *Hebrews, James, 2 John, Jude* and the *Apocalypse* (though also those of the *Epistle of Barnabas*). In the Old Testament part of this same work, only the "protocanonical" books are dealt with, though the names occurring in the "deuterocanonical" parts of *Daniel* are included. In the preface, St. Jerome declared he had "gone through the individual books in the Scriptural order."

Not only during the "precritical" period of St. Jerome's writing, but throughout his entire literary career he makes use, as canon-ical Scriptures, of the New Testament books according to the list in the letter to Paulinus; and in addition, whatever doubt he there casts on the *Epistle to the Hebrews* is cleared up by most emphatic personal affirmation later on. The extent of use varies, naturally; and for the *III Epistle of John* we should have to appeal to letter 146 of St. Jerome, whose date is unknown. The *II Epistle* of St. John is cited under the apostle's name in the same letter 146, in letter 123, 8 (A.D. 409), and in the *Commentary on Aggeus,* II, 1ff., from about the same time as *de viris illustribus* itself. But from the treatments of Peter, James, and Jude in the latter work, as well as from the *Liber de nominibus hebraicis,* we learn that St. Jerome acknowledges a collection of *seven* Catholic Epistles; and the more frequent references to *James, II Peter* and *Jude* make it plain that he treats the collection as canonical without distinction. In *adversus Jovinianum* I, 39, a long extract from *II Peter* is cited in controversy, in the year A.D. 393.

To confine ourselves for the rest to St. Jerome's later writings, we may cite the following: *James* 2:10 is explained, as from "James the Apostle," in *adversus Pelagianos* I, 19 (A.D. 415); and a whole series of testimonies drawn from the same Epistle are to be found *ibid.,* II, 5, 13, 15, 18, 19, 23; III, 14. *Jude* 8 is quoted as from *apostolus Judas* in *Commentarius in Hieremiam,* V, 64 (A.D. 414–?). *II Peter* 2:19 is quoted *ibid.,* I, 23; [16] III, 62. Finally, from letter 140, 8 (A.D. 414, Cavallera) we note that the question of authenticity and that of canonicity are kept separate, for in preparing for a citation of *II Peter* 3:8–9, introduced by *scribit autem Petrus hoc modo,* Jerome tells us the text is taken *ex epistula quae nomine Petri apostoli scribitur,* which at least modifies the concept of St. Peter's authorship.

For the *Epistle to the Hebrews* we need not multiply citations; it was always a favorite source with St. Jerome. The key passage is in letter 129, 3 (A.D. 414) wherein we find: "The Vessel of Election says to the Hebrews," followed by a summary of most of chapter XI of the Epistle. The authority of this source is then discussed as follows:

For our own people, let this be said: this Epistle written to the Hebrews is accepted as of the Apostle Paul, not only by the churches of the East, but by all church writers of the past in the Greek language, though many (*plerique*) think it to be of Barnabas or of

Clement. And it makes no difference whose it is, since it is by a churchman and is honored in the daily reading of the churches. But if Latin usage does not receive it among the canonical Scriptures, neither do the churches of the Greeks accept the *Apocalypse* of John with equal readiness; yet we accept both, following in this not at all the present usage, but the authority of the ancient writers, who for the most part make use of citations from both, not as they are wont to do occasionally for the apocrypha—in fact they use illustrations even from pagan literature, though rarely—but as canonical church texts.

When we pass to the question of St. Jerome's treatment of the Old Testament canon during the period following the *Prologus galeatus*, we find that the two books *adversus Jovinianum* and the *Apologeticus ad Pammachium* (*Ep.* 48–49) which is connected with them (A.D. 393) show us a practice hardly different from that of the earlier period. A favorite quotation from *Wisdom* 6:6 (7) has already been mentioned as occurring here. In addition we find that the freeing of Susanna is given (*adv. Jovin.*, I, 25) as a possible reason why *Daniel* was already well known (to Ezechiel, cf. *Ezech.* 14:14–20) as a young man. It is by no means surprising that *Proverbs* should be quoted freely from the Septuagint, since St. Jerome's own rendering of this book from the Hebrew had not yet been made. But in *adversus Jovinianum* II. 2. 4 *Job* also is quoted extensively according to the Septuagint,[17] although in *Ep.* 49, 14, *Job* 18:14–15 is given according to the Vulgate. In *adversus Jovinianum* II, 3 we have *Ecclus.* 27:6 and 2:1. The episode of Habacuc bringing food to Daniel is cited *ibid.* II, 15, though with a qualification (*licet hoc in hebraicis voluminibus non invenerimus*). *Wisdom* 1:11 is cited *ibid.*, II, 31. And Esther's prayer is used (*Esther* 14:11, Vulg.), from the Septuagint tradition of course, in *Apologeticus ad Pammachium, Ep.* 49, 14, just as it had been cited earlier in *Comm. in Ep. ad Galatas* (see note 7, above). The use of *Isaias* 38:19 according to the Septuagint in *adversus Jovinianum* I, 5 and 25 is of a different character, since it is in effect an *argumentum ad hominem*, and the difference from the Hebrew is noted.

Let us now ask ourselves, if the practice remains so little changed both for the use of the Septuagint generally, and for the citation of its "deuterocanonical" books, what motive underlay St. Jerome's theoretical acceptance of what is in fact a Jewish Old Testament canon? It is often said, and Rufinus said it among the first, that Jewish influence was responsible. This is, of course, true as far as it goes; but it is not always made clear on what basis the Jewish influence made itself felt. That St. Jerome had an apologetic purpose in view in relation to the Jews is brought out in a number of passages. As a Christian priest, it was his responsibility to place the claims of Christ before his Jewish neighbors as well as before all other men. But since the Jews possessed the Scriptures of the Old Testament in their original language, they could not be expected to acknowledge those claims unless they were founded on the text they knew and treasured. The Christian claiming to possess the Scriptures could hardly enter with profit into discussion of Christian teaching with a believing Jew unless he could found his arguments on a revealed source acknowledged by both. This is brought out in more than one passage. It is the whole basis for the preparation of the *Psalterium juxta hebraeos*, which was called forth by the actual difficulties of Jerome's friend Sophronius in attempting to quote the Psalter in such discussions. "It is one thing," says St. Jerome, "to recite the Psalms in the churches of those who believe in Christ; but another thing to reply to the Jews who cavil at each separate word." [18] The same motive is alleged in the preface to *Isaias*: "(Christ) knows that I have sweated over the learning of a foreign tongue to this end, that the Jews may no longer mock His churches for the falsity of their Scriptures." It has also been suspected that when St. Jerome takes over the formula for describing the "deuterocanonical" books as *ad aedificationem plebis*, he uses the term by contrast to books which can be used as authority in establishing the truth of Christian doctrine for the Jews in particular. This cannot be the entire scope of such statements,[19] but it is clear that such a preoccupation was in his mind during this time.

What further explanation for St. Jerome's change of position may be required is to be derived, in the present writer's opinion, from the nature of the Septuagint text itself with which he had to deal in his Old Testament studies. In his preface to the Four Gospels, dating from the spring of A.D. 384, St. Jerome outlines an attitude toward the text which is quite different from his theory at a later date. He speaks of the *Graeca . . . veritate* of the New Testament, in the same fashion as later he will stress the *Hebraica veritas* of the Old. "Nor am I discussing," he continues, "the Old Testament which the Seventy elders translated into Greek and which comes to us at second hand. . . . Let that be the true interpretation, which the Apostles approved." The restriction that Latins have the Septuagint at second hand is the only one he makes on the authenticity and dependability of that version. This attitude toward the Septuagint is reflected again in the preface to the books of *Paralipomenon* (from the Greek), addressed to Domnio and Rogatianus (A.D. 389–92?). Here we are told that the barbarous corruption of proper names to be found in the Latin codices of these books was due to the fault of copyists, and was "not to be ascribed to the Seventy translators, who, filled with the Holy Spirit, rendered what was true." The function of the *obelus* is to introduce what the Seventy interpreters have added to the Hebrew text "either for the sake of ornament or on the authority of the Holy Spirit." Something of this attitude still survives in the later preface (A.D. 396) to the rendering of the same books of *Paralipomenon* from the Hebrew: "If the edition of the Seventy interpreters were still current in its pristine form as they rendered it into Greek, you would not have reason to urge me, my dear Chromatius, most holy and learned of bishops, to render the Hebrew scrolls into Latin." The point is then made that the Septuagint text current in his day is not in all cases the text of the Apostles, and with a reference to his letter (57) *de optimo genere interpretandi* this is supported by instances which go beyond the books of *Paralipomenon* and leave the question open for the entire Old Testament. The letter itself (A.D. 395) both limits the Apostles' use of the Septuagint to cases where the latter does not disagree with the Hebrew, and speaks of the great number of additions and omissions with which the Septuagint can be charged.

But before A.D. 393, St. Jerome had already finished an undertaking which could scarcely fail to undermine his confidence in the right of even the primitive Septuagint text to be considered adequate for all the books of the Old Testament. In his preface to the *Comm. in Ecclesiasten* (*PL*, 23, 1009–12) he indicates as follows the manner in which he then (up to c. A.D. 387) built up his text for that book:

I note, briefly, that I have followed no one's authority, but in translating from the Hebrew I have adapted myself to a great extent to the usage of the Seventy Translators in those points at least which were not very different from the Hebrew. Occasionally too I have made reference to Aquila, Symmachus and Theodotion, so as neither to discourage the reader's interest by excessive novelty, nor on the other hand to forsake the source of truth against my own conscience and follow the streamlets of opinion.

This would be all very well for a book like *Ecclesiastes*, in which the Septuagint rendering is late, hence somewhat slavish, and not very far removed from the Hebrew text. But the making of a fairly literal rendering from the Hebrew for other Old Testament books would soon show by experience that the Septuagint is a very fallible guide indeed. And we can find traces of this experience recorded in the successive prefaces which he composed to the four Major Prophets.

We may surmise that in the beginning St. Jerome conceived of his task in rendering the Old Testament from the Hebrew as being one of providing a standard against which the existing Latin renderings might be measured, so that men of Latin speech could discern, without the need of recourse to either Greek or Hebrew, the state of their own codices, and which of these had truly a claim to represent the original. In fact the preface to *Isaias* says little more than this: "Nevertheless, as the Greeks read Aquila, Symmachus and Theodotion after the Seventy Translators, either out of a desire for their teaching or so as to understand the Septuagint the more by comparison with them, so I ask my dissatisfied readers that they too will deign to have at least one interpreter after their earlier ones." There is no particular reason to suppose that St. Jerome's attitude toward the Septuagint during the earliest years of his final stay in Palestine was in any essential way different from that of St. Augustine. The latter made a special point of urging his far-away correspondent to keep to that venerable version as the basis of his work, and thereby to restore a *"Latina veritas"*; while at the same time he conceded in language which can in no way be improved upon even with the perspectives of today, to what an extent the Latin texts then in circulation were confused and untrustworthy: "The Latin text in different codices is divergent to an almost insufferable degree, and so suspect of not being in harmony with the Greek that one hesitates to quote or to argue from it at all." [20] In fact, of course, the divergence between the Old Latin and the fourth-century Greek codices was not always to the disadvantage of the former; but this, had it been noted, could hardly have lessened the confusion.

Origen was committed to the criticism and repair of the Septuagint for the very reason that he wrote in Greek for a Greek world; and that abundant materials lay ready to his hand for the work of comparison and restoration, in the later Greek versions which (especially that of "Theodotion") he freely employed. St. Jerome at first followed in the footsteps of Origen, his guide in the technique of textual criticism: and in both the *Psalterium gallicanum* and his rendering of *Job* from the Greek it was essentially a Hexaplaric text which he put into Latin. This will undoubtedly have been true also of the rest of his revision based on the Septuagint, which has perished. The case of *Job* must have been a particularly striking experience for the sage of Bethlehem. From what he tells us in his preface to Job from the Hebrew we can see that the only Latin text known to him before his own activities was a pre-hexaplaric text of that book; for it lacked some seven or eight hundred lines, and was "shortened, slashed and corroded." Yet even when he found himself called upon to fill up gaps of this sort as Origen had done—and St. Jerome must have recognized that the inserts were Theodotionic in character—we do not find him affirming that the defect is traceable to the original Greek Septuagint translators. Nor is it necessary to suppose that at this point he was maintaining a prudential silence in the face of his critics. Discovery of the basic weakness and of the quite uneven character of the Septuagint would come rather from a direct and full knowledge of the Hebrew text than from study centered on the Hexapla; and, as has been said, in the prefaces to the Major Prophets from the Hebrew we can trace the progress of this discovery on St. Jerome's part.

What is said of the limitations of the Septuagint text in the preface to Isaias cannot be regarded merely as a rhetorical device to prepare the reader for surprising differences in the new Latin rendering from the Hebrew. The Septuagint translators are thought to have observed a kind of *disciplina arcani* in view of the clear presentation by Isaias of the mysteries of Christ and His Church. "And so I surmise that the Seventy Interpreters were in their day unwilling to disclose the mysteries of their faith clearly to the gentiles, lest they should 'give what is holy to the dogs, and pearls to swine'—for when you read this edition you will see that they hid these mysteries." There is no suggestion in this of the basic fact that the Greek translator of *Isaias* was simply unequal, in many ways, to the task he had set himself. The premise accepted by St. Jerome that the Septuagint was in some sense produced under the influence of the Holy Spirit hardly leaves room for admission of such a fact before all alternatives have been exhausted.

In the preface to *Jeremias*, our attention is called to the "altogether confused order of the visions among the Greeks and Latins," by contrast with the Hebrew; and to the fact that the Hebrews have not the book of *Baruch*. For *Ezechiel*, however, we are told in its preface: "The current edition of it is not very different from the Hebrew. Therefore I rather wonder what the reason was, if we have the same translators in all the books, for their translating in some books the same elements, in others, different ones." Here we have clearly implied a divergent value for the Greek (and the dependent Latin) renderings of the different books; and this critical approach, which now shows clearly for the first time, is accentuated in the preface to *Daniel*. In the latter we read: "The churches of our Lord and Savior do not read the prophet Daniel according to the Seventy Translators, but use the edition of Theodotion. Why this has happened, I do not know. Whether, because its diction is Aramaic and differs in some of its characteristics from our manner of speech, the Seventy Inter- preters were unwilling to preserve the same sentence-structure in translation; or whether the book was made public in their name by some unknown person whose knowledge of Aramaic was in- adequate; or whether there was some other reason, I know not. This only I can say, that it is considerably out of harmony with the true text, and the judgement that rejected it was correct." Here, then, is the discovery which St. Augustine, for instance, was never in a position to make; and here we may find the most pro- found motive for St. Jerome's loss of confidence in the Greek translation.

The only secure basis, therefore, for an authentic text, becomes the *Hebraica veritas*; not merely because the Greek codices, like the Latin, disagree among themselves, but because whole books are to be found in which the Septuagint rendering is inadequate. There is then left only one final court of appeal. This, too, is said explicitly, in *Ep.* 71, 5 (A.D. 398): "For as the dependability of the Old Testament books must be tested by reference to the Hebrew scrolls, so that of the New Testament books calls for their Greek text as the norm." If this is true for the nature of the text, it is easy to employ the same principle to determine what books and parts of books the text should properly include, and thus to formulate a criterion of canonicity. It is true that St. Jerome was in a position to secure Semitic texts, some of them presumably originals, even for certain "deuterocanonical" writings: *Ecclesi- asticus, I Maccabees, Tobias, Judith*. Of these, however, at least *Ecclus.* and *Tobias*, when confronted with the available Greek texts and Latin codices, must necessarily have engendered doubts as to how the different traditions were to be reconciled; and since he could get no guarantee from those who supplied him with his Semitic texts for these books, their position was not really different from that of *Wisdom*, or *Baruch*, or *II Maccabees*. St. Jerome therefore builds up an academic theory, based on Jewish practice and on academic testimonies, as to the extent of the canon. In the preface to *Esdras* and *Nehemias* (A.D. 394), he defends this theory on the ground we have indicated as basic:

And let no one be disturbed because we publish this as a single book, nor let anyone revel in the dreams of third and fourth *Esdras*, for in the Hebrew copies too, the words of *Esdras* and *Nehemias* are confined to a single scroll; and what is not contained in the Hebrew, or numbered among the twenty-four Elders,[21] is to be altogether rejected. And should one appeal to the Seventy translators against you —the copies of whose work prove by their very diversity that they have been slashed and destroyed, for what is in discord surely cannot be declared true—send him to the Gospels, in which many passages are cited as from the Old Testament which the Septuagint translation does not contain . . .

Once this theory has been enunciated, it is maintained consistently, as the preface to the Solomonic books (see note 19, above) and the letter to Laeta indicate.

Throughout his work of translating from the Hebrew, St. Jerome had constantly to defend himself against the charge of working to the prejudice of the Septuagint and its Latin derivatives. His reply to this was an unvarying denial; and he had very strong evidence to support his position. First of all, he had himself been responsible for a complete revision of the Old Latin rendering on the basis of the Hexaplaric Greek text. Secondly, he was able to assert, both in his preface to *Paralipomenon* from the Hebrew (A.D. 396),[22] and in his apology against Rufinus (A.D. 401),[23] that the Greek tradition regularly formed the basis of his instructions and sermons in his own monastery.[24] In addition, his commentaries on the Prophets make it a regular practice to furnish not only the new Vulgate, but also the Septuagint understanding of a given passage; and the longest reflections, along with the spiritual applications, are often built upon the Septuagint form of text. Once, indeed, the choice of material from the Septuagint is a calculated procedure—the third book of the apology against Rufinus opens with two citations from *Proverbs* and a third from *Isaias*; the first and third are from the Septuagint, the second from the Vulgate. Then at the end (43) of the work, St. Jerome proceeds to belabor his opponent with a chain of forty quotations from *Proverbs* according to the Septuagint. But the obviously controversial motive behind this procedure is altogether exceptional; and when the language of the older version comes to the Saint's lips or pen during these later years, even in passages taken from the rejected books and sections, it is clearly as something long known and loved, and chosen for its own sake.

Yet despite this continuing use of the Septuagint, and despite the need for great care in the expression of any criticism of that rendering which his enemies might pounce upon, St. Jerome does make it plain that his estimate of the version has changed radically. In the preface to *Paralipomenon* (A.D. 396) we find rejected one of the elaborations on the story of how the Septuagint was composed:

If then it was lawful for others not to hold to those [the Seventy translators] whom they had once received, and if after the seventy separate cells which are popularly referred to on no one's authority, they have each opened cells of their own, and the result is read in the churches, why should not my Latin brethren receive me, who without doing any violence to the older version have so prepared my new one that I can guarantee my result on the authority of the Hebrews, and what is more, of the Apostles.

Rufinus, in his own *Apology*, II, 33 (A.D. 400), says, "The Seventy-two translators, each in his separate cell, produced a single, consistent version, under the inspiration, as we cannot doubt, of the Holy Spirit." Not only the first part, but by implication the last as well, of this statement is directly countered in Jerome's preface to *Genesis*, which he introduces into his reply, *Apol. Adv. Rufin.*, II, 25:

I do not know who was first responsible for setting up the lie about seventy separate cells at Alexandria in which [the translators] are supposed to have put together an identical text, since Aristeas, Ptolemy's defender, and Josephus at a much later date, gave no such report, but tell us that they translated, not prophesied, in a single hall. For it is one thing to be a prophet, another to be a translator: in the one case the Spirit foretells things to come, in the other, learning and fluency of language render what the translator understands—unless Cicero is to be supposed to have translated the *Oeconomicos* of Xenophon, the *Protagoras* of Plato, and Demosthenes' speech on behalf of Ctesiphon under the influence of a rhetorical spirit; and unless the Holy Spirit cites passages from the same books one way through the Seventy translators and another way through the Apostles, so that these latter falsely declare to be written what the others passed over in silence. What then? Do we condemn the old texts? By no means; but we work in the Lord's house as best we can after the endeavors of these predecessors. They interpreted before the coming of Christ and put forth in hesitant statements the things of which they were ignorant; after His Passion and Resurrection we write not so much prophecy as history.

He then alludes to the spiritual gifts mentioned in *I Corinthians* 12:28, and makes the point that Apostles rank before Prophets, while interpreters rank almost last. He prefers, therefore, to follow the Apostles rather than the Seventy translators; and he concludes by asking prayers, that he may be enabled to translate the remaining books into Latin "in the same Spirit by Whom they were written." There may still be a sense in which the Septuagint was prepared under the influence of the Holy Spirit; but it leaves room for ambiguities and omissions, if not errors. We have come a long way from St. Jerome's attitude in the prefaces to the Four Gospels, to *Paralipomenon* from the Greek, and to *Isaias*. That transition, more than the existence of earlier testimonies on the subject, more even than an apologetic interest in the Jews, explains his acceptance of a canon based on the Hebrew.

St. Jerome's own current use of books he excludes from the canon, and his varied treatment for different texts, at different times, within the material he rejects, may be illustrated as follows. The two books of *Wisdom* and *Ecclesiasticus* are quoted fairly frequently, rather rarely with any qualification, and sometimes in such a way that it becomes plain St. Jerome has difficulty in keeping their teaching distinct, in his well-stocked memory, from that of *Proverbs* or *Ecclesiastes*. Thus in *Ep.* 133, 13 (A.D. 415) the saint announces his intention of refuting the Pelagians in a work based on God's word in Holy Writ. In the actual treatise *adversus Pelagianos*, II, 11, he then quotes *Wisdom* 1:11 as "written in another place," after a citation from *Psalm* 115:2. Again, in the same treatise (I, 33) he builds up a chain of argument in which admitted and "deuterocanonical" testimonies are strangely interwoven. "Is it from me that you exact explanations of the decree and ordinance of God?" he says. "A book of Wisdom gives the answer to your foolish question." This is followed by *Ecclus.* 3:22; then *et alibi* introduces *Eccles.* 7:17 (after the Septuagint); and finally, *et in eodem loco* connects the foregoing with *Wisdom* 1:1. "You will perhaps deny the authority of this book," St. Jerome continues; and to forestall this eventuality he quotes several passages from the New Testament and one more from *Ecclesiastes*, "a book in regard to which there is no room for doubt." Most probably he intends in the first instance to refer his chain of citations to the book of *Wisdom*; *Ecclesiastes* is certainly excluded. In the commentary on *Jeremias* (A.D. 414–) we find *Wisdom* 1:4 quoted as "Scripture" (in *Hieremiam*, IV, 8). Yet already against Rufinus (II, 17; A.D. 401) St. Jerome had used *Wisdom* 1:4–5; but here the citation came between two others drawn from profane texts, and it appears that this collocation may have been purposeful, as the book is referred to as the *Wisdom* "which we read under the name of Solomon." In replying to Vigilantius, A.D. 406, he not only repudiates the apocryphal *Fourth Book of Esdras*, declaring that he has never read it, but in the same context (*adv. Vigilant.*, 6) repudiates equally the "second Solomon"—almost surely either *Wisdom* or *Ecclesiasticus* —whom Vigilantius has quoted. The reflection "What need is there to take up a book that the Church does not receive?" is by implication applied to this "second Solomon"; and the scorn for Vigilantius' use of sources goes so far as to suggest that he next make use of heretical writings, pretended revelations, and drinking songs.

His reference to *Ecclesiasticus* in these years shows again St. Jerome's habit of dwelling on favorite texts: *Ecclus.* 2:1, used against Jovinian (see above), recurs in *Ep.* 118, 4 (A.D. 406); the same letter (118, 1) cites as Divine Scripture *Ecclus.* 22:6, found also in *Ep.* 102 four years earlier. Similarly, *Ecclus.* 7:40 occurs both in *Ep.* 127, 6, A.D. 413, and in *Ep.* 140, 18 in the following year. The former of these places dates the text "many generations later" than *Psalm* 43, 22, which has been cited as prophecy inspired by the Holy Spirit; and with the text from *Ecclus.* is coupled one from Persius' *Satires,* V, 23. Toward the end of St. Jerome's literary career *Ecclus.* is used often enough: *Ecclus.* 27:28 in *Ep.* 125, 19 (A.D. 412); *Ecclus.* 10:9 in *Ep.* 133, 1 (A.D. 415); and *Ecclus.* 48:17–49:7 in *comm. in Hieremiam,* IV, 34 (after A.D. 414), besides passages already cited.[25] Yet when it comes to the letter given as 148 in the editions, if there were no other reason to challenge its authenticity, the very fact that in it *Ecclus.* is used not in an incidental manner, but six times, always as *scriptura* or *divina sententia,* would be sufficient to establish that this was not written by St. Jerome.

The portions of *Daniel* for which no Semitic original exists receive rather divergent treatment in St. Jerome's later writings. In the preface to *Daniel,* he indicates the absence of the Susanna narrative, of the hymn of the three youths, and of the stories of Bel and the Dragon from the Hebrew. Admitting that they are "spread all over the world" he states that he has supplied them, preceded by an obelus which is their death-warrant (*easque jugulante*—the obelus was dagger-shaped), "so that we may not seem to the untrained to have lopped off a goodly part of the scroll." He then quotes "one of the Jewish rabbis" for a series of objections against each section in turn, and concludes by "leaving a decision on this circumstance to the judgment of the reader." The *Apology against Rufinus* (II, 33; A.D. 401) stresses the fact that he has not given this series of indictments as his own opinion; but even here he does not indicate acceptance of the parts in question, and surely the reader's judgment was left free in the earlier preface only as to the validity of the Jewish testimony, and not regarding the conclusion which it tends to support. The prayer of Azarias and the hymn of the three youths in the fiery furnace (*Dan.* 3:24–90) are marked off in the Vulgate text both at the beginning and the end of the section by indications that they are not to be found in the Hebrew and that they have been rendered from Theodotion. Yet at least they are not relegated to an appendix to the book, as has been done with parts of *Esther*. In the commentary on *Daniel* (A.D. 407) they are dealt with in the same manner as in the text itself: with a twofold indication that they are being commented on only briefly, "so that we may not appear to have passed them over altogether." The comment ends with the remark, "From here on we follow the *hebraicam veritatem*." In *Ep.* 120, 12 (A.D. 407) it is noted that the Jews do not accept *Dan.* 3:86; yet in the same year, *Ep.* 121, 8, furnishes a free adaptation of *Dan.* 3:29–33. Subsequently, *Ep.* 130, 10 (A.D. 414) draws on details from *Dan.* 3:47–50.

For the person and the story of Susanna, St. Jerome retained a pronounced sympathy, at least for some years. In the preface to *Daniel* he speaks of the *Susannae . . . historiam*, while Bel and the Dragon are *fabulas*. The suggestion of Greek origin for the narrative, based on the word-plays which it contains, he attributes in this preface to the rabbi whose objections he cites. In *Ep.* 54, 10 and 58, 1, both from A.D. 394–5, he alludes to the Susanna narrative; and in *Ep.* 65, 2 (A.D. 397) he is led by the occurrence of a similar word in the title to *Psalm* 44 to speak of the meaning of Susanna's name, "Lily," and its aptness to signify the chastity in wedlock of which she is the type. In the prologue to his commentary on *Daniel*, however, St. Jerome in A.D. 407 meets Porphyry's objection to the book as a whole by dissociating the Susanna narrative from the rest of the book; the saint himself calls it a *visio*, but refers to Origen, Eusebius and Apollinaris as calling it a *fabula* with "no authority as sacred Scripture." Then at the end of his commentary he joins it with the Bel story, and instead of giving any explanation of his own, merely proposes to excerpt from Origen's writings what the latter has to say of these *fabulae*. That the term is intended to have pejorative implications is made plain in the commentary on *Jeremias* (V. 67), where in discussing *Jer.* 29:21–23 St. Jerome quotes the Jews as identifying the false prophets spoken of by Jeremias with the elders in the Susanna story. Between the two cases there are discrepancies, which they settle to the prejudice of the Susanna narrative, "For which reason many, including nearly all the Jews, do not receive it, *quasi fabula*, nor do they read it in their synagogues." The Bel narrative is not drawn upon for quotations; in the commentary, a single note challenges its canonicity—more likely on Jerome's own authority than on Origen's. The Dragon story (*Dan.* 14:22ff.) is passed over in complete silence at the end of the *Daniel* commentary (contrast note 9, above, for the earlier period).

What is to be said regarding the other books can be summarized much more briefly. St. Jerome renders *Tobias* and *Judith* from Semitic texts, "judging it better to displease the judgment of Pharisees and to obey the behests of bishops" for *Tobias*; and, "because the Nicene synod is alleged to have counted this book among the Holy Scriptures" for *Judith*.[26] *Judith* is drawn upon, *Ep.* 54, 16 (A.D. 394–5), as a type of chastity, with the qualification, "if anyone is of the opinion that the book is to be received as canonical"; in *Ep.* 79, 10 (A.D. 400) she becomes a type of the Church. *Tobias* is cited in the prologue to the commentary on *Jonas* (A.D. 396), "because, though it is not in the canon, it is made use of by churchmen" (*PL*, 25, 1119). In the non-Hebrew parts of *Esther*, St. Jerome discerns rhetorical exercises (*Praef. in libr. Esther*); a rhetorician himself, he views them with distrust (though he cites *Esther* 14:16 in *Ep.* 130, 4, A.D. 414). While St. Jerome did not finish his commentary on *Jeremias*, the prologue (ii) tells us explicitly that he had resolved not to comment on *Baruch* or on the "Letter of Jeremias" (*Baruch* 6), which latter he styles a *pseudepigraphon*. Yet *Baruch* is elsewhere quoted directly on at least three occasions.[27] The *Books of the*

Maccabees are given as references several times in the commentary on *Daniel*, and 2 *Macc.* 5:17 is alluded to in *adversus Pelagianos* II, 30 (A.D. 415). But St. Jerome's citations include also the passage about the bee in *Proverbs* 6:8 (in the Septuagint and not in the Hebrew or the Vulgate; *Ep.* 125, 11, A.D. 412), and a quotation from one of the Three Pages in 3 *Esdras* (4:59; *Ep.* 65, A.D. 397), which book is now designated as *extra seriem canonicorum librorum* (appendix to the Clementine Vulgate). There is perhaps in this a parallel to his use in *adversus Pelagianos* III, 2 (A.D. 415) of the "Gospel according to the Hebrews," along with the *Epistle of Barnabas*, 5:9 (cited under the name of Ignatius!); having given the texts, he adds, "If you do not accept these citations as authoritative, at least in view of their antiquity, take them as evidence of what has been the view of all churchmen."

The final criterion for the canon of the Scriptures, like that for any other point in the *depositum fidei*, is the teaching and practice of the Church. In St. Jerome's time the teaching had not been reduced to a formula of universal acceptance; and the practice was obscured by hesitations over certain books in certain regions, and by doubts on academic grounds. The practice of the Church did not hinge, as St. Jerome came to expect that it should, on the existence of an authoritative Hebrew or Aramaic original for all books or parts of books in the Old Testament. St. Jerome himself went beyond any such theoretical standard, as we have seen. His friend Epiphanius concurred perfectly with him regarding the theory of the Old Testament canon. Yet in A.D. 394, when both had already given some expression to their theory, Epiphanius cited *Wisdom* 2:23 in writing to John of Jerusalem, for one of "seven proofs from Holy Scripture"; and the citation is translated and preserved for us (*Ep.* 51, 6, 7) by Jerome in the collection of his own letters. The panegyric of Paula (*Ep.* 108) after her death (A.D. 404) shows St. Jerome's most cherished pupil as seen by himself; her favorite Old Testament texts are counted over, and we find that it is the Septuagint form of text to which she is attached. In keeping with this, she quotes *Ecclesi-*

asticus (3:33) among other books (*Ep.* 108, 16)—it is hardly surprising that the text is one we find employed by St. Jerome himself on at least two occasions (*Ep.* 66, 5, A.D. 398; *Ep.* 79, 5, A.D. 400). In this same letter, St. Jerome calls *Ecclus.* 13:2 "Scripture," and alludes to *Wisdom* 2:24 (*Ep.* 108, 18, 21). It was for hearers like Paula that the spiritual interpretation of texts in his commentaries was based on the Septuagint form; and if the Church has come, in the matter of the canon, to sanction Paula's practice rather than his own theory, St. Jerome would be the last to regret it.

NOTES

[1] *Psalterium breviarii romani . . . secundum novam e textibus primigeniis interpretationem latinam, Pii Papae XII auctoritate editum: editio typica vaticana* 1945.

[2] Pope Pius XII, encyclical letter *Divino afflante Spiritu,* 30 Sept. 1943, no. 22.

[3] *Honorabile connubium in omnibus, et torus immaculatus,* Vulgate.

[4] An incidental use of Wisdom 4:8 in *Ep.* 58, 1 (A.D. 394-95), where it is ascribed to "Solomon," suggests that St. Jerome may have thought he was quoting from Proverbs on this occasion. The case is not unique (cf. *in Hieremiam prophetam,* V, 63, ed. S. Reiter, CSEL, 59, Vienna, 1913, p. 352, for Wisdom 8:2, and *ibid.* I, 4, p. 8, for our same Wisdom 4:8, introduced this time by *alio enim propheta loquente didicisti,* in A.D. 414); but no general theory can be built on such lapses of memory as occur in St. Jerome's work.

[5] That the so-called *Decretum gelasianum* was drawn up by Pope Damasus at a Roman synod under the influence of St. Jerome in A.D. 382 has been affirmed, but seems unlikely at the best. Cf. for acceptance of this position Howorth, H. H., "The Influence of St. Jerome on the Canon of the Western Church," I., *Journal of Theological Studies* 10, 1908-09. The entire series of articles (*ibid.,* 10, 1908-09, 481-96; 11, 1909-10, 321-47; 13, 1911-12, 1-18) is of interest for our subject.

[6] *Loc. cit.,* 10, 1908-09, 493.

[7] For example, in *Comm. in Ep. ad Galatas,* Esther 14:11 (Vulg.) in the comment on Gal. 1:6 (*PL,* 26, 319); Wis. 4:22, 12:1 under Gal. 3:1-2 (*ibid.,* 348, 350); II Macc. 7 under Gal. 3:14 (*ibid.,* 362); I Macc. 2 under Gal. 4:19 (*ibid.,* 384). In *Comm. in Ep. ad Ephesios,* Wis. 11:23 is cited under Ephes. 1:6 (*ibid.,* 450); Wis. 2:24 under Ephes. 2:5 (*ibid.,* 467); Wis. 7:21 under Ephes. 3:5ff. (*ibid.,* 480); Wis. 9:15 under Ephes. 4:2 (*ibid.,* 493); Ecclus. 27:12 under Ephes. 4:2 (*ibid.,* 495); Ecclus. 10:24 under Ephes. 4:27 (*ibid.,* 512). Here and elsewhere, verse numbers are those of the Vulgate unless otherwise specified.

[8] Susanna (Daniel 13) 56 is cited in the commentaries on Nahum 3:8ff. (*PL,* 25, 1263), and on Soph. 1:11, 2:8ff. (as "Daniel"), 3:8-9 (*ibid.,* 1349, 1366, 1378). Ecclesiasticus is referred to as follows: 6:7 under Mich. 7:5-7 (*ibid.,* 1219); 4:25 under Mich. 7:14ff. (*ibid.,* 1228); 1:2 under Hab. 3:11ff. (*ibid.,* 1323); 3:20 and 22:32 under Soph. 2:3-4 (*ibid.,* 1358-9);

8:6 and 27:28 under Soph. 3:19–20 (*ibid.*, 1385). I Macc. 2 is referred to under Nahum 1:1 (*ibid.*, 1232).

[9] *quamquam apud Hebraeos haec ipsa non legatur historia. Igitur si quis recipit Scripturam illam, sive non recipit. . . .*

[10] Cavallera, F., S. *Jérôme sa vie et son oeuvre* I, 2 (Paris, 1922), 28f.

[11] Stummer, F., *Einführung in die lateinische Bibel* (Paderborn, 1928), 92–93. Stummer gives in an appendix to his book the full text of the various prefaces (not that of the *Psalterium juxta Hebraeos*, however), of the letter to Paulinus and of the articles from *de viris illustr.* which were normally carried in the Vulgate manuscripts.

[12] *Paulus apostolus ad septem scribit ecclesias, octava enim ad Hebraeos a plerisque extra numerum ponitur.* It might be well to say at once that for St. Jerome *plerique* need not mean "most"; it is used by him in the sense of "a good many," without any reference to the idea of a majority. Cf., *e.g.,* S. Reiter, in the *index verborum* to *CSEL,* 59 (above, note 4), p. 555, s.v. *plerique.*

[13] Jerome's revision of the commentary of Victorinus on the Apocalypse is from the period A.D. 397–400.

[14] Cf. especially, *Of Measures and Weights,* 23. The assumption that the Septuagint arrangement of the Prophets found support in Jewish testimony from contemporaries of Epiphanius and Jerome is not supported by the known facts.

[15] Nothing illustrates this better than the section (59) where St. Jerome refers to the presbyter Caius, and speaks of his denial of Pauline authenticity to the *Epistle to the Hebrews.* The section ends with a sentence which has every appearance of being a personal affirmation by St. Jerome: *sed et apud Romanos usque hodie quasi Pauli apostoli non habetur.* The force of this as a statement of the actual case at Rome or in the West generally in St. Jerome's time is considerably lessened when we discover that it is a literal rendering of what Eusebius affirmed for his own time, in St. Jerome's source, *Hist. eccl.,* vi, 20. Unless we take the phrase "heavenly Jerusalem" in *Ep.* 14, 3 to be a deliberate use of Hebr. 12:22, the first certain quotation of Hebrews by St. Jerome is in *Ep.* 18A, 5, written from Constantinople in A.D. 380–81.

[16] Not indicated in Reiter's edition.

[17] Job 9:20, 30–31 in II, 2; in II, 4, Job 4:17ff.; 7:1; 40:16, 22, 21, 41:5, 26, 40:30; and in another group, 40:31, 17, 41:16, 19, 22, 23, 26. Substantially it is St. Jerome's own Hexaplaric rendering that is used.

[18] *Praefatio in psalterium juxta Hebraeos, PL,* 28, 1223–28.

[19] Cf. *Praef. in Samuel et Malachim: Sicut ergo Judith et Tobi et Maccabaeorum libros legit quidem Ecclesia sed inter canonicas Scripturas non recipit, sic et haec duo volumina [Jesu filii Sirach liber et alius pseudepigraphus qui Sapientia Salomonis inscribitur] legat ad aedificationem plebis, non auctoritatem ecclesiasticorum dogmatum confirmandam.* Besides, he applies the expression *ad aedificationem ecclesiae* to the *Epistle of Barnabas* in *de viris illustr.,* 6, while at the same time classing it as apocryphal. Compare Balestri, J., *Biblicae Introductionis Generalis Elementa,* Rome, 1932, 324.

[20] Cf. Augustine's letter of A.D. 403, no. 104 in the collection of St. Jerome.

[21] Apocalypse 4:4ff.; a Christian turn given by St. Jerome to the Jewish grouping of the books based on the number (22) of letters in the Hebrew alphabet. The same computation is given in the *prologus galeatus.*

[22] *quos (Septuaginta translatores) in conventu fratrum semper edissero.*

[23] *Apol. adv. Rufin.*, II, 24.

[24] This is illustrated by the collected material in *Anecdota Maredsolana,* III, ed. G. Morin (Maredsous, 1895–1903): *S. Hieronymi presbyteri . . . commentarioli in Psalmos; . . . tractatus sive homiliae.*

[25] These references are not intended to be exhaustive; see however the discussion to follow regarding Paula, and for the letters between A.D. 395 and 400, add: Ecclus. 25:12 in *Ep.* 57, 1; Ecclus. 4:25 in *Ep.* 66, 6; Ecclus. 13:1 in *Ep.* 71, 3; Ecclus. 11:27 in *Ep.* 77, 6.

[26] The oft-cited complaint over St. Jerome's hasty rendering of Tobias in a "single day" is uncalled for. He was a competent and experienced translator working from a text which could not have been wholly new to him, with the help of a Jewish translator for the Aramaic, and the service of secretaries. A careful combing of the Greek texts, which he did not profess to be supplanting, yields little indeed that is not contained in the Vulgate. The chief geographical difficulties with the Vulgate text are resolved when it is recognized (cf. M. M. Schumpp, *Das Buch Tobias,* Münster i. W., 1933, 63–64) that *Rages* is not a genuine Vulgate reading in Tob. 3:7. The short space of time mentioned by St. Jerome for a number of his writings seems to have been a point of pride with him; some of these are important original compositions (cf. *Ep.* 75, 108, 127; *adv. Vigilant.*). In the case of the three books, Proverbs, Ecclesiastes, Canticle of Canticles, which we are told were done in three days, we know that St. Jerome had been occupied with the Hebrew text of Ecclesiastes fourteen years previously. Even the process of rendering into Latin what he was told in Hebrew was the meaning of the Aramaic original is not unexampled in St. Jerome's other work. He had the monastic rule of St. Pachomius translated from Coptic into Greek for him in A.D. 404, *viva voce,* while he furnished a Latin rendering from the Greek. In the case of Tobias, he had a check on the translator from Aramaic in the previously extant Latin text, of which internal evidence shows he made considerable use in preparing his own rendering (cf. Schumpp, *ibid.,* xxix–xxxiii). That he took incidental liberties with the wording may be admitted: for example, only in the Vulgate has Tob. 13:5 been retouched on the basis of Psalm 6:5. Judith is even closer to the Old Latin than is Tobias.

[27] Baruch 5:5 in *Ep.* 77, 4 (A.D. 400); Baruch 3:12 and 3:38 in the *Tractatus (Anec. Maredsol.,* III, 2, pp. 411, 181) of unknown date.

Contributors

CHANOINE GUSTAV BARDY ("St. Jerome and Greek Thought") is professor of positive Theology at the Grand Seminaire of Dijon, contributor to the Fliche-Martin *Histoire de l'Eglise* and author of innumerable books and articles on the first six centuries of the Church.

EUGENE BURKE, C.S.P. ("St. Jerome as a Spiritual Director") is Associate Professor of Dogmatic Theology at Catholic University, the author of a book on the Ecclesiology of St. Leo the Great.

FERDINAND CAVALLERA, S.J. ("The Personality of St. Jerome") is doyen of the Faculty of Theology at the Institut Catholique of Toulouse, editor of the *Revue d'Ascetique et Mystique*, and of the *Dictionnaire Spirituelle*, author of a definitive *Saint Jérôme, sa vie et son oeuvre*, and recipient of a recent *Melanges offerts au R.P. Cavallera*.

LOUIS N. HARTMANN, C.SS.R. ("St. Jerome as an Exegete") is chairman of the Commission for the Confraternity of Christian Doctrine's translation of the Scriptures into English, and Secretary of the Catholic Biblical Society of America.

M. L. W. LAISTNER ("The Study of St. Jerome in the Early Middle Ages") is John Stambaugh Professor of History at Cornell University; Hon. Fellow of Jesus College, University of Cambridge.

FRANCIS X. MURPHY, C.SS.R. ("The Irascible Hermit" and "St. Jerome as an Historian") is the author of *Rufinus of Aquileia* and a contributor to *Thought, Traditio, Speculum,* etc.

Jean-Remy Palanque ("St. Jerome and the Barbarians") is a professor on the Faculty of Letters at Montpellier and at Aix, author of *Saint Ambrose et l'Empire Romain,* and contributor to the Fliche-Martin *Histoire de l'Eglise.*

Edwin A. Quain, S.J. ("St. Jerome as a Humanist") is Professor of Classics and Dean at the Graduate School of Arts and Sciences at Fordham University and an Editor of *Traditio.*

Patrick W. Skehan ("St. Jerome and the Canon of the Holy Scriptures") is associate professor of Sacred Scripture and Oriental Languages at Catholic University and an editor of the *Catholic Biblical Quarterly.*

Index